The Planet Kings

1976
1

1977

D1610243

The Player Kings

Richard Findlater

Weidenfeld and Nicolson
5 Winsley Street London W1

301839

SBN 297 00304 6

Printed in Great Britain by
Bristol Typesetting Co Ltd, Barton Manor, St Philips, Bristol

Contents

Foreword in warning 9

Part One

Panorama: 1600-1900 19

1 David Garrick 24
2 John Philip Kemble 49
3 Edmund Kean 72
4 William Charles Macready 94
5 Sir Henry Irving 120
6 Sir Johnston Forbes-Robertson 147

Part Two

Panorama: 1900-30 167

7 Sir John Gielgud 173
8 Sir Laurence Olivier 204
9 Sir Michael Redgrave 238
10 To be concluded 264

Postscript 278
Index 281

List of Illustrations

Between pages 112 and 113

David Garrick: from the studio of Sir Joshua Reynolds (*National Portrait Gallery*)

Garrick as Hamlet (*Enthoven Collection, Victoria and Albert Museum*)

Garrick as Abel Drugger: after Zoffany (*Enthoven Collection*)

John Philip Kemble: engraved in 1799 by Heath from a miniature by Chinnery (*Enthoven Collection*)

Kemble as Rolla: caricature by Dighton, 1799 (*Enthoven Collection*)

Kemble as Coriolanus: after Lawrence (*Enthoven Collection*)

Edmund Kean: by Samuel Cousins (*Enthoven Collection*)

Kean as Shylock in 1814 (*Print Room, British Museum*)

Kean as Overreach (*Enthoven Collection*)

William Charles Macready: engraved from a miniature by Thorburn (*Mander and Mitchenson Theatre Collection*)

Macready as William Tell: after Inman (*Enthoven Collection*)

Macready as Macbeth, 1851: after I. H. Wilson (*Enthoven Collection*)

Henry Irving in the 1870s (*British Theatre Museum*)

Irving as Mathias (*Enthoven Collection*)

Irving as Mephistopheles: by Phil May (*By permission of the Savage Club*)

Johnston Forbes-Robertson: by Spy, 1895 (*Enthoven Collection*)

Forbes-Robertson as Hamlet, 1913 (*Enthoven Collection*)

Sir John Gielgud, 1970: photograph by Nicolo Vogel

Between pages 208 and 209

Gielgud as Hamlet, 1929: photograph by Pollard Crowther
(*Mander and Mitchenson Theatre Collection*)

Gielgud as John Worthing, 1939: photograph by Angus McBean
(*Mander and Mitchenson Theatre Collection*)

Gielgud as Raskolnikov, 1946: photograph by Wilson (*Mander and Mitchenson Theatre Collection*)

Gielgud as Angelo, 1950: photograph by Angus McBean
(*Mander and Mitchenson Theatre Collection*)

Gielgud as Prospero, 1957: photograph by Angus McBean
(*Shakespeare Memorial Theatre*)

Sir Laurence Olivier, 1970: photograph by Neil Libbert (*By permission of* The Observer)

Olivier as Titus Andronicus, 1957: photograph by Angus McBean

Olivier as Othello, 1964: photograph by Angus McBean

Olivier as Archie Rice, 1957 (*Keystone Press*)

Olivier as Macbeth, 1955: photograph by Angus McBean
(*Shakespeare Memorial Theatre*)

Sir Michael Redgrave, 1970: photograph by Franco Nero

Redgrave as Uncle Vanya, 1962: photograph by Angus McBean

Redgrave as Andrew Aguecheek, 1938

Redgrave as Antony, 1953: photograph by Cecil Beaton

Angus McBean's photographs are now in the possession of the Harvard Theatre Collection.

Film still of Sir John Gielgud as Hamlet on the front of the jacket loaned by the Mander and Mitchenson Theatre Collection, reproduced by kind permission of the British Film Institute from the film ' A Diary for Timothy ', directed by Humphrey Jennings and produced by Basil Wright for Crown Film Unit in 1945.

Foreword in warning

In the publicity machines of contemporary show business great actors seem to be commonplace: dozens of them have come and gone in the film studios during the past forty years. Greatness, in this world, is recognized by winning (or just failing to win) an Oscar (or something like it); by breaking box-office records; by signing an inflationary contract. Yet that little word 'great' – 'the most telling monosyllable in criticism', as a veteran reviewer has described it – is an accolade that may be jealously reserved in the theatre for less than a dozen actors and actresses in four hundred years. Reviewing Olivier's Oedipus in New York, back in 1946, John Mason Brown wrote: 'For everyone's sake, for the well-being of the art involved, in the interests of criticism, out of respect for the language, and in defence of standards, "great" is an adjective which ought to be kept buried in the deep freeze. It cannot, it should not, it must not, be squandered lightly . . .' Agreed: it is with that approach that the adjective is used in the following chapters.

All attempts to define the qualities of the great actor, in any but the widest terms, seem doomed to failure. You can list the qualities acclaimed in those players who have generally been recognized as great: stamina, single-mindedness, and tireless energy; the capacity to mobilize that energy at a moment's notice, to strike twelve at the drop of a hat; the ability to surprise – in the right place; mesmeric eyes of unusual brilliance; physical grace and good looks; the impersonative power of self-transformation; authority and presence; the talent to make an audience frightened, make them laugh, make them cry, make them love you; a rare vocal range, depth, volume and control. All these may be marks of great acting. Yet they are also, singly, marks of very good acting, or merely very successful acting, and some of them are conspicuously missing from the assets of the nine actors picked out in this survey. Greatness cannot be measured only by voltage any more than by footage; and it would be as unwise to assume that all great actors must be vocal clarinets or physical Proteans as to suppose that they are all alcoholics, illegitimate, and five feet four. Cleverness can get in the way of great acting: so can charm, beauty, technique and intellectuality. Great actors may be short and plump. Their voices may be harsh and mannered. Outside the theatre their minds might well be dismissed by dons as *beta*. They may always look much the same. They may give bad performances. Great acting is what great actors often do: but fine actors sometimes seem to manage it.

The simplest – if not the only – clue to the mystery, I believe, is still provided by the dictum of the Victorian critic, G. H. Lewes, that ' the greatest artist is he who is greatest in the highest reaches of his art '. In the British theatre the summits of the actor's art are still the Himalayan heroes and villains of Shakespeare. No one – with the hypothetical exception of Burbage – has triumphed in all the great roles (stage history disproves Henry Irving's maxim that ' a great actor can do nothing badly ' and Max Beerbohm's even shakier assertion that ' the great artist is always at his best'). A man who flops in Macbeth, Antony, Lear and Richard III may still win homage for his Hamlet and Othello. But a man who has not identified himself with at least one of the titanic parts must still, surely, be classed as an actor of the second rank, whatever he can do outside Shakespeare. He may seem to reach the top in lesser roles – like, for example, Garrick as Ranger, Kean as Overreach, Irving as Mathias and Olivier as Archie Rice – but his crucial test as an artist is collaborating with the superb. In every generation Shakespeare demands great acting; he may not get it, though great reputations may nevertheless be made; but while his servants may behave as his master, or may (however dedicated) fail to meet the challenge that he sets, the best of them show their own sorts of greatness in the work.

For the better part of three hundred years the corruption and exploitation of Shakespeare has overshadowed the contemporary drama as a mainstream enterprise of the British stage. He is the bane of British playwriting still. Yet the plays, however mangled, have provided and continue to provide not only the greatest dramatic literature but also the greatest gymnasium for actors (if not actresses) in the world. In trying to take their measure or to fit the plays to themselves British actors through the centuries have maintained, remade and sometimes enriched a changing tradition which may – with warrantable inference though little factual evidence – be traced back to Shakespeare's lifetime.

Fashions in acting shift with fashions in personalities and play-making, and all are influenced by the size and shape of the stage, the methods of theatrical lighting and production, the audience's taste and social composition, the trade's organization and society's general climate. Of course, tests of greatness change as well. So does the demand for it. Great actors – puritans have argued – are the enemies of good drama, the mini-gods of a personality cult whose rituals of worship block the lines of communication between living dramatists and their potential audience, and paralyse the progress of the theatre. Their undemocratic, para-noiac, anachronistic insistence on big parts denies the *Zeitgeist* – so one set of current objections might be summarized – by a romantic, pre-Freudian, pre-Marxist glorification of solipsistic experience and undemocratic authority: 'the player king' stands self-condemned as an anomaly. The survival of such stars (for this argument does not distinguish between the real and the fake) is an historical fluke, like the exaltation of the conductor. Their iconography is at best time-wasting fantasy: at worst, corrupting and reactionary propaganda for an exploded view of history, society and human nature. To put it at one extreme, in the words of Dr Timothy Leary (writing in *The Politics of Ecstasy*): 'Pitiful Shakespeare! All those grim, suffering, ham-actor heroes sweating out the failure of ambition, the torments of jealousy, the agony of wounded pride, the passions of unre-quited love. The Western world has been on a bad trip, a 400-year bummer.' Yet for millions 'pitiful Shakespeare' remains – supremely and indestructibly above all transient fashion – as the springboard into new oceans of theatrical experience and self-knowledge; and the great actor is the one who can make you jump higher, take you deeper and keep you going longer than any other kind of actor, in any other kind of play.

The reader will draw his own conclusions from the following chapters about what greatness is. Here are some suggested clues. Great acting seems to combine an intermittent mastery of magic and technique, hard labour, passionate determination and exceptionally good luck, magnetism and scholarship, realism and a kind of ecstasy or possession. The great actor is a man in full command of a great part of his audience and of himself; he is also a man who can lose himself at the moments when (in the old actor's phrase) the god descends. Whatever he does must seem inevitable, as if it had to happen, and yet surprising, as if it has happened for the very first time. By the standards of everyday behaviour he may look and sound outrageously unnatural, yet he is, in essence, *us*: he may be beyond naturalism, yet never beyond nature. He is 'beside himself', as a mad king or an avenging prince, and yet he is deep *inside* his self and our selves – or so it seems, in the moment of communion. The mystery lies in the harmony of actor and character, illusion and reality, con-trick and sacrament, being and seeming. Great acting is the exaltation of Life but it is also the apotheosis of Theatre, annihilating any antithesis between them. And it is still, to me, a great enigma.

This is a book about great acting in the last 250 years and, incidentally, about the history of the British theatre. It is a book about men only, and Englishmen at that, on the stage: three restrictions dictated by considerations of space and shape, rather than by prejudice against women, foreigners and films. Inevitably it depends upon hearsay and second-hand evidence which is, again inevitably, often contradictory, usually patchy and always open to doubt. So it is bound to be unfair, dogmatic and presumptuous, begging a host of unanswerable questions. Is Olivier as great as Garrick? Was Kean's Shylock better than Irving's? How great was Gielgud's Hamlet? In which year? On which nights? Any attempt to evoke and assess the acting of the past which employs that slippery, devalued criterion of 'greatness' is condemned to run into a morass of posers like these. After all, any description of even contemporary first-rank acting can only be, at best, an approximation to an unverifiable truth. The excellence of what Olivier or Gielgud did the day before yesterday is already a matter of argument: it is hard even to be sure, in the theatre of memory, what precisely happened. To dogmatize about the merits of long-dead artists is dangerous enough. It is worse to sit in judgement on the living, before their careers are completed, without having seen all their performances in all their roles many times over. As the recorded history of acting in this century is, in general, the history of first nights, how can we hope to recapture in print the best performances of our time when, for so many leading actors, their first nights are their worst nights? Again, while some great names from the past linger on as legends unconfirmed by circumstantial evidence, others survive in a review or an essay, caught in the act for posterity, but possibly in the wrong act on an off-night. Getting the right kind of memorial is a matter of chance. A fine actor in opposition to contemporary fashion, without a Hazlitt or Lewes to mirror him, may be denied the honour due to him, even after death. Where, to take two recent names at random, do Donald Wolfit and Wilfrid Lawson live to the full in print? Going two centuries back, what were Charles Macklin and John Henderson really like? What did they all owe to the authors, directors, and colleagues?

To the actors singled out in the following chapters many readers may well add and subtract several names; but there are two special omissions of reputations which are usually classified without challenge among the half-dozen actors recognized as great, and they are omitted because there is little fact, though much generality and guesswork about their performances. One is Thomas Betterton, who led the stage for nearly half a century between 1660 and 1710. For evidence of his greatness – indeed, for any evidence of a specific kind – we rely largely upon the loaded testimony of two junior colleagues, Colley Cibber (sweet) and Anthony Aston (rather sour), writing about him when he was over fifty, and upon the praise of Addison and Steele. Betterton was middle-sized, ' inclining to the corpulent ', with a big head, a short, thick neck, a broad face, small eyes and short arms, but ' a commanding mien of majesty.' He apparently combined unusual power with unusual control. His voice – ' low and grumbling ', said Aston – was, said Cibber, ' of the kind which gave more spirit to terror than to the softer passions; of more strength than melody '. He could time it, according to Aston, by ' an artful climax, which enforced universal attention, even from the fops and orange-girls '. Betterton created about 130 characters, including Valentine in Congreve's *Love for Love* and Jaffier in Otway's *Venice Preserv'd*, but he was at his best in Shakespeare: ' the one was born alone to speak what the other knew only to write.' It was claimed in 1708, indeed, by John Downes, that

Betterton learned both Hamlet and Henry VIII, in effect, in direct succession from Shakespeare; and although this is no more than hearsay, it is likely that Sir William Davenant – Betterton's first manager – instructed him in the way that roles were played in the pre-1642 theatre, in so far as the old school did not clash with the new fashion.

As Brutus, Betterton had 'an unruffled temper', with a 'hasty spark of anger' quite different from the 'fierce and flashing fire' of his Hotspur; his wide range in tragedy and comedy included Falstaff, Macbeth, Henry VIII and Othello, in which Addison praised his 'wonderful agony'; but his prime success appears to have been Hamlet. He was at his best in the 'To be or not to be' soliloquy, in the closet-scene, in his grief for Ophelia, and in his encounters with the Ghost, whom he made 'equally terrible to the spectator as to himself.' He was still playing Hamlet when he was nearly seventy, and yet he seemed – or so Steele asserted – 'a young man of great expectation, vivacity and enterprise.' He could hush the noisy Restoration audience, and keep it hushed: 'to have talked or looked another way, would have been thought insensibility or ignorance,' declared Cibber; yet he 'never prostituted himself to the low ambition of a false applause.'

The voice of a singer is not more strictly tied to time and tune, than that of an actor in theatrical elocution; the least syllable too long or too slightly dwelt upon in a period, depreciates it to nothing; which very syllable, if rightly touched, shall . . . give life and spirit to the whole. I never heard a line in tragedy come from Betterton, wherein my judgment, my ear, and my imagination, were not fully satisfied . . .

We know little more of substance about Betterton, and much less about Richard Burbage, for whom Shakespeare apparently wrote his major roles. Burbage, born about 1567, was the younger son of the ex-joiner who built the first permanent playhouse in Britain since the Romans, the Shoreditch Theatre of 1576, and later rebuilt the Blackfriars. He became leader of the fellowship of players with whom Shakespeare worked, the outstanding troupe of the day; and he was, almost certainly, the first Hamlet, Lear, Shylock, Romeo, Macbeth, Brutus, Richard III, Pericles and Othello (said to be his finest part). His portrait shows that he had big eyes, a big nose and a trim beard. He was praised for his capacity 'for so wholly transforming himself into his Part, and

putting himself off with his Cloathes, as he never (not so much
as in the Tyring-House), assum'd himself again until the Play was
done ':

> A delightful Proteus that could
> Transform himself into what shape he would.

Burbage was said to be short, he was certainly famous, he was
called 'the best' by Ben Jonson, and when he died in 1619
several people wrote glowing epitaphs full of not very informative
hyperbole. That is roughly all we know of the man who, it is
sometimes assumed, must have been the greatest actor in the
history of the English stage.

Yet in spite of the awesome difficulties of finding it, defining
and describing it, great acting on the stage – past and present –
offers a tantalizing and irresistible challenge to the writer: to the
playgoer it offers one of the most exalting and elusive experiences
available in the arts.

In such a survey as this, where constipation of detail is a
grave occupational risk, many names, points and performances
have been regretfully omitted: in the contemporary chapters
gaps of this kind may seem to gape especially badly, but without
ruthless concentration on the central figures – at the expense of
discussing their leading ladies, directors, authors and colleagues –
the book, already bulky, would be doubled in size. The principal
sources among the hundreds on which this book draws have been
summarized in a final note and book-list, instead of being
itemized in clogging page-by-page annotations: this is hopefully
designed for the general reader rather than the theatrical scholar.
It is intended not as a final inventory or evaluation – an impossible
dream, of course – but as a beginner's guide for all those who
want to know more about great actors in the eighteenth and nineteenth centuries – what they did, how they developed, what kind
of theatre they worked in – and about great acting now or in the
recent past.

The six actors selected in Part 1, which attempts to cover the
period up to 1914, are already the subject of a substantial theatrical library, and here their careers have been telescoped, summarized and simplified. The perspective is different in Part 2,
which concentrates on the past forty years, less thoroughly
charted in book-form: the evidence about the acting of the three

knights under review is scattered in hundreds of newspapers, magazines and memories. In trying to piece some of that evidence together I have given more detail to their performances than to those of their great predecessors. I have also, perhaps, given first-night reviewers more weight than they deserve. But in the absence of fuller-scale theatrical criticism their testimony is indispensable, and the proximity of the players makes it unavoidably hard to view them with quite the same degree of historical detachment, especially as their careers are by no means ended.

Two main sources must be recorded here: my own books *Michael Redgrave – Actor* (Heinemann, 1956) and *Six Great Actors* (Hamish Hamilton, 1957), both out of print. The bulk of Part 1 draws on the latter book, in a revised and extended form.

Part One

Panorama: 1600–1900

'There can be no serious school of acting without a dramatic literature to feed it,' declared Henry James a hundred years ago, comparing English players to their disadvantage with the priests of his adored Comédie Française. In the British theatre no recognizable 'school' of acting, in the sense of an institutional *conservatoire*, has ever been tolerated; pedagogues and ideologues have (until recently) been noticeably scarce; and for long stretches of our theatrical history, actors have found no new dramatic literature of any substance to feed on. Yet despite the perennial poverty of the contemporary drama 'serious' acting has thrived – in the school of experience, and on the experience of Shakespeare in particular. The actors for whom he wrote at the beginning of the seventeenth century helped to shape the working lives of their professional posterity, through many styles and fashions.

Shakespeare's fellowship of players worked under very different conditions from those expected by today's Equity members. They often acted in daylight, without actresses, against a rowdy, restless, popular audience, in which all classes joined, most of it standing in the open air. On the South Bank they took for granted as the normal accompaniment to theatrical performances the cries of tortured animals from the nearby pleasure-grounds of Paris Garden, the brawls among the groundlings standing under the stage, the interruptions of gallants sitting actually on the stage. These Elizabethans enjoyed a bit of violence. Sackerson the star bear was nearly as popular for a time as Burbage the star actor, and the Londoners for whom Shakespeare contrived the blinding of Gloucester were accustomed to such treats as the whipping of blind bears at the stake, the bloody duel of the cockfight, or the public execution and disembowelling of criminals. But they also revelled in the sound of words: Shakespeare wrote for good listeners – and good declaimers. The range of his language indicates the range of the techniques at the command of his fellow-actors. They were singers, dancers and acrobats as well as orators, and their theatre mixed spectacle and poetry, pantomime, history and melodrama, ballads, jigs and processions, together with arias of verse and set-pieces of comic cross-talk. Although they worked, for the most part, in the public playhouses, on bare, wide platforms thrust deep into the audience, they were also used to acting on small 'private' stages by candlelight, or in the round at Whitehall before a royal gathering, or – on provincial tours – in guildhalls, inn-yards and banqueting halls.

Nobody can tell, for sure, exactly what Elizabethan actors did or just how good the best of them were: Hamlet's speech to the players, for instance, suggests that there was known to be room for improvement. But although they lacked the aids of a darkened auditorium, elaborate scenery and the picture-frame to concentrate the attention of their public, it seems as if they could, at their best, dominate the audience by presence, skill and technique. In gesture and speech their style in poetic drama would no doubt appear to us elaborate and formal, closer to opera than to the conversational compromises of contemporary naturalism. Yet they were accustomed to quick adjustments in scale, from rhetorical set-pieces to comic knockabout, and to wide-ranging characterization. There was living-space in the drama for legendary clowns like Tarleton and Kempe, whose counterparts in later ages were segregated in the pantomime or music hall. Under pressure of stage conditions Shakespeare's company used their voices and their bodies far more fully than contemporary actors are required to do, stretched as they were by the far-reaching ambitions of their authors and the flexibility of an open stage. They worked hard, very hard, with little time for rehearsal: they often played four or five parts in a day, and perhaps twenty in a week, for the company was small, the continually changing repertoire was large, and the dramatists felt no obligation to keep their characters or scenes to a workable economic minimum. They also worked together, for years, as a team. As a team, they were in charge of productions; as a team, they commissioned and published scripts; as a team, they shared the profits and organized the training of novices and the pensions of veterans. It was for them, as a team, that the greatest plays in the history of the drama were written.

Their London public was, proportionately, not only bigger but probably more representative of the nation, as a social cross-section, than at any other time in our history (excluding the public for Christmas pantomime in its heyday). When *King Lear* was written London playgoers numbered perhaps ten per cent of the population, then around 160,000, compared with around two per cent in Garrick's time, when it was about 60,000. When Shakespeare died in 1616 there were at least six playhouses devoted to the drama; but for nearly two centuries after the Puritans shut them down, the capital had to make do with half that number for a steadily growing population. Not until late Victorian times was there any approach in London to the intensity, depth and range of Elizabethan theatrical activity.

The acting fellowships, the public stages and their popular audiences did not return after the Restoration. The drama finally went indoors as the pleasure of a minority, at first largely run as a sport for the court, and then in the following century, increasingly, as an entertainment for the middle class. From 1660 onwards the actors were joined by actresses. Companies no longer worked as a team but as the employees of a manager (although the fellowship system lingered for generations among the ragged strollers of the provinces, the acting proletariat). The turnover of new plays dropped sharply, compared with the feverish productivity of Shakespearian days – Garrick, for instance, staged only seventy-five in twenty-nine years – but the turnover of parts, old and new, was still far higher than contemporary actors can contemplate: Garrick, again, had ninety-six roles in his repertoire.

From 1660 to 1860 English acting was generally empirical, swayed by a Quin or a Garrick, a Kemble or a Kean, a Macready or a Phelps, who were argued over as exponents of the ' classic ' or the ' natural ' approach. It usually reached its peaks in Shakespeare, however, ' improved ', bowdlerized and butchered. Its flexibility was inevitably limited by the frontiers of the repertoire and the conventions of the stage; and in tragedy there was a persistent tradition of sonorous, generalized declamation, a kind of incantatory formalism which was described at its tail-end as, among other things, ' the actor's Gregorian '. Serious acting was, on the lower slopes of the profession, identified with the ' poetry voice ' and the ' tragedy face ', a ponderous tread and statuesque attitude, putting voice and manner before truth and meaning.

For most of those two hundred years up to 1860 the British theatre was not noticeably concerned with such objectives as *ensemble* acting, historical consistency, psychological truth, visual unity, scenic realism or total illusion. Until the end of the eighteenth century, at least, actors wore pretty well what they liked – John Henderson boasted in the 1770s that he wore the same costume for ten successive roles – and often did what they liked when not actually standing to deliver. Players came to specialize in such stock lines of 'business' as First Old Man, Second Low Comedian and Singing Soubrette. Elderly juveniles were not unknown, as ageing leads struggled to hold on to roles acquired in their salad days. Big speeches were delivered at the front of the stage, where the candles were clustered at their brightest in the centre. Such incongruities were accepted as conventions – like the handful of canvas flats which served as décor, over and over again, in different productions.

During this period conditions of acting were influenced by such general trends as the dominant romanticism and theatricalism of the contemporary drama; the supremacy of verse; the slow and spasmodic progress towards historical accuracy and neo-realism in staging; the gradual retreat of the play behind the picture-frame arch, as the apron stage – which in Garrick's day still projected about a dozen feet into the audience – was whittled away; the change from candles to gas light, and to greater control of light in the auditorium as well as on the stage; the growth of 'minor' theatres in London, and of a chain of Theatres Royal outside it. One of the prime factors in conditioning acting style was the inflation of the 'patent' theatres, Drury Lane and Covent Garden (see page 25), to meet the demand of the growing metropolitan audience. Drury Lane trebled in size in fifty years; by 1800 both houses could seat over three thousand people. The bigger they grew, the less important was the 'straight' drama. Intimacy and subtlety became almost impossible. The legitimate actor had to mug harder, exaggerating speech and gesture, to project his performance across the vast space of these ornamental barns, which became increasingly dedicated to spectacular show business. The mechanical, ranting conventions of the pseudo-classic school were encouraged. A hallmark of the old tragedian was his resonant declamatory tone. As the dramatist

Tom Robertson wrote in the 1860s, ' The habit of addressing distant galleries gives a fearful distinctness to their utterance. They are terribly impartial to each letter of every word they utter . . .' By then a new generation of acting had emerged, with a style to match the smaller scale and greater realism of the drama, the reduced size of the playhouses, and the changing expectations of the audience . . .

David Garrick

In the flickering candlelight of a small, half-empty theatre in the East End of London, watched by a restless audience of periwigged playgoers, a short, dark and alert young man – wearing a temporary hump upon his shoulder – stepped out from the wings into history. Pulling his plum-coloured velvet robe about him, he limped across the strip of green baize cloth, six foot square, which was always laid down for the performance of tragedies, and took up his stand at the front of the stage. Fixing his bright and piercing eyes upon the backless benches in the pit, whose occupants still laughed and chattered, he launched into Gloucester's opening speech in *Richard III*.

> Now is the winter of our discontent
> Made glorious summer by this sun of York . . .

Soon the usual playhouse noise was hushed; the Monday night chill wore off; for this unknown young man was doing something which had never been seen before on the stage of Goodman's Fields or any other theatre in the year of grace 1741: he was acting a character in a classical play as if he were a contemporary person talking from experience.

The rebel player, like the original author, was not named upon the bills, where he was described as 'A Gentleman (Who never appeared on any Stage)'. Although this was not strictly accurate, for he had already acted at Ipswich that summer under a pseudonym and had made one secret appearance on this very stage in the mask and costume of a harlequin, this young man wearing Gloucester's hump had received no kind of training as an actor. He was a wine merchant of twenty-four, who had spent most of his life in the quiet cathedral town of Lichfield. At first the audience watched him in silence, astonished by his daring, but their enthusiasm mounted as the play went on. (Only half of it was by Shakespeare: the rest was supplied by Colley Cibber, whose 'improved' version held the stage for 150 years.) They were startled into applause by the passionate sincerity with which he courted Anne at her father-in-law's funeral, a scene 'thrown away' by the current favourites of the stage, but the turning-point of the evening came after Crookback dismissed the mayor and alderman and flung his prayer-book to the ground. More surprises followed: the fierce relish of Gloucester's 'Off with his head! So much for Buckingham!'; the 'rage and rapidity' of his outburst:

> The North! what do they in the North,
> When they should serve their sovereign in the West?;

his fear and terror in the tent-scene; and the agonies of his death after the desperate fight with Richmond. Instead of declaiming the verse in a thunderous, measured chant, this actor *spoke* it with swift and 'natural' changes of tone and emphasis. Instead of patrolling the boards with solemn pomp, treading heavily from pose to traditional pose, he moved quickly and gracefully. Instead of standing on his dignity and marbling his face into a tragedian's mask, his mobile features illustrated Richard's whole range of turbulent feelings. He seemed, indeed, to identify himself with the part. It was all so *real*. The next day the wine merchant wrote to his disapproving brother: 'Last Night I Play'd Richard the Third to the surprise of Every Body and as I shall make very near £300 per annum by it, and as it is really what I doat upon, I am resolv'd to pursue it.' The letter was signed D. Garrick.

There was no great crowd to see Garrick's début, on the historic night of 19 October, 1741. Débuts of stagestruck amateurs, announced anonymously in this way, were frequent and often disastrous. Although the evening's entertainment began at six, the play itself was presented 'gratis' in the interval of a 'a concert of vocal and instrumental music' (prices: one, two and three shillings). This was one of the many absurd evasions into which determined men were driven in the eighteenth century by the government's restrictions on theatrical enterprise. Only two London playhouses were then officially allowed to open during the season (from September to May): they were the 'patent

houses' of Covent Garden and Drury Lane, which enjoyed until
1843 a joint monopoly – by virtue of royal patents issued by
Charles II – over the drama of the spoken word. Around their
rivalry revolves the history of the pre-Victorian stage, yet all their
differences were forgotten at any challenge to their privilege; and
in 1741 they were soon obliged to recognize the challenge
delivered at Goodman's Fields. On that October night in Whitechapel a revolution had begun, unheralded but irresistible, with
this performance of *Richard III* – acted by an amateur, between
two parts of a musical concert, at a theatre without a licence, in
defiance of the law.

Within a few weeks David Garrick was the talk of London.
Hundreds were turned away from the little theatre every night. A
fashionable audience was often in its place by five o'clock, ready
to endure the legal camouflage of the concert for the sake of
seeing the new tragedian, and sometimes the stage itself was so
crowded with spectators that they blocked the view from the
boxes and the pit. Pope, who had given up playgoing, was one
of the many celebrities who made the expedition to the East End:
he came three times. 'That young man,' he said, 'never had his
equal, and will never have a rival.' Pitt avowed that this novice
from the Midlands was the best actor England had yet produced.
Although Thomas Gray was exaggerating when he wrote of 'a
dozen Dukes of a night at Goodman's Fields', peer after peer
invited the young actor to dinner, in the safe knowledge that in
spite of his calling he was a gentleman. 'I believe nobody (as an
Actor) was ever more carress'd,' wrote Garrick to his brother,
'and my Character as a private Man makes 'em more desirous of
my Company.' The enthusiasm was not unanimous, especially in
the green-rooms of Covent Garden and Drury Lane. James Quin,
the leading actor of the day, dismissed Garrick's popularity as a
merely modish novelty. 'Garrick,' he said contemptuously, 'is a
new religion; the people follow him as another Whitfield, but
they will soon return to church again.' To this, the newcomer
replied in rhyme:

> When Doctrines meet with general approbation,
> It is not Heresy, but Reformation.

History – and the audience – were on Garrick's side: reformation
seemed long overdue. 'If the young fellow is right,' Quin

26

announced, ' I and the rest of the players have been all wrong.'
That, in fact, was the verdict of the town, and of posterity.
Although this triumphant Richard was only the first sketch of a
great performance, although ' the young fellow ' was without training or experience, he leapt at once to the top of the profession.

Offstage, David Garrick was a man of uncommonly complex
temperament and physical grace. A born mimic, he could – and
would – act at the drop of a hat: by nature both cautious and
mercurial, shrewd and generous, something of a chameleon in his
very gregarious social life, he excelled as both artist and admini-
strator. Agile and light in build, he was only five feet four in
height, with small hands and feet, and unusual muscular control.
His firm chin, big broad nose, expressive mouth and dark, piercing, lustrous eyes were set in a round and somewhat heavy face.
His light tenor voice, of notable sweetness, was at the time of his
début perhaps still coloured by the accent of his Midland home.
He was born in Hereford, on 19 February, 1717, while his father
– an officer in the dragoons – was on a recruiting campaign; and
he was brought up in the garrison-cathedral town of Lichfield,
to which Captain Peter Garrick retired for some years on half-
pay. On neither side of the family were there stage connections.
Too much should not be made of the ' typically French ' build of
David and his brother George, yet some credit for the actor's
un-English mobility of features and eloquence of gesture may
perhaps be taken by his grandfather, a Huguenot who fled to
England when the Edict of Nantes was revoked. With six brothers
and sisters, David enjoyed a childhood which was – unlike that of
many famous players – apparently happy and secure, emotionally
if not financially. His parents found it difficult to make ends
meet and to keep up appearances, but they clung firmly to their
gentility, and Garrick later set great store by his status as a
gentleman's son. When he first began to act the stage was still
socially beyond the pale, yet Captain Peter's training as a gentlemen helped him not only to establish his authority in the theatre
but also to wield an influence outside it.

When he was fourteen, economic pressures at home became so
severe that his father rejoined his old regiment on full pay and
went off to Gibraltar, where he remained for five years, leaving
David as the virtual head of the family. During the crucial years

of his growth into manhood, the ' English Roscius ' was thus plunged into both freedoms and responsibilities of unusual scope. In spite of the separation from his well-loved father, in spite of the genteel poverty of their life in Lichfield, and in spite of the drudgery of the local grammar school, Garrick seems to have made the most of his adolescence. Witty and charming even as a boy, he was so much of a favourite with the officers of the Lichfield garrison, so the legend goes, that they sometimes took him to London on visits to the theatre, and on his return he would keep them amused for weeks with his imitations of Cibber, Quin and the other stars of the day, for he was already an acute mimic with remarkable powers of memory and observation.

Stage-struck from an early age, Garrick was among the first in the house whenever the strolling players came to Lichfield. This hobby was shared by the tall, ugly son of the bookseller Michael Johnson. While David Garrick dreamed of being an actor, Samuel Johnson – seven years his senior – laboriously planned a tragedy in blank verse. It was to Johnson that Garrick was sent to learn Greek and Latin, at his ill-fated ' private academy ' in the nearby village of Edial. When Captain Garrick came home in 1736, he resolved that David should settle down and take life seriously. He must be a lawyer. But first of all, the young man needed coaching, for he had learned little enough at the grammar school or at Edial, and so he was sent in 1737 to Rochester, where he was to imbibe ' mathematics, philosophy and humane learning'. Samuel Johnson, his companion on the road, went to London to sell his tragedy and make his fortune. Within a few years these two ill-assorted provincials from Lichfield climbed to the commanding heights of contemporary culture.

After a year at Rochester Garrick came of age, inherited a thousand pounds from his Lisbon uncle, and gave up all pretence of studying for the law. With his brother Peter, who had inherited a small sum from their father (he had died a few weeks after David left Lichfield) he decided to go into the wine trade. They rented premises off the Strand in Durham Yard, and while Peter stayed in Lichfield, David acted as London representative. He could scarcely have picked a better way of indulging his hobby, even if at first he did not set out deliberately to train himself for the stage. Among the main sources of custom for a wine merchant were the coffee-houses, then the centres of male social life in a

small, compact metropolitan culture. The best coffee-houses were
across the Strand from Garrick's office, in the neighbourhood of
Covent Garden; and Covent Garden was the heart of the theatre
world, for most of the actors lived in the surrounding streets, a
few minutes from their work in the two ' patent houses ' nearby.
Garrick soon became known as a good companion, even if he was
not a good salesman. These were his years of apprenticeship:
watching histrionic form at Covent Garden and Drury Lane,
joining in the post-mortems next morning over coffee, eaves-
dropping on backstage gossip, observing the passing show. He
studied the methods of actors and dramatists, and assiduously
practised the writing of plays and prologues. At that time, and
for over a century to come, an evening at the theatre included
at least one farce, ballet, pantomime, or other ' after-piece ', as
well as the main five-act tragedy or comedy, and throughout the
season the programme was changed from night to night. There
were no ' long runs '. New plays did well if they were staged nine
times in their first season, but if successful they remained in the
repertoire of both theatres for years to come. Nor were there
frequent changes of cast: supporting actors often stayed in the
service of the Lane or the Garden for over twenty years, and stars
continued to appear in their early successes long after they had
outlived them.

In the spring of 1740 Garrick had the pleasure of seeing his
comic sketch *Lethe* on the stage of Drury Lane. It was produced
on a benefit night – that is to say, one of the nights towards the
end of the season given up to a particular player or group of
players, who received all the box-office takings minus the nightly
house charge (the manager's estimate of the running costs). This
was a recognized form of salary supplement which persisted for
over a century, although it was sometimes known to result not
in a bonus but a loss. On the occasion of *Lethe*'s premiere it was
the benefit of Henry Giffard, an Irish friend of Garrick who
owned the new little theatre in Goodman's Fields (then closed
under the Licensing Act of 1737). Another Irish friend was
Charles Macklin, a noisy, belligerent actor who helped to clarify
Garrick's own ideas by his harangues on the decline of the theatre,
his programme of reform, and his revolutionary performance of
Shylock, eight months before Garrick's own début at Giffard's
theatre. For forty years *The Merchant of Venice* had been repre-

sented by a version in which Shylock appeared as a comic buffoon, with the red wig and ill-fitting clothes of the stage clown; but Macklin persuaded Charles Fleetwood, manager of Drury Lane, to revive most of the original Shakespearian play, and he himself, dressed in the red hat and black gaberdine of Venetian Jews in the sixteenth century, acted the character with savage pathos and villainy. The triumphant success of Macklin's performance (which he repeated for some fifty years) may be said to prefigure the advent of Garrick. For Macklin not only brought Shylock to life: he challenged those conventions of contemporary acting which Garrick was, in his own performances, to destroy.

Until Macklin's Shylock and Garrick's Crookback burst upon the stage in 1741, English ' serious ' acting was dominated by the fossilized style accredited to the great Restoration player Thomas Betterton – a formalized, rhetorical and statuesque mode of stage behaviour, in which manner was all, and the means had become confused with the end of playing. Energy, emotion and passion were suppressed as vulgar; an elaborately artificial code of expression (or ' *Theatric* way of speaking ') was confused with ' classical ' art; and actors stood tiptoe on their dignity throughout the play. With deep solemnity, tall plumes of feathers nodding above their periwigs (traditional head-dress of the tragic hero), Quin and Cibber moved into stereotyped attitudes and boomed out the verse with predictable sonorities (Macklin was dismissed from Covent Garden for refusing to talk in what he called ' the hoity-toity tone '). As Dr Johnson wrote, some years later:

> From bard to bard the frigid caution crept,
> Till declamation roared, while passion slept.

Garrick explained to a friend that ' when first setting out in the Business of an Actor ' he ' endeavour'd to shake off the Fetters of Numbers . . . I hate your Roarers '. At its best when applied to stage heroes in the pseudo-Roman mould, such as Addison's Cato, this technique reduced other characters to a common measure of ' dead, insipid pomp ', stifling individual truth with generalized grandeur. Yet the burly Quin, for one, was clearly an actor of talent and power, particularly in comedy, and even as Macbeth – one of the roles in which his ' method ' was least congruous – he won high praise from Garrick himself. That is one reason why ' little Davy ' chose so well for his début at Goodman's Fields, after careful discussions with Macklin and other friends. Not only was the role of Crookback well suited to his height, but – especially as corrupted by Colley Cibber – it gave Garrick a fine opportunity to show off the very qualities in which he surpassed the old guard: emotional range, expressive facial by-play, variety in speech, intensity and unity in characterization. One critic noted with surprised approval, in 1741, that: 'When three or four are on the stage with him, he is attentive to whatever is spoke, and never drops his character when he has finished a speech, by either looking contemptuously on an inferior performer, unnecessary spitting, or suffering his eyes to wander through the whole circle of spectators ' – a revealing comment on current practice among the stars.

Not only did Garrick establish his dominion in tragedy, during that first astonishing season of 1741, but he showed his skill in comedy, too; and here there was equal need of reform. Although Garrick shocked and dismayed many admirers of his Crookback by ' condescending ' to such parts as Costar Pearmain in *The Recruiting Officer* and Lord Foppington in *The Careless Husband*, the subtlety, grace, and realism which he brought to them seemed no less remarkable than the merits of his tragic acting. Only one of these roles – Bayes in the Duke of Buckingham's *The Rehearsal* – remained in Garrick's repertoire in later years, but they demonstrated at once that he was a great all-rounder. As Bayes, his excellence lay partly in the complete solemnity with which he played this jackass author (hitherto acted in broad, grinning caricature), and partly in the mimicry with which he had once delighted the Lichfield garrison. In the scene where Bayes coaches the players in a rehearsal of his own tragedy, Garrick burlesqued the leading actors of the day – Quin, Delane and Ryan – ridiculing with exact detail their sing-song voices, their heavy tread, their clumsy and deliberate gesture (Quin moved his arms, it is said, as if he were heaving ballast into the hold of a ship). This was a part of Garrick's frontal attack on the acting values of his time, in order to make way for his own brand of theatrical truth, and although he later dropped these imitations at the insistence of the indignant victims, his sabotage had already been successfully completed, as far as his own acceptance was concerned. When Garrick's first season at Goodman's Fields ended in May 1742, he had acted nearly twenty characters and had given about 150 performances, appearing almost every night (including Christmas Day). Never again did he act so much, for so little reward: within a few months, his salary rose from six guineas a week to the five hundred guineas which Fleetwood paid him to appear at Drury Lane the following season – the highest salary yet earned by an actor. (After Garrick left, Giffard's little theatre in Whitechapel never opened its doors again: the ' patent houses ' made sure of that.)

During the next five years, Garrick increased his reputation, widening his repertoire and his technique, in both London and Dublin (then the favourite summer rendezvous of stars from Drury Lane and Covent Garden). The old and new styles were on view at the opposing houses, and in the London season of 1746-7 they were actually seen together upon the same stage, when Garrick and Quin agreed to share the honours at Covent Garden. Each played his best roles in friendly rivalry, watched by an audience which followed acting form and admired technical display, applauding 'points ' and effects with the kind of eager partisanship now more noticeable at a football match or a jazz concert. Although Quin's supporters rallied to his Cato, and his Falstaff triumphed over Garrick's weak Hotspur, the theatre was half-empty when he rashly tried *Richard III;* and there was little doubt of the winner in this strange contest on that memorable evening when both men acted together in Rowe's *The Fair Penitent*. In the opposing roles of Lothario, the gay amorist, and Horatio, the noble-hearted husband whom he wronged, Garrick and Quin dramatically illustrated the clash between their generations. The playwright Richard Cumberland wrote of Quin many years later:

> With very little variation of cadence, and in a deep full tone, accompanied by a sawing kind of action which had more of the senate than of the stage in it, he rolled out his heroics with an air of dignified indifference . . . When, after a long and eager expectation, I first beheld little Garrick, then young and light and active in every muscle and feature, come bounding on the stage – heavens, what a transition! It seemed as if a whole century had been stepped over in the transition of a single scene.

This Covent Garden season, which included some of Garrick's most famous roles in comedy and tragedy, confirmed his leadership as an actor; and before it ended, he signed an agreement which put him into power as a manager. In partnership with James Lacy, at an immediate cost of £8,000, Garrick became master of his own theatre and monarch of the English stage, after only five years in the profession. (The full price was £12,000: for this Garrick would receive £500 a year, share the profits, and be paid 500 guineas for his acting.) His home was Drury Lane – a musty, intimate, square-shaped old theatre, still much as it was when designed by Sir Christopher Wren in 1664. It held about 1,260 until 1762, when its capacity was nearly doubled; and in 1775 it was redesigned by the Adam brothers. Its ' apron ' stage projected about thirteen feet into the auditorium, which on good nights was filled with a restless, noisy and at times belligerent crowd of all classes in boxes, pit and galleries. Garrick's big scenes were played upon this apron with the audience around him, and not behind the picture frame of the proscenium arch. Until 1765 light came from seventy-two candles, in six large chandeliers above his head, and from a row of footlights or floats. After 1765 he abolished the chandeliers, introduced – under French influence – side-wing lights, and improved the footlights. Candlelight also illuminated the auditorium at full strength (such as it was) throughout the performance: not until over a century later was the house darkened during the play; yet, by modern standards, Garrick's audience endured a kind of hot, stuffy and murky twilight, for the candles might be said to give more heat than light and ate up the oxygen greedily. In this theatre, moreover, there was no attempt at realism in scenery, properties or costumes, for the audience was interested in the display of technique rather than in the hypnosis of illusion. The lack of those aids which the modern player takes for granted makes all the more notable Garrick's long dominion not only over their minds but also over their emotions.

Garrick remained supreme at Drury Lane for nearly thirty years, as successful in management as in acting. In his private life, too, he achieved a lasting partnership. After a stormy three years with one of his leading ladies, Peg Woffington, in 1749 he married a young Viennese dancer, Eva Maria Veigel, known on the stage as Mlle. Violette. Having given up her career for love, Mrs Garrick settled down in a remarkably happy and peaceful marriage, which endured until her husband's death. Rich, happy and eminently respectable, the darling of all classes and the leader of the stage, Garrick took the fortunes of Drury Lane and the prestige of the whole theatre to unprecedented heights. ' He raised the character of the profession,' as Burke said, ' to the rank of a liberal art.'

To keep on his pinnacle was no sinecure. Other actors – Mossop, Powell, Barry, Henderson – threatened his place as the first player: his most famous duel occurred in 1750, when he played Romeo for twelve consecutive nights against Barry at Covent Garden, and in spite of his physical handicaps as a stage lover almost equalled the impact of his more handsome and romantic rival. Violent riots broke out when the audience took arms against some of his stage reforms and his ' foreign ' novelties. Discontented players and frustrated playwrights conducted a spasmodic resistance movement against his rule, in pamphlets, newspapers and whispering campaigns. There were feuds, intrigues and betrayals. His old friend Macklin became one of his most relentless critics. He was charged with being a miser, a bully, a hypocrite, with writing most of his own favourite notices and bribing the authors of the others, with ruining the chances of other artists. As anyone who wanted to make his way as an actor or an author depended upon either Drury Lane or Covent Garden, it is scarcely surprising if the actor-manager of one theatre for so many years was the focus of so much resentment, contempt, and envy; and his vanity, evasiveness and snobbery supplied his many enemies with ammunition. His unpopularity in some sections of his profession was increased by his preference for the company of writers, painters, and, above all, peers. Garrick dearly loved a lord. Some of his happiest hours were spent at Chatsworth and other great country houses, writing verse to his hosts, entertaining them with the kind of witty small talk in which he was so proficient, and doing his party pieces – notably, the dagger scene from *Macbeth*, Hamlet's ' start ' at seeing the ghost, and the madness of King Lear. Yet although he may have chased, he was also pursued. In admitting him to dinner, his aristocratic admirers prepared the way for a recognition of the fact that his less captivating colleagues also had human rights. Their patronage, and what was more, their friendship, not only flattered ' little Davy's ' abounding vanity (the life force of most actors), but also helped him to keep the English theatre in health and high esteem. ' Inimitable Shakespeare! but more matchless

Garrick!' wrote the Earl of Chatham. 'Always as deep in Nature as the Poet, but never (what the Poet is too often) out of it.'

To be fashionable for thirty years (with an occasional un-modish interregnum) demands greater powers than a talent for bribing the press and toadying to the nobility. Garrick was, first of all, a shrewd and resourceful manager, adept in compromise, alert to the demands of the box-office, but always insisting upon high standards of production and performance. From his first Drury Lane season onwards, he demanded stricter attendance at rehearsals and sharper attention to discipline and work. He paid more heed to casting and to unity of style than was common in the eighteenth century, supervising two generations in the 'natural' acting with which he had ousted the 'formal' style of Quin and Cibber. 'I have seen you, with your magical hammer in your hand,' wrote the actress Kitty Clive to him, thirty years later, '*endeavouring* to beat your ideas into the heads of creatures who had none of their own . . .' Yet unlike some stars of later days, he did not surround himself with mediocrities to make his own light shine more brightly. As a good manager, Garrick had the shrewdness to engage the best talent available, which included such artists as Barry, Woodward, King, Shuter, Parsons, Weston, Powell and Bensley, with Mesdames Pritchard, Clive, Cibber, Woffington, Yates, Pope, Abington, and – not least – Siddons. He trained two generations of actors, many of whom went out to build and run new theatres in the provinces. His own appearances were carefully rationed: during his last decade at the Lane he acted only some twenty times a season, instead of the centuries he scored in early years.

Garrick also attempted, with some success, to reform the manners of the audience. In his first season he showed his mettle by banning visitors backstage during the performance (unsolicited callers in green-rooms and dressing-rooms, not to mention the knots of spectators in the wings, had been a considerable nuisance for many years), and by requiring the occupiers of boxes to pay as they came in (it had been a popular amusement of young bloods to dodge payment at the end of the first act by playing hide and seek round the theatre). Some years later he succeeded, despite hooligan protests, in clearing the stage on benefit nights, when the player's friends took their places on tiers of wooden benches behind the actors; but he failed to stop the practice of allowing people in at half price after the third act of the main production. Here, as in other things, Garrick had to move cautiously, for actors were still treated as servants of the public, and signs of insubordination were sometimes punished by violent demonstrations among the audience.

Again, although Garrick was unconcerned about historical accuracy or unity of effect in dress and scenery, he took pains to provide rich spectacle and costumes, and introduced many improvements in stage lighting and effects. After 1765 both the auditorium and the stage of Drury Lane were illuminated much more clearly and evenly. He improved the comfort and appearance of the house, and increased the size of the company to over a hundred performers. Within a few years the nightly running costs jumped from £60 to £90, without a corresponding rise in the price of seats, yet Drury Lane continued to flourish. Pantomimes and after-pieces kept the treasury full. For staging such entertainments Garrick has often been attacked, yet he himself explained the situation once and for all in the prologue by Dr Johnson which introduced his first season at Drury Lane:

> The drama's laws, the drama's patrons give,
> For we that live to please, must please, to live.

In Garrick's time, the majority of the drama's patrons wanted pantomime, spectacle, and farce: to keep his theatre open, he gave them what they wanted. It was his duty – and his pleasure. The profits were used to finance his productions of Shakespeare and other dramatists, old and new. Here, too, Garrick comes under heavy fire, for his crass ' improvements ' of *Hamlet, The Winter's Tale, A Midsummer Night's Dream, King Lear* and many other plays. As Romeo, he woke up Juliet in the tomb: ' Bless me! how cold it is,' she observed, in awakening; and he wrote in some sixty-five lines such as these for Romeo:

> 'Twixt death and life I'm torn, I am distracted:
> But death is strongest.

(This ' improvement ' endured on the stage till the 1880s.) He cut the rude mechanicals and the love scenes of the young Athenians in *The Dream;* he cut the first three acts of *The Winter's Tale;* he cut the graveyard scene and the fencing match from *Hamlet*. (' Rubbish ', he called it.) Instead, Hamlet suddenly stabs Claudius, the queen dies of a seizure off-stage, Laertes stabs Hamlet, and – with the Prince's blessing – remains alive to share the government of Denmark with Horatio. It may be hard for us to understand or forgive a man who sliced and mangled some of the greatest plays ever written, substituting his own pedestrian verse for Shakespeare's superb poetry, while declaring:

> 'Tis my chief wish, my joy, my only plan
> To lose no drop of that immortal man.

Yet Garrick was a man of his age. Actors are probably shackled more securely to the values of their time than any other artists. And until recent times all actors have shown the same calm but by no means ignorant assurance that they know better than Shakespeare what their public will accept. Thanks to Garrick's genius as an actor, and his understanding of his audience, a surprisingly large amount of the work of 'that immortal man' was kept alive on the English stage.

When Garrick retired in 1776, having sold Drury Lane to Sheridan for £35,000, he was still at the height of his popularity. Three years later he died. He was buried in Westminster Abbey, with five peers among the pall-bearers, and posterity has kept his memory bright ever since. If, as Dr Johnson sneered, 'more pains have been taken to spoil the fellow than if he had been heir-apparent to the Emperor of India'; if 'little Davy's' name is remembered when so many of his renowned contemporaries in politics, war, religion and literature have been lost in oblivion; then there is good reason – and the best reason of all, of course, was his acting.

In 1761 Sir Joshua Reynolds painted his friend Garrick standing, undecided, 'between tragedy and comedy'; he was, as Dr Johnson once acknowledged, 'a master' in both; no other English actor (with the possible exception of Betterton) has been in the same position, and no other (except, perhaps, for Olivier) has equalled the width of Garrick's range, in light and broad comedy, 'juvenile lead' and 'character part', romantic drama and Shakespearian tragedy. Although he was overwhelmed with manuscripts from aspiring playwrights during his long managerial career, and although he staged some seventy-five new plays (excluding after-pieces) in twenty-nine years, few provided him with good acting parts in either tragedy or comedy, and none allowed him to exercise his full powers. He turned continually to the drama of the past, often altering the stock pieces of the repertoire without scruple, and on occasion he wrote the plays himself (in all, twenty-one pieces). As an author Garrick had a flair for plagiarism, borrowing situations from other men's plays, fitting stock roles to his colleagues and himself, and editing the result into a vehicle for their talents. The gouty old Lord Chalkstone, in his own *Lethe*, was one of his most popular 'character' parts: he kept it in the repertoire for twenty-four years. Another was Fribble in *Miss in her Teens*, which he adapted from a Parisian success. Exploiting his own littleness, as in *The Rehearsal*, by perching a hat that was much too small for him on top of his wig, he presented Fribble as a mincing, effeminate dandy, a familiar species in the coffee-houses of Covent Garden. ' Naturally monkeyish ', as one critic phrased it, he is said to have imitated eleven men of fashion so distinctly that each victim recognized his reflection on the stage. Helped by Harry Woodward's Captain Flash, Garrick made *Miss in her Teens* a box-office hit in the Covent Garden season of 1746-7. Garrick always excelled as a romantic amorist in the comedy of manners, and in that same season he introduced one of the most successful portraits in this gallery – Ranger in Dr Benjamin Hoadly's *The Suspicious Husband*, a well-made comedy of intrigue which retained its popularity on the stage until mid-Victorian times. ' It is one of the few *living* comedies,' wrote Percy Fitzgerald in 1868, ' is written with extraordinary animation and reads now almost as freshly as on the day it appeared.' Ranger, a somewhat chaster heir of the Restoration rakes, is an amorous law student of inexhaustible effrontery and appetite (' as every woman, who is young, is capable of love, I am very reasonably in love with every woman I meet '). To him a rope ladder at a bedroom window is a challenge (which the author gives him plenty of scope for meeting), but although he does his frank best to seduce three young ladies, virtue triumphs in the end and Ranger's own honest heart is pinned firmly on to his sleeve. This gave Garrick an excellent opportunity to relax in his own personality, exerting his infectious gusto and radiant charm in the kind of lightweight role with which some modern actors make their one pigeon-holed reputation.

In a different kind is Sir John Brute, the bullying drunkard of Vanbrugh's *The Provok'd Wife,* a part in which Garrick successfully challenged Quin's much coarser and broader study. In his most riotous excesses, he was still a gentleman. This is how he appeared to G. C. Lichtenberg, an Austrian visitor, who saw Garrick in 1775:

In the beginning, his wig is quite straight, so that his face is full and round. Then he comes home excessively drunk, and looks like the moon a few days before its last quarter, almost half his face being covered by his wig; the part that is still visible is, indeed, somewhat bloody and shining with perspiration, but has so extremely amiable an air as to compensate for the loss of the other part. His waistcoat is open from top to bottom, his stockings full of wrinkles, with the garters hanging down, and, moreover – which is vastly strange – two kinds of garters . . . In this lamentable condition he enters the room where his wife is, and in answer to her anxious enquiries as to what is the matter with him (and she has good reason for inquiring) he, collecting his wits, answers: ' Wife, as well as a fish in the water '; he does not, however, move away from the doorpost, against which he leans as closely as if he wanted to rub his back. Then he again breaks into coarse talk, and suddenly becomes so wise and merry in his cups that the whole audience bursts into a tumult of applause. I was filled with amazement at the scene where he falls asleep. The way in which, with shut eyes, swimming head, and pallid cheeks, he quarrels with his wife, and, uttering a sound where ' r ' and ' l ' are blended, now appears to abuse her, and then to enunciate in thick tones moral precepts, to which he himself forms the most horrible contradiction; his manner, also, of moving his lips, so that one cannot tell whether he is chewing, tasting, or speaking: all this, in truth, as far exceeded my expectations as anything I have seen of this man.

In another popular scene the drunken Sir John attacks the watch, in women's clothes, and it was in this costume that Garrick later sat to Zoffany, the famous painter of theatrical portraits and conversation pieces, wearing a lace cap with pink ribbons and a yellow satin brocaded dress.

Zoffany also painted Garrick in what was perhaps the most famous of all his comic roles – the small part of Abel Drugger, the oafish tobacconist's apprentice in *The Tobacconist,* his own version of Ben Jonson's *The Alchemist.* He had studied this almost as carefully as he did the Prince of Denmark, giving private rehearsals in the presence of such friends as Macklin before he brought the character to Drury Lane in 1744. With the brown shock-haired wig and grubby smock, Garrick seemed to assume the identity of this knowing simpleton, wiping his own personality clear of its authority, grace and intelligence, and wearing a vacant stare as if it were his natural expression. His predecessor in the Jonson role, Theophilus Cibber, had made a stock buffoon of Drugger; his contemporary, Thomas Weston, presented 'a comic face of stupid awe and petrified astonishment, which excited universal mirth by its stolidity'; but Garrick let his face record a flood of feelings, in a *tour de force* of by-play and mime. When this Drugger first spoke to the tricksters Face and Subtle, said one witness, his face seemed 'all caution; timorous, stammering and inexpressible'; and then, as Subtle examined his chin, teeth and little finger for auguries, his features mutely expressed, in eloquent succession, fear, greed, vanity, delight, hope and simplicity. Again, when the mock-astrologers spelled out the name of Abel Drugger in the stars as the name of a man who would be great, Garrick made him 'keep his joy to himself, for to blurt it out before everyone would be lacking in decency. So Garrick turns aside, hugging his delight to himself for a few moments, so that he actually gets those red rings round his eyes which often accompany great joy, at least when violently suppressed, and says to himself: "That is my name." The effect of this judicious restraint is indescribable, for one did not see him merely as a simpleton being gulled, but as a much more ridiculous creature, with an air of secret triumph, thinking himself the slyest of rogues.' Whether Jonson intended that effect or not (he did not write the line concerned), there was no doubt of Drugger's popularity. Fanny Burney, who saw Garrick in this role after watching his Lear, wrote at a later date: 'Never could I have imagined such a metamorphose as I saw, the extreme meanness, the vulgarity, the low wit, the vacancy of countenance, the appearance of *unlicked nature* in all his motions.' The same note is struck by the actor-dramatist, Arthur Murphy: 'He represented the tobacco-boy in the truest comic style: no grimace, no starting, no wild gesticulation. He seemed to be a new man.' Here was an example of that transubstantiation which marks one kind of greatness in acting: the visible erasure of one identity by another, the radical change of being. Weston, whom some

people thought to equal Garrick in the role, was funny in himself,
'one of the drollest creatures on whom I have ever set eyes,' said
Lichtenberg. As soon as he appeared, in whatever role he played,
he set the house in a roar. But it was always the same joke: the
rich absurdity of being Weston. Garrick was a different man
every time.

In ' serious ' drama Garrick had a superb gift for pathos, excel-
ling as a victim and a repentant sinner. Persecuted and harried to
death, he brought tears to eighteenth-century eyes for thirty years
by his sufferings on the stage. In blackface he triumphed as
Oronooko, the noble savage in captivity who gave his name to
Thomas Southerne's play, and he also appeared as Osmyn, the
no less noble Moor in captivity from Congreve's *Mourning
Bride*. Other roles included Jaffier, the half-hearted revolutionary
in Otway's *Venice Preserv'd* (an actor's favourite for some two
hundred years); Chamont, the romantic avenger of the same
author's *The Orphan; Hastings in Rowe's Jane Shore;* Beverley,
the doomed hero of Edward Moore's *The Gamester;* and old
Lusignan in *Zara,* adapted by Aaron Hill from Voltaire. Yet it
was, of course, in Shakespeare that Garrick scored his greatest
triumphs. Benedick was his only role in Shakespearian comedy;
he failed as Antony, Hotspur and Othello; he was somewhat miscast as Romeo (which he played till he was forty-four, although
his technique outside the love scenes made it one of his most
popular parts); but as Macbeth, as Hamlet and as Lear he was
acclaimed as the best actor of his age.

With the century's disregard of historical accuracy, he appeared
as Macbeth in the scarlet coat of an officer in the army of George
II, with a wig, a silver-laced waistcoat, and breeches of contemporary cut – the Thane of Glamis in modern dress. He retained
the singing witches and dancing furies with which Sir William
Davenant had turned the play into a melodramatic Restoration
pantomime (although instead of ' flying ' them, he kept them
grounded), and he wrote in a long dying speech, borrowing from
Marlowe's *Faustus,* in order to give himself scope for some of his
favourite effects. Yet this *Macbeth* was first billed ' as written by
Shakespeare ', and was indeed closer to the original than any
version staged since the Restoration. It was also probably better
acted – when Mrs Pritchard appeared with Garrick – than at any
time in the play's history. Quin had played the first two acts in his

best blustering style, but after that his performance seems to have collapsed and the play itself was thought to be responsible. It was left to Garrick to show, even in this tailored draft, the pity, horror and poetry of the rest. Some critics found him too melancholy, with ' an excessive dejectedness of mind ', in present-ing Macbeth's guilt. Yet few were unmoved in the dagger scene. As Macbeth stared at the vision, his face seemed to blanch and contract with terror, giving the audience a ' sense of real *seeing* '. After the murder, with the real dagger in his bloody hands, ' he was absolutely scared out of his senses; he looked like a ghastly spectacle, and his complexion grew whiter every moment, till at length, his conscience stung and pierced to the quick, he said in a tone of wild despair:

> Will all great Neptune's ocean wash this blood
> Clean from my hand . . .'

In the banquet scene one night, so the story goes, when Garrick came to the line ' There's blood upon thy face ', he spoke it with such urgency and looked so intently at the first murderer that the actor put his hand to his face with a start and said: ' Is there, by God! ' When the ghost of Banquo rose, said an admiring observer, ' how repeatedly astonishing [was] his transition, from the placidly merry to the tremendously horrific! ' He died on-stage, and Noverre, the great French dancer, testified to the effect:

The approach of death showed each instant on his face: his eyes became dim; his voice could not support the effort he made to speak his thoughts. His gestures, without losing their expression, revealed the approach of his last moment; his legs gave way under him, his face lengthened, his pale and livid features have the signs of suffering and repentance. At last, he fell . . . he clawed the ground and seemed to be digging his own grave, but the dread moment was nigh . . . The death rattle and the convulsive movements of the features, arms and breast, gave the final touch to this terrible picture.

It was in rapid transitions and graduations of feeling and facial expression that Garrick particularly scored, and Drury Lane was small enough for the audience to see every phase of his facial play. ' He falls from fury into tears with a breath; and is pure and entire in both sensations.' Never was this power more strik-ingly exemplified, perhaps, than in *King Lear*. He himself thought this ' the finest tragedy ', although much of what he admired was the work not of William Shakespeare but of Nahum Tate, whose version held the stage for over 150 years. In this *King Lear* there is no Fool or King of France: Edgar and Cordelia marry and become co-monarchs of the realm; Gloucester and Lear survive in a comfortably happy ending. One of Garrick's great moments, indeed, was in his stage battle with the ruffians who try to murder Lear and Cordelia: his face glowed with exultation which, a moment later, faded into the fatigue of old age. Even in print, Shakespeare's original shocked Dr Johnson to the core, and would have been unthinkable on the stage. Cordelia's death made demands which eighteenth-century playgoers would not accept. Like the poetry, the agony of *King Lear* was thought to be primitive and irregular. Both needed levelling and improvement by more civilized minds. But even with the terror and the pity so carefully diluted, Tate's *King Lear* – as played by Garrick – harrowed the house. Actors and spectators wept freely. Boswell, for instance, shed ' abundance of tears '. At one performance even a soldier on duty (for many years two redcoats stood guard beside the stage every night) was seen to break down and weep. In eighteenth-century England, with all its worship of the golden mean, it was not thought ' common ' to reveal your feelings; and emotions, in the theatre at least, seemed much more inflammable than in the neutral audience of today.

Garrick first took on the role at Goodman's Fields at the age of twenty-four, and it became one of his most popular performances in tragedy from the beginning of his regime at Drury Lane. He wore a grey and rather fluffy wig, but allowed no beard to mask his facial by-play, unhampered by an excess of ' old man ' make-up. He walked with a crutch, and appeared in virtually modern dress, with the ermine-trimmed coat which was prescribed for most stage kings. ' I never see him coming down from one corner of the stage, with his old grey hair standing, as it were, erect upon his head, his face filled with horror and attention, his hands expanded, and his whole frame actuated by a dreary solemnity,' wrote one playgoer, ' but I am astounded, and share in all his distresses; one might interpret from the dumbness of his gesture.' One of his great moments was the curse on Goneril. Flinging away his crutch, he fell suddenly on to one knee, stretched out his arms, clenched his fists, threw back his head, and began to speak – trembling with anger in ' a broken, inward, struggling utterance ' – with increasing speed and volume and ' such a combination of painful, enraged feelings, as scarce any countenance but his own could describe '. ' It seemed,' said Macklin, ' to electrify the audience with horror ', till he ended in a burst of tears. Garrick had full command of pathos, too: not only in the final scene did he draw the audience's tears, with:

> Do not laugh at me,
> For as I am a man I think that lady
> To be my child Cordelia.

and:

> Did I not, fellow?

but also, less aptly, in such speeches as:

> I will do such things –
> What they are I know not . . .

And the Tate version gave him a triumphantly happy ending with:

> Old Lear shall be a king again,

a cry in rapture which, it seems, usually brought the house down. It was in Lear's madness, however, that Garrick excelled. ' He had no sudden starts, no violent gesticulation,' wrote Arthur Murphy, ' his movements were slow and feeble, misery was depicted in his countenance; he moved his head in the most deliberate manner; his eyes were fixed, or, if they turned to any one near him, he made a pause, and fixed his look on the person after much delay; his features at the same time telling what he was going to say before he uttered a word. During the whole time he presented a sight of woe and misery, and a total alienation of mind from every idea, but that of his unkind daughters.'

From contemporary evidence, Garrick appears to have tackled the problems facing the actor of this great role – the combination of age and strength, pathos and terror, madness and reason – by emphasizing the weakness, tearfulness, feebleness of the king, with the indispensable help of Nahum Tate in scaling down Lear's size: ' a little, old, white-haired man . . . with spindle-shanks, a tottering gait, and great shoes upon his little feet.' He showed, another admirer noted, ' in the very whirlwind of passion and of madness, such an exact attention to propriety, that it is still the passion and the madness of a king.' Garrick's tall and handsome rival, Spranger Barry, also exhibited a regal dignity in the role, together with the gift of pathos that helped to make him so great a favourite; but in the words of a contemporary wit:

> A king – ay, every inch a king,
> Such Barry doth appear;
> But Garrick's quite a different thing,
> He's every inch King Lear.

The third (and most popular) of Garrick's major Shakespearian successes was Hamlet. He dressed, during the early part of his career, in a simple, black contemporary suit, with a plain neck-cloth, so that the Prince of Denmark looked something like an English parson; but the actor later preferred less austere contemporary attire, a court suit of black velvet. Although there were frequent corruptions and cuts in the text (he omitted, for example, the 'Now I might do it pat' soliloquy), this was closer to Shakespeare than the Macbeth or Lear, and Garrick discarded some of the 'traditions' that had grown up in the past seventy years – notably, the slow music which accompanied Hamlet's entrances. He needed no such aid. 'When Garrick entered the scene,' Arthur Murphy wrote, 'by the force of deep meditation he transformed himself into the very man. He remained fixed in a pensive attitude, and the sentiments that possessed his mind could be discovered by the attentive spectator. When he spoke, the tone of his voice was in unison with the workings of his mind . . .' – a practice obvious enough to modern playgoers but then audacious in its novelty. In the 'To be or not to be' soliloquy, said Murphy, 'his voice and attitude changed with wonderful celerity, and, at every pause, his face was an index to his mind.' But it was at the entrance of the ghost that Garrick's silent facial miming made its most celebrated effects. A picture of that scene has been preserved for us by the invaluable Lichtenberg, in 1775:

The theatre is darkened: the whole audience of some thousands are as quiet, and their faces are as motionless, as though they were painted on the wall of the theatre; even from the farthest end of the play-house one could hear a pin drop. When Horatio says, 'Look, my lord, it comes!' Garrick turns sharply, and at the same moment staggers back two or three paces with his knees giving way under him; his hat

45

falls to the ground and both his arms, especially the left, are stretched out nearly to their full length, with the hands nearly as high as the head, the right arm more bent, the hand lower, and the fingers apart; his mouth is open; thus he stands, rooted to the spot, with legs apart, but no loss of dignity, supported by his friends . . . His whole demeanour is so expressive of terror that it made my flesh creep even before he began to speak. The almost terror-struck silence of the audience probably did much to enhance this effect. At length he speaks, not at the beginning but at the end of a breath, with a trembling voice, ' Angels and ministers of grace, defend us ', words which supply anything this scene may lack, and make it one of the grandest and most terrible which will ever be played on any stage . . . As the ghost goes off the stage a few moments later, Hamlet still remains motionless, his sword held out so as to make him keep his distance, and at length, when the spectator can no longer see the ghost, he begins slowly to follow him, now standing still and then going on, with sword still upon guard, eyes fixed upon the ghost, hair disordered, out of breath, until he too is lost to sight. You can well imagine what loud applause accompanies this exit. It begins as soon as the ghost goes off the stage, and lasts until Hamlet also disappears . . .

This was the scene which so terrified the simple countryman Partridge, in *Tom Jones,* that he ' fell into so violent a trembling that his knees knocked upon each other '. Boswell once asked Dr Johnson: ' Would not you, sir, start as Garrick does if you saw a ghost?' ' I hope not,' replied the Doctor. ' If I did, I should frighten the ghost.'

To prove that Garrick was a great actor is, of course, impossible, and some people believe that he has been overvalued by posterity. He seemed great, they say, only by contrast with the marionettes who preceded him. The very rarity of his versatility has made others cry him down as a tragedian. It is unnatural, such critics imply, for a man who excels as Abel Drugger to triumph as Lear: success in comedy can only be won by lower natures, for comedy is a lower order of creation. In Shakespeare, snobs suggest, Garrick was little more than an accomplished but superficial ' character actor '. Eighteenth-century audiences knew no better. Yet was it not, then, an extraordinary feat to keep his ' novelty value ' through thirty years and two generations and to take in not only the English but the French as well? All his triumphs, say other conscientious objectors, were made in ' actor-proof' parts: he edited every role to fit his own range. But what other player in our history has encompassed a range so magnificently wide with such enduring strength and diversity? Others, again, point out that although Garrick might appear to be 'natural' beside Quin, he would look elaborately artificial beside Olivier. Even in 1763 he was criticized for being at times 'too stiff and prolix' in colloquial and narrative passages. Like all actors, moreover, he had his mannerisms: he resorted to a 'start' too persistently, he employed 'a sort of hesitating stammering', especially in his death scenes, and his pauses were sometimes 'a trap for applause where he could reasonably expect none'. Yet Garrick never ceased to develop and to change his performances. After his long holiday abroad in 1765 there seems to have been a particularly noticeable evolution in his style towards greater easiness and informality, and he 'entirely dropt that anxious exertion at the close of a speech, both in look and behaviour, which is called by the comedians a clap-trap'.

All these comparisons between eighteenth-century 'artificial' and twentieth-century 'natural' are irrelevant. Garrick acted for his audience, not for posterity. If he were alive today, he would act, as he had to, in the manner fit for the time. He was no doctrinaire in 'naturalism' or 'theatricalism'. Like all artists of the theatre he worked in collaboration with the public, as their servant, their ally and their master. He gave them more than they expected or perhaps understood, but he knew what they wanted and how they felt, or refused to feel: they were one of the most important conventions of his art. He stood for order, for an arrangement of experience and a mode of being more regular and complete than those in the offstage world, in an age which exalted the orderly, the well-proportioned, the harmonious. Yet from the moment he set foot upon the stage, Garrick held the audience in thrall; he pulled them with him into the extremes, as they were measured on the eighteenth-century scale; and he would do the same for us. 'Do not sacrifice your taste and feelings to the applause of the multitude', he wrote to a young actor, 'a true genius will convert an audience to his manner, rather than be converted by them to what is false and unnatural.' The 'natural', in Garrick's time, was what Garrick did: he 'converted' the multitude by his own reflection of 'nature', in the mirror of his body and mind. With a voice that could 'pierce the heart, as the sound of a trumpet' and eyes that 'looked into the very soul' he kept command of the stage for over thirty years – in both tragedy and comedy. He had the unmistakeable authority, the irresistible truth, the irrefutable intensity of a great artist, a great entertainer and a great actor.

◇◆◇ 2 ◇◆◇

John Philip Kemble

Long before the doors of Drury Lane Theatre opened, on the evening of 30 September 1783, a large crowd had gathered in the street: and at half-past five there was a fierce rush up the gallery stairs and into the pit, where people fought for places on the benches. In the candlelight the famous playhouse looked and smelt and sounded much as it had done throughout the last hundred years, with the whiff of stale beer, sweat, and oranges, the cries of women selling fruit and playbills, the blur of gay colours in the boxes. Impatient for the programme to begin, the hot-faced, loud-mouthed customers in the upper gallery whistled and howled and stamped, much as they had often done in the days of Betterton and Garrick. Behind the scenes and below the stage, in dressing-rooms, green-rooms and corridors, there were the usual last-minute fidgets, rumours and small disasters. The play was *Hamlet*, but there was the pervasive excitement of a first night. In the boxes, ranged in three tiers of varying elegance, there was already by half-past six an unusually large and punctual parade of fashionable society, and the throng of carriages outside was as chaotic as on the evenings when Mrs Siddons, the talk of London, was playing.

On stage, at the end of the traditional procession, as the courtiers filed into a rather tatty throne-room, the audience saw a tall and handsome man of twenty-six. He wore the formal attire required at the court not of Claudius but of George III – 'rich black velvet, with a star on the breast, the Garter and pendant ribbons of an order – mourning sword and buckles, with deep ruffles.' (Later he broke away from this tradition of contemporary dress and took to 'Old English' costume, as it was called: a kind of fancy-dress anthology of Tudor and Stuart details). He moved

49

slowly, with deliberate grace; he took up attitudes, with statuesque composure; he declaimed the verse, with measured dignity.
His long, stern face was sorrowful and his bearing was royal.
'How like his sister', they said to each other all around the
theatre, at the Prince of Denmark's first appearance, and they
waited for the thunderclap of genius. For this was the brother of
Sarah Siddons, who had made an instant success in tragedy the
previous autumn at the Lane, and it was rumoured that he was
also her equal. John Philip Kemble had come to town.

Although billed 'as originally written by Shakespeare', this
Hamlet was edited with traditional ruthlessness. Kemble also
curiously omitted – like Betterton, but unlike his successors –
the instructions to the players, 'upon the modest principle, that
he must first be admitted a master in the faculty, before he
presumed to censure the faults of others'. Yet compared with
other plays in the Shakespearian canon *Hamlet* was treated with
relative respect on the eighteenth-century stage, and Kemble had
better reason for other amendments, which were mostly to the
'business' of playing. His 'new readings' were followed alertly.
Critics noted that he kneeled when the Ghost disappeared
(through a trapdoor), and at 'Slanders, sir', in replying to
Polonius, he tore the page out of his book. One detail which
excited a special buzz of comment was that in following the
Ghost he turned his left hand towards the spectre, and trailed
his drawn sword behind him in his right hand, whereas every
Hamlet hitherto had unfilially presented the point of his sword
towards his dead father. It was not only in business, however, that
John Philip Kemble was recognized as an innovator. Here, for the
first time, was the gloomy Dane. Instead of the relaxed and
flexible style of acting associated with the 'Garrick school', he
presented a grave, intense but sculptural formality, with sudden
dips into more passionate or colloquial mood: he was, for
instance, rebuked for being too 'familiar' in his manners with
Rosencrantz and Guildenstern. 'How original', said some con-
noisseurs in the pit: 'how unnatural', said their neighbours –
and at once an argument began that was to continue for most of
Kemble's life.

He was not, perhaps, quite equal to his sister Sarah, and the
thunderclap of genius apparently never came – on that night, at
least. Yet with this performance at Old Drury he launched a

London career that was to establish him, in his time, among the great English actors. Drury Lane had lacked a tragedian of the first rank since Garrick, and the newcomer – unlike his principal rival, plump John Henderson of Covent Garden – appeared to have the face and the build for tragedy. By the end of *Hamlet* (and it ended, as in Garrick's time, before the entry of Fortinbras), it was obvious that he also had the mind for it. Too much mind, said some objectors, from the start. For thirty years he was in command, but Black Jack – as his enemies called him – was always a controversial artist, and posterity has not unanimously voted him a place on Olympus.

John Philip Kemble was born on 1 February 1757 at Prescot, a few miles from Liverpool, where his parents had stopped to act for a night or two. Roger and Sarah Kemble were strolling players, performing in the villages and towns of the West Midlands, and John Philip was their first son. Born into the theatre and brought up in a hamper, as it were, he was often required to act with the family in childhood. In those days there were no restrictions on juvenile labour, and children went on the stage in infancy. The steadily increasing clan of Kembles shared the usual hardships and humiliations of the stroller's life – nine of the twelve were born in different towns – but although they must have had no illusions about the glamour of the stage, and although Roger Kemble forbade them all to make acting their career, most of them obstinately tried to follow in their father's footsteps, and three at least arrived at the top of their trade.

As the son of a Roman Catholic actor, John Philip learned a double isolation in childhood. Acting had not yet become one of the liberal professions outside London, and the prestige won by Garrick did not extend to strollers, who were often treated as social pariahs. Roman Catholics, moreover, were denied elementary rights by law. This status of being an 'outsider' had an obvious influence on Kemble's life and work, and it was confirmed by his education. Having attained a certain settled prosperity Roger Kemble determined to turn his eldest son into a Catholic priest, and sent him at the age of ten to a Catholic seminary in Staffordshire. From there, at fourteen, John Philip went to Douai. For two centuries this had been a nursery of the priesthood and a headquarters of the Catholic underground, and it was the nearest university open to an English boy brought up in the old faith. Even if Roger Kemble had been wealthy enough to think of Oxford and Cambridge, they were closed to non-Protestants.

At Douai John Philip demonstrated a prodigious memory and a skill in rhetoric, which earned him leading roles in the college theatricals. This may have served to inflame his secular ambitions, but certainly he discovered by the time he was eighteen that he had no vocation for the priesthood. His proud spirit rebelled against the rigid discipline and self-mortification required, and he longed for the egocentric splendours and miseries of the world into which he was born, a world he was resolved to conquer. Instead of humbling the will, as it was intended to do, Kemble's Jesuit training intensified his single-minded determination to dominate the English theatre: and it provided him with a classical education which, in setting him apart from his colleagues, helped him to lead them. Such an educational background was so uncommon that William Smith, one of the very few graduates of a public school (Eton) and university (Cambridge) on the stage, was generally known as 'Gentleman' Smith.

In the winter of 1775 Kemble ran away from Douai and came back to England. Landing at Bristol, he tramped through the West Midlands in search of his parents, whom he found in Brecknock – his sister Sarah's birthplace – a few days before Christmas. The season of goodwill made no impression upon Roger Kemble. Whatever John Philip may have hoped, his father was furiously angry. After so much money had been spent on his education, the young blockhead had thrown it all away – to be an actor. It was an unforgivable waste of opportunities. Disowned by his father, he set out to make his living as a strolling player with only a few guineas in his pocket, collected by a whip-round in the family troupe.

Even for a veteran, life ' on the hoof ' in midwinter was often very hard. For an inexperienced boy, accustomed to the sheltered austerity of Douai (he liked it well enough to send his favourite brother Charles there, in later years) that apprenticeship must have seemed unexpectedly grim. But he was resolved to prove that Roger Kemble was wrong: he *had* to be an actor. There are many legends of his bitter poverty in this period of initiation.

At one time he toured the villages delivering moral lectures in the best Douai style, accompanied by an equally desperate fellow-actor who gave conjuring tricks, and the pennies they took from the yokels often paid for food and shelter. Sometimes he had to exist on raw turnips, grubbed up in the fields as he tramped through the countryside: sometimes he had to act without a shirt; in Worcester he suffered the shame of being jailed, because he had failed to pay for a new suit. This proved, however, to be the turning-point of Kemble's career, for when he appealed for help to his sister Sarah she came to the rescue and brought him to Liverpool, where she was leading lady in the local theatre. Thanks to her influence, he was engaged by the manager in minor roles, and set his foot upon the ladder of fame – after only eighteen months of roughing it.

Kemble began his acting life with four great advantages, although not all were immediately apparent. He had a genius for a sister, who paved the way for his own success; he was tall, handsome and knew how a gentleman should behave; he had an inexhaustible capacity for hard work – on himself; and he knew exactly where he was going. His progress was, by the standards of the time, unusually rapid. After only a year at Liverpool he moved up another rung to Tate Wilkinson's company, which played in prosperous theatres in Hull, York, Leeds and other cities, and was probably the best of all provincial troupes. Within a short time Kemble was taking roles away from the leading man. He also began a bout of literary activity. What he wrote was ephemeral nonsense, for the most part, but it helped to establish him as that rare prodigy – an educated actor – among the *literati* of York and later of London.

York at the turn of the century was still something of a regional capital, with a relatively strong, self-contained culture of its own. Dublin was even more independent and important, especially in the world of theatre, and there Kemble went in the autumn of 1781. He had learned a great deal from Wilkinson, but there was still considerable room for improvement in this rather clumsy and aloof young man. Kemble was disappointed with the 'idleness, drunkenness and dirt' of the little playhouse in Smock Alley, and with the personality of the manager, Richard Daly. Daly was, in turn, disappointed with the acting of Kemble, to whom he was paying the high salary of five guineas a week, but who failed at first to impress the Dublin public. Within a few weeks, however, the tragedian was taken up by Captain Robert Jephson, a dramatist and local celebrity, who groomed him for the starring role in his own play *The Count of Narbonne,* a version of Horace Walpole's famous novel *The Castle of Otranto.* Jephson went so far as to hire a drill-sergeant and a dancing-master ('No Actor in the World,' Kemble wrote to him, 'stands more in need of Improvement than I do '), and made the training of Kemble's voice his personal responsibility, (he had theories about voice-production and delivery). As a result of this patronage, it seems, Kemble's acting was much improved, and in *The Count of Narbonne* he scored a personal triumph, followed – again under Jephson's tuition – by *Macbeth.* It is noteworthy that it was not on the stage that Kemble first engaged the Captain's attention, but at the dinner-table where his classical education and gentlemanly manners won friends and influenced people throughout his career. By the end of his season at Smock Alley, Kemble showed the practical results – he was earning ten guineas a week.

Dublin was the last station in Kemble's progress to the capital. In October 1782, his sister Sarah – returning to Drury Lane after seven years in the provinces – gave a performance as Isabella, in the Garrick-Southerne *Isabella: or, The Fatal Marriage,* which made her the idol of London: and she did not fail to advance John Philip's claims to consideration. Before long the talent scouts were in Dublin, and Kemble was approached by the managements of both Drury Lane and Covent Garden. Not surprisingly, he signed a contract with Old Drury, his sister's theatre, and this was how he came to act in *Hamlet* on that auspicious autumn night in 1783.

In spite of the success of this performance, Kemble's advance was checked at first by theatrical etiquette. The senior actors in the company had acquired prescriptive rights in most of the leading parts in the repertoire, and the newcomer – however ambitious he might be – had to bide his time until Tom King (the manager) and 'Gentleman ' Smith (a favourite in comedy) surrendered their roles through retirement or death. Had Kemble electrified the town, in the way of his sister, his seniors might have been induced to capitulate more quickly, but the very gravity and unfamiliarity of his playing meant that his progress was made more slowly; and although his following grew steadily, there was an articulate opposition in the press to his 'new readings' and his formal style. All the while, however, he established himself in the theatre, won influential friends outside it, and developed his technique. Old Tom Sheridan, the proprietor's father, coached him for *King John,* and he studied the methods of John Henderson (the only actor, he said in later life, from whom he had ever learned anything of value). In that first Drury Lane season he played Hamlet twelve times, and took twelve other roles, including Sir Giles Overreach, Richard III and Shylock (in all of which he was thought inferior to Henderson, as in later years to Cooke and Kean). Thirteen roles in nine months is by modern West End standards, an unimaginable variety, yet Kemble was relatively unemployed, for he appeared only fifty-five times during the season. In the 1784-5 season he appeared even less frequently, but in his third season he had an unpredictable stroke of luck. Gentleman Smith decided to retire, Kemble was allowed to play some of King's roles, and – what was even more decisive – the sudden death of Henderson, at the age of thirty-nine, removed his chief rival as tragedian of the day and heir to Garrick. From now on Kemble sometimes appeared as often as six times a week in repertoire, playing such roles as Macbeth and Othello, and the change in the balance of power was registered by a noticeable swing in his favour among the critics (some of whom were converted to the Kemble style with suspicious promptitude). He did not forget, moreover, the importance of being earnest, if he was to gain the allegiance of the élite. In 1786 he published an essay on the character of Macbeth, which Hazlitt later dismissed as 'literary foppery', but which served to consolidate his reputation as a gentleman-scholar among the aristocratic patrons of the stage.

In the autumn of 1788, when Tom King retired in disgust from the management of Drury Lane, John Philip Kemble seemed a natural choice as his successor. Although he was only thirty-one, and it was but five years since his début in London, he had ability, authority, education and family connections which no other candidates could claim. And he set out, with high hopes, to reform this 'Slaughter-House of Dramatic Poetry' – as one visiting Frenchman called it – in spite of the problem represented by its chief proprietor, Richard Brinsley Sheridan, a problem whose enormity was, in the end, to drive John Philip and his sister from the theatre.

Sheridan's brilliance as an orator (most notable in the trial of Warren Hastings) and as a dramatist (in *The School for Scandal* and *The Rivals*) was not accompanied by an aptitude for theatrical management. He neglected Drury Lane for Parliament and Carlton House, yet kept control of backstage affairs in his own capricious and inefficient hands. It required uncommon patience and persistence to get Sheridan to keep appointments and make decisions, yet he would not delegate his power. Tom King complained that he had no authority to hire or dismiss actors, even to order so much as the cleaning of a costume. Only Sheridan could authorize spending at Drury Lane, and it was almost impossible, at times, to make him pay the company and staff. Wages were often weeks in arrears, for Sheridan used the treasury to finance his own heavy expenditure as a Whig politician in high society. Stage-hands and actors had to make do, somehow, until he could be cornered and persuaded – sometimes under the threat of a strike by the stars – to disgorge a few pounds. Yet for many years disaster was mysteriously kept at bay by ' Sherry's ' notorious charm, which not even Mrs Siddons could withstand, and by the talents of the Kemble family.

Kemble could do nothing about reforming the finances of Drury Lane, when he succeeded King as manager in 1788, but he did his best to improve the standards of performance and production. He was still at the mercy of Sheridan's whims, but the proprietor gave him greater liberty than he had permitted King to enjoy. From the beginning, Kemble insisted on taking rehearsals seriously and introduced a much stricter discipline than had been known for years. Taking no pains to be popular backstage, he soon gained a reputation as a martinet and a reformer. Kemble's reforms were most conspicuous in the management of minor players and crowds (' the whole tribe of mobs, whether civil or military plebeians ') and in the costume and scenery of his Shakespearian revivals. He set out to stage the classics on a grand and ' appropriate ' scale, combining scholarship and spectacle, and is said to have spent as much upon one of these productions as his predecessors spent on an entire season. Instead of allowing actors to wear, in effect, what they liked, Kemble supervised the details of their dress and at times insisted upon a kind of archaeological accuracy. (He fined Mrs Crouch, the singing star of his company, five guineas for refusing to appear in the dress allotted to her.) Instead of bringing out the old stock scenery ('nothing could be less accurate, or more dirty, than the usual pairs of low flats,' notes his devoted biographer James Boaden), he engaged the painter William Capon to create special decor; and Capon applied himself to stage design with a romantic antiquarian passion that matched Kemble's own, and an unprecedented care for detail.

In the first month of his first season at Drury Lane Kemble produced seven Shakespearian plays, in all of which he starred, and during his career he staged twenty-five of the canon. His devotion to Shakespeare was indeed the outstanding feature of his management. Every season he read as many as a hundred new plays, but few indeed were ever produced, and these were seldom of any merit. Kemble saw well enough that, as Boaden writes, 'the elder dramatists alone afforded him sufficient scope', and he told Boaden (himself an aspiring author) that he was not interested in new work. 'What could be expected now in the way of the regular drama,' he asked, 'that previously had not been better done?' It is a question that reverberates in the history of British acting. Under his command Drury Lane was a temple of the classics, presented with lavish showmanship and processional pomp (he hired nearly 150 extras for *Coriolanus*), and subsidized by the pantomimes, musical farces and operatic spectacles which shared the bill and drew the crowds.

By modern standards both Kemble's reforms and his scholarship may seem ludicrously inadequate. Like Garrick he mangled the texts of which he was supposed to be the custodian. He used Dryden's operatic version of *The Tempest*, the Cibber 'improvement' of *Richard III*, the ruined *King Lear* of Nahum Tate and James Thomson. Even in his greatest Shakespearian success – *Coriolanus* – he employed a clumsily edited and rewritten text. In his choice of costume and scenery, moreover, he was still deeply influenced by stage convention. He played Benedick and Othello in the uniform of a British army officer of the day. As Macbeth he wore the traditional tragedian's plume of black feathers, until Sir Walter Scott – one of his closest friends – tore it from his bonnet and placed there the appropriate eagle quill (a gesture which, Kemble said, meant more to him than three rounds of applause). Mrs Crouch, as one of the singing witches in that play, wore 'powdered hair, rouge, point lace and fine linen', and a critic noted that the minor characters in some productions appeared in 'a motley assemblage of dresses, such as perhaps were never seen in any age or nation'. In the Kemble *Coriolanus* there was 'a pretty exact representation of Hanover Square, and some very neat Bond Street shops appeared two or three times, as parts of Rome'.

Yet it must be remembered that the demand for complete realism on the stage is a relatively recent development, and one which Kemble himself helped to foster by his pioneering revivals of Shakespeare. He entertained a generation which lacked our own self-conscious sense of the past, and which did not expect the total illusion, the historical consistency or theatrical unity which we have come to take for granted. When the green carpet was still laid down for tragedy, and the scene was changed by stage hands in full view of the audience, who cared if Elsinore, Cyprus and Rome all looked much alike, and all were populated by eighteenth-century Londoners (sprinkled with visitors from a fancy-dress ball)? Kemble taught people to care a little more, to look with fresh eyes at the stage pictures, so preparing the way for the next advance in scenic reform; and he in turn, like Garrick in his time, kept the Shakespearian repertoire alive, with his great sister's help, for the new audiences of an expanding London.

Even that hostile witness Leigh Hunt, who later waged a press campaign against Kemble's domination of the London theatre, wrote that 'were it not for Mr Kemble's exertions the tragedies of our glorious bard would almost be in danger of dismissal from the stage: and it does him infinite credit to have persevered in his exertions in spite of comparatively thin houses; to have added to the attractions of his poet by a splendour of scene as seasonable as well-deserved; and to have evinced so noble an attachment, and helped to keep up so noble a taste, in an age of mawkishness and buffoonery.' As a director he was recognized as being 'wonderfully thorough and impressive', and a contemporary theatrical scholar, G. C. D. Odell, justly describes him as 'certainly the first great producer of Shakespeare on the English stage'. It may well be true, in the words of William Robson (author of *The Old Playgoer*), that ' he never had the means to do all that his genius and his love for his art inspired . . .'

As an actor, during his thirty-four years on the London stage, Kemble was most popular and at his best – outside Shakespeare – in neo-classical drama (such as Addison's *Cato*) and the fashionable romantic German drama of Kotzebue. The Stranger, in the play of that name (' Silent record of unutterable anguish'), and Rolla in Sheridan's adaptation of *Pizarro,* were among his greatest triumphs. Other successes were Pierre, in Otway's *Venice Preserv'd;* Penruddock, the morose misanthrope in Richard Cumberland's *The Wheel of Fortune;* Zanga, the baleful blackface Iago of Edward Young's *The Revenge;* ' the stricken, murmuring, lost Octavian ' in George Colman's *The Mountaineers;* the remorseful villain, De Montfort, in Joanna Baillie's play; and Norval in Home's *Douglas.* Forgotten plays, most of them, they gave John Philip Kemble scope for his special virtues in depicting the suffering of strong men and the strength of heroes. In Shakespeare, Hamlet remained one of his most popular roles. He scored as Wolsey in *Henry VIII*, as Henry v, as King John, and as Macbeth; but his Othello was – said one of his most fervent admirers – ' at most, only a part very finely played ', he failed as Richard III, and his Lear was apparently inferior to Garrick's. Kemble liked to act in comedy, but most witnesses found him ludicrously inept in light entertainment, although Charles Lamb, who could not ' disembarrass the idea of Hamlet from the person and voice of Mr Kemble ', also admired his talents in Congreve and Wycherley. Boaden insists that ' out of the management . . . he was the gentlest of all great actors . . . He would do *anything*.' But what he could do was limited.

As manager of Drury Lane, John Philip Kemble had to face many problems apart from the feckless and dangerous irresponsibility of his employer. Two years after Kemble took over from Tom King, Sheridan decided that it was time to pull down the old theatre in which Betterton and Garrick had acted; and the new Drury Lane, opened in April 1794 with *Macbeth,* was twice the size of the old. It was, in fact, the largest playhouse in Europe, and held over 3,600 people. The ' Grand National ' of Sheridan's dreams, however, cost far more to build than he had estimated (a hundred times as much as the original theatre) and from the beginning it was saddled with a burden of debt. Inevitably,

Kemble found even greater difficulties in making Sheridan pay up, and the size of the theatre had a decisive effect on his career as a manager and his style as an actor. Intimacy and subtlety of playing were impossible in such grandiose barns as the new Drury Lane (and Covent Garden). ' Our theatres are fit for nothing,' Coleridge said, with pardonable exaggeration. ' They are too large for acting and too small for a bull-fight '; and Richard Cumberland noted that Garrick's effects would evaporate ' in their passage through the misty void, and he would have found himself understood only in the neighbourhood of the orchestra '. This architectural inflation, itself the result of the absurd ' patents ' which restricted the spoken drama to the Garden and the Lane, promoted the declamatory, statuesque acting of Kemble and his followers, and also confirmed the need for spectacular staging of the classics. Yet, even so, Drury Lane needed other baits to draw the town, and Kemble was obliged to present, on an increasing scale, what he sombrely called ' shewy after-pieces and laughable farces '.

There are, of course, many squalls in the life of a manager, especially one as imperious and violent as Kemble, who lacked Garrick's evasive diplomacy. He had to cope with temperamental leading ladies who harassed him by their absenteeism, intrigues, and civil wars. He fought a duel with one of his actors, who complained of Kemble's conduct at rehearsals (' Black Jack ' contemptuously fired his pistol in the air, and nobody was hurt). He attacked a girl in her dressing-room, and had to make a public apology in the press. He rebuked the rowdy audiences for their grosser exhibitions of bad manners: although he was accustomed (like all his contemporaries) to a deal of noise, his Roman dignity was offended when apples or bottles landed on the stage. And he was exposed to a constant war of nerves by the theatre's creditors, including most of the company. In 1796 he at last resigned the management, and when he resumed that responsibility four years later it was only on the understanding that Sheridan would sell him a share in Drury Lane – he hungered for a theatre which was all, or even partly, his own. Not long after this deal fell through. John Philip Kemble left Drury Lane for ever. He was tired of having to beg for money, of having to fight Sheridan's battles, of tasting only the shadow not the substance of power, and towards the end of the 1802-3 season he had his final quarrel with Sheridan. This time he was impervious to the proprietor's charm: his patience was at last exhausted.

Kemble set out for a grand tour of Europe, in a specially constructed carriage, with his banker as travelling companion. It was during the brief lull in the Napoleonic Wars caused by the Peace of Amiens, and he was fêted in Paris by the great French actor Talma and his colleagues of the Comédie Française. Soon after he returned, in April 1803, it was announced that all the Kembles were moving to Covent Garden, after twenty years at the rival house. He had agreed to pay £22,000 for a sixth share in the theatre, of which he paid £10,000 in cash; and he was to receive £200 a year as manager, and £37 16s a week as actor. The playhouse was renovated in white and gold. Sixteen new private boxes – rented at £300 a season – were opened, for the aristocratic patrons who were rightly expected to follow Kemble and his sister from Drury Lane. And Kemble inaugurated his new regime, as he had begun his London career twenty years before, with *Hamlet*.

In 1803 it seemed, no doubt, as if he was opening a new and glorious chapter in his career. At forty-six he was still the acknowledged head of the English stage. No likely claimant to the title was in sight. His most dangerous competitor, George Frederick Cooke, who had come to Covent Garden in 1800, was a superb stage villain of great passion and power. In certain roles such as Richard III and Sir Giles Overreach (in Massinger's *A New Way to Pay Old Debts*) he easily eclipsed Kemble, to whose patrician dignity he opposed plebeian energy. But Cooke had no staying power as a man and no conscience as an artist. With an earlier success, and even half Kemble's will-power and self-criticism, he might have reached the top. But it was not until his mid-forties that he was 'discovered' by London, after twenty-four years of provincial slogging, and by that time he was a confirmed alcoholic. He was often too drunk to appear (the programme had to be suddenly changed in such emergencies) and was often hissed or laughed off the stage. At his best his acting was erratic and disorderly, like that of many 'instinctive' players who depend not on technique but on 'inspiration'. In spite of his popularity with London audiences he was no match for Kemble, especially when – from 1803 onwards – he was obliged to work under Kemble's management. Yet John Philip was both shrewd and generous in his treatment of Cooke, who was allowed to keep such prize roles as Richard III and Shylock.

Free at last from the burdens of Drury Lane, Kemble – so it must have appeared in 1803 – could now enjoy the independence which his proud spirit had craved so long: Covent Garden was not only solvent but profitable, and he could confidently look forward to a prosperous future. On a provincial tour he could earn as much as £1,400 in four weeks, and unlike his surtaxed successors in the modern theatre he could keep a good deal of it. He was at liberty to consummate his ambitions as a scholar-artist by entertaining his aristocratic friends at his house in Great Russell Street (later absorbed by the British Museum); by continuing to enlarge his huge and valuable library (which included many rare Elizabethan quartos); and by producing the 'best' plays with what he called 'a union of propriety and splendour', beyond the resources of Sheridan. Yet everything went wrong for Kemble after he left Drury Lane.

The first setback to his hopes came in December 1804 when Master William Betty, the Infant Roscius, arrived in London. This thirteen-year-old boy, who strutted and squeaked his way through a small part of the classics repertoire, came to town in a cloud of glory at unprecedentedly high pay. Both Covent Garden and Drury Lane paid him £50 a night, with a clear benefit every week (worth about £250 a time), but they reaped their reward, for Master Betty nearly doubled their takings. The capital was at his feet. Nobody had ever cheered John Philip Kemble with this wild enthusiasm. Fox, for one, thought the boy's Hamlet 'finer than Garrick'. In one season, he is said to have earned nearly as much as Kemble had paid in cash for Covent Garden. John Philip and his sister withdrew from the stage, with understandable but discreet hauteur, while the Betty cult endured. Within four months, the boy prodigy was out of fashion, and the Kembles were back in power. Yet this extraordinary infatuation was something more than an outbreak of hysteria: its violence was fired by a revolt against the reigning stage dynasty. The audience was bored with John Philip Kemble. For twenty years, so it seemed to them, his tall aristocratic figure had dominated the stage, striking noble, classic attitudes in noble, classic roles; his slow, rather hoarse voice, with its eccentric pronunciations, had droned round pit, box and gallery; and it was always the same

Kemble, in the same plays. In those twenty years the London audience had changed: Kemble, it seemed, had not. He had made himself into an institution. The adulation of Master Betty, in the season of 1804-5, was the first public demonstration that the public wanted something more.

Three years after Master Betty disappeared, Kemble suffered a much more damaging blow. In the early morning of 20 September 1808, Covent Garden Theatre caught fire and was burned out in four hours. Twenty-two people were killed, and most of the theatre's scenery, wardrobe, manuscripts and records went up in smoke. The loss was estimated at over £150,000, and only a small part of this could be met by the insurance companies. For Kemble, in particular, it was a disaster: after only five seasons his theatre was destroyed, and he had to start again from scratch. Worse followed when the new Covent Garden was opened a year later, on 18 September 1809. To build it, a public subscription had been launched, headed by the King and the Duke of York, and the Duke of Northumberland – one of Kemble's admirers – contributed £19,000. Yet the cost of this vast theatre, built in grandiose, pseudo-classical style, was disproportionately high (about £300,000) and the proprietors decided to pass some of the cost on to the consumers. A week before the gala opening they announced that the prices would be raised from six to seven shillings for the boxes and from three-and-six to four shillings for the pit. It also became known that twenty-six private boxes had been built, at the expense of the galleries, and that the famous soprano, Madame Catalani, was engaged to sing at £50 a night. The result was an extraordinary explosion of popular anger, known as the O.P. or Old Price Riots, directed against the management for daring to put up the prices in order to subsidize a foreign opera singer and promote upper-class immorality (for the private boxes were regarded by pit and gallery as arbours of aristocratic vice).

On the first night of the season, when John Philip Kemble stepped proudly out on the stage of his new theatre for the first time, he was greeted with a tempest of hissing, shouting and whistling that drowned his prologue. The ' torrent of execration ' continued throughout *Macbeth*, with continual yelling of ' Old Prices ' and ' No Catalani ', and Mrs Siddons and her brother were shouted down with particular violence. Most of the women

in the private boxes left early in the evening, but the theatre was
still crammed with rioters, who stood in shouting ranks with
their hats on and their backs to the stage. The actors went
doggedly on through the tragedy and the musical farce which
followed it, but scarcely a word could be heard for the noise.
When the programme was over, and the audience refused to
move, Kemble made the first of many mistakes: he sent for the
police. The sight of two constables walking on to the stage roused
the rioters to wild frenzy, and their temper grew even more
ferocious when – after the constables' tactful withdrawal to Bow
Street – fire engines were brought forward to threaten the house.
It was not until two o'clock in the morning that the theatre at
last began to clear, after a good-humoured chorus of ' God Save
the King.'

That was only the beginning. Every night, week after week,
the well-organized riots continued. No damage was done to the
theatre, and none of the company suffered any physical violence,
but from the second night onwards the audience paraded banners
and placards with increasingly abusive slogans; they danced the
' O.P. dance ', stamping rhythmically up and down as they
chanted; they wore O.P. hats and O.P. brooches; and all the
while they kept up an unearthly din with horns, gongs, bells,
rattles, whistles and their own stentorian howling, as the unfortunate actors went through their repertoire in dumb show at high
speed. Most of the press, including *The Times,* was on the
rioters' side, and ballads, broadsheets and caricatures appeared in
profusion. Kemble was, not surprisingly, the main target. He
ordered the trap doors on the stage to be opened as a defence
against the audience, and hired professional bruisers to attack
the demonstrators – actions which whipped up public hatred of
him to boiling point. When the theatre's accounts were inspected
by an independent committee, which approved the proposed
increase in prices, the crowd's fury was unabated: Kemble was
then charged with corruption and profiteering, as well as brutal
tyranny and oppression. Every discreditable incident in his life
that could be discovered (or invented) was used by the O.P.-ites
in a vicious campaign against the great tragedian. Towards the
end of this astonishing affair threatening mobs often gathered
outside his house in Great Russell Street. His windows were
smashed, and his wife had ladders at the ready, in case their home

was taken by storm. He was, for a time, the most hated man in town.

The rights and wrongs of the O.P. riots are, like its causes, complex; but it is plain that the violence of this anti-Kemble feeling was due to more than the rioters' immediate grievance against the Covent Garden management. Never deeply loved by the audience, Kemble had been deeply feared and respected; but the respect turned into resentment of his autocratic self-sufficiency, his insulation and rigidity. He was attacked as a principle of authority. Londoners saw him as a Coriolanus of the stage, icily contemptuous of those he was supposed to serve, and they were determined to humiliate the pride of this ' upstart ' player. In the end, of course, they had their way. After three months of rioting, Kemble was obliged to accept the O.P. terms and to make a public apology from the stage. When, at the beginning of the next season, he foolishly tried to break his promise by maintaining half the private boxes, the riots began all over again. This time he had learned his lesson: at the first crack of the whip the theatre closed and the necessary changes were made. There was no doubt now who was the master.

When peace was at last concluded, Kemble enjoyed an Indian summer of public favour at Covent Garden. Cooke had gone to America. Mrs Siddons retired, and he was alone in the field. Yet the applause of these crowded houses did not reconcile the proud actor to his humiliation. ' My lord,' he said to Lord Mountjoy, ' Christ was crucified, De Wet was assassinated: so much for the world and its people.' He was an embittered and ailing man, whose powers were in decline and whose dreams of independent management had evaporated. Asthma and gout (and a quarrel with the proprietor) soon drove him from the theatre. After a leisurely absence of nearly two years he returned in the winter of 1813, and once again drew the crowds to his Cato and Coriolanus; but the final disappointment came a few weeks later, in January, with the sensational success at Drury Lane of Edmund Kean, who was hailed at once on all sides as the greatest actor of the age, with what seemed a revolutionary style of playing. ' We wish we had never seen Mr Kean,' wrote Hazlitt. ' He has destroyed the Kemble religion; and it was the religion in which we were brought up.' This aloof patrician seemed something of an anachronism in the new industrial Britain – no longer a representative figure of the drama, but a symbol of the *ancien régime*. Kemble knew that his reign was over, and he made his plans accordingly. After preparing an eight-volume edition of the classic drama, as staged under his management, he embarked on his final season in the winter of 1816; and he made his farewell performance as Coriolanus on 23 June, 1817. Having sold his library and his wardrobe, he set off abroad – to Paris, Toulouse and at last to Lausanne, where he died on 26 February, 1823.

Although the mysteries of acting remain, ultimately, impervious to intellectual analysis, one serviceable key to the looking-glass world may be found in the distinction between the 'personality' and the 'character' actor, redefined by Louis Jouvet in the terms *acteur* and *comédien*. Broadly speaking, the *comédien* is a Protean player who sinks his personality in the part, apparently creating a new self from role to role, whereas the *acteur* sinks the part in his personality, allowing each new role to irradiate another aspect of his unchanging ego. This was, in part, the difference between Garrick and Kemble, as it was between Garrick and Quin. Kemble's effective range of parts was narrow; he lacked plasticity and flexibility; his long face, Roman nose, and jutting chin, his stately walk, dignified carriage and slow delivery, were always uncompromisingly unconcealed. That is one reason why audiences grew tired of his long domination, and why his acting has probably been more rigorously analysed than that of any comparable figure in the English theatre. *Acteurs* are always more vulnerable to criticism than are *comédiens;* if their mannerisms and mistakes are more obvious, their skill is likely to be underrated. Kemble's weaknesses, moreover, were highlighted by the contrast of Kean's 'romantic' style, and it is his misfortune that there were no Hazlitts or Hunts to record his earlier triumphs. It is the Kemble of late middle age, when his style appeared to be fixed and even fossilized, that survives in the essays from which people take their opinion of his acting: here – as in many other things – he was unlucky. He was a classicist marooned among the romantics, an aristocrat in an increasingly democratic culture, and the best writers were in the opposition camp.

All such considerations aside, it seems clear that John Philip Kemble – judged as a great actor – had serious limitations. His face could express only a small compass of intense emotions, his eyes lacked the mesmeric lustre of a Kean or Garrick, and the look of patrician dignity which he brought to many of his roles seemed, at times, like 'a man who is just going to sneeze'. In action, he was consistently statuesque, and was known to introduce a Turveydrop passion for deportment into the most incongruous situations: he played Hamlet, according to Hazlitt, like a man in armour. At his worst, to quote Leigh Hunt, 'it was not the man, but his mask; a trophy, a consul's robe; or, if you please, a rhetorician'; and Mrs Siddons observed that even in his most 'impetuous bursts', her brother was 'always careful to avoid any discomposure of his dress or deportment'. 'In every part,' said William Robson proudly, 'he was a *gentleman*.'

Kemble suffered throughout his life from asthma and a cough which became 'almost habitual', and he therefore had to discipline his voice (and his audience) into a slow and elaborately careful delivery. He paced through the blank verse of his favourite roles with measured stride and prolonged pause, 'enunciating every letter in every word', as Macready put it. But his voice lacked range, volume and melody: Macready called it 'husky and untunable', at the end of his career, and in the year of his retirement the German writer Ludwig Tieck described it as 'weak and tremulous, though full of expression, and every word is sounded with knowledge and feeling, only with too much emphasis: between every second and third word a significant pause is made, and most lines end on a higher pitch.' Tieck found this declamation 'a real hindrance to genuine acting, in fact [it] made it almost impossible.' That is why Kemble's most bitter critic, Leigh Hunt, could dismiss him as 'a teacher of elocution rather than an actor and not a good teacher, on that account'.

His pronunciation, too, was pedantically eccentric. In the teeth of public ridicule, he obstinately insisted on his own extraordinary variants: 'beard' became 'bird', 'rode' was 'rod', 'virtue' was 'vartue', 'earth' became 'airth' and – most notorious Kemble-ism of all – 'aches' was pronounced as 'aitches'. Unwaveringly confident in his own scholarship, Kemble ignored the critics and the audience. Charles Mathews met him backstage one night, while the audience was still hissing his pronunciation, and Kemble imperturbably took a pinch of snuff and sniffed, 'Umph! how those good people think they're right.' This innovation was part of what Hunt called his 'laborious and almost universal preciseness':

> He strives by niceties to strike the mind;
> For meaning too precise, inclin'd to pore,
> And labour for a point unknown before;
> Untimely playing thus the critic's part,
> To gain the head when he should smite the heart.

Smiting the heart was not, however, Kemble's forte. He awed, but he did not usually kindle. He impressed but he did not often overwhelm. Even in his best roles he seemed, at times, to be keeping his distance from the character and the audience. 'He sacrifices too much to decorum,' said Hazlitt; and it was the weakness of his method that when he was below par, or when he was not trying, the effort and calculation should seem most conspicuous. At the end of his life, Macready believed, 'in all he did the study was apparent.'

> Stiff, pompous, stern, each haggard feature groom'd:
> Each step predestin'd, and each look foredoom'd:
> Precise in passion, cautious ev'n in rage,
> Lo! Kemble comes, the Euclid of the stage:
> Who moves in given angles, squares a start,
> And blows his Roman beak by rules of art.

And so the evidence against Kemble accumulates. If that were all, then he would scarcely merit a place among the great actors of our stage; but if that were all, then he could not have commanded the London theatre for over thirty years, nor enjoyed the friendship and respect of so many members of the Georgian social and cultural élite, nor established a 'school' of acting which dominated the stage for many years after his retirement, nor survived in print with such abundant, complex and controversial vitality. He has, indeed, been judged too narrowly by the standards of naturalism, an approach to acting which he would have despised. He is condemned for failing to provide something which he deplored as vulgar – 'nature'. His prime talent was for the 'supernatural', in the phrase of Byron – who called him 'the most supernatural of actors' – and he exercised it on the outsize heroes and villains of the classic and pseudo-classic drama. 'Give him only the *man* to play, why, he is nothing,' said Hazlitt. 'Give him the paraphernalia of greatness, and he is great.'

Kemble's art was deliberately stylized, declamatory and sculptural; it belonged to an age of oratory, an age which worshipped the classical ideals of harmony, proportion, repose and order; but it was exhibited in an age in love with the Gothic and Romantic, in huge theatres dedicated to pantomime and spectacle. Yet his acting was, in a sense, the product of an architecture: it was meant to be seen at a distance. This was, as his biographer Herschel Baker says, ' a style of long, sweeping lines and detached, almost impersonal grandeur. It was a histrionic counterpart of what Sir Joshua Reynolds demanded in painting: a marmoreal loftiness and zealous avoidance of the minute, the particular, the personal.' His performances were, said one admiring witness, ' ANIMATED PAINTINGS '. This is how he appeared as Coriolanus (in a scarlet robe, with built-up heels on his sandals):

In his first encounter with the rabble, it is impossible not to admire the noble proportions and majestic contour of his figure; the expression of his face, naturally of the Roman character; his right arm erected in conscious authority; his chest thrown forward, and his head slightly back; his right leg fearlessly advanced, and firmness in all his attitude, together with the exact adjustment and tasteful folds of the classical drapery with which his person is invested, compose a most superb and commanding *tout ensemble* of the human form.

With less enthusiasm, Hazlitt explains the success of Kemble's Cato: ' There was nothing for him to do in this character, but to appear in it. It had all the dignity of still-life. It was a studied piece of classical costume – a conscious exhibition of elegantly disposed drapery – that was all: yet, as a mere display of personal and artificial grace, it was inimitable.'

Yet Hazlitt was less than fair: there was more than a tasteful disposition of drapery in this performance, which was – with Coriolanus – the most popular in Kemble's repertoire. There was also, another critic noted, ' a regular and magnificent declamation, supported throughout with majesty, and occasionally varied with the energy of a simple passion. In this style of speaking and acting Mr Kemble is without an equal or a rival.' Oratory and sculpture were here combined, in a carefully designed series of effects, projected with theatrical expertise, keen intelligence and studied intensity. Kemble was indeed a master of the grand style, in spite of his eccentricities of voice and manner. He had the physical advantages of a strong and handsome face, a head of

heroic cast, a dignified carriage, and a royal authority. Hazlitt
described him as ' the only one of the moderns who both in figure
and action approaches the beauty and grandeur of the antique ',
and Macready wrote of his Cato that ' in face and form he
realized the most perfect ideal that ever enriched the sculptor's
or painter's fancy . . .'

Kemble's range was small indeed, but within it he was incomparable. Lacking flexibility, he was at his best – as Hazlitt said –
' in the development of some one solitary sentiment or exclusive
passion . . . where all the passions move round a central point,
and are governed by one master-key, he stood unrivalled ' – as in
Penruddock, Cato, The Stranger and Coriolanus. Both Hunt
and Hazlitt, critics of the Kemble school, thought Penruddock
' perfect'. Yet in *Hamlet* and *Macbeth* (the best that Hunt and
Hazlitt saw) Kemble also scored great triumphs in his prime,
and although he was obliged to act in lesser plays he was content
with nothing less than masterpieces. (His Macbeth was heroic,
emphasizing the ' Bellona's bridegroom ' side of the soldier's
character, ' touching in crime and noble in infamy '.) For all his
dignity, he could move the audience to tears. ' The distinguishing
excellence of his acting,' Hazlitt wrote, 'may be summed up in
one word – *intensity;* in the seizing upon some one feeling or
idea, in working it up, with a certain graceful consistency, and
conscious grandeur of conception, to a very high degree of pathos
or sublimity.' He exploited, moreover, the theatrical virtues of
contrast: against the general, formal pattern of his declamatory
delivery he would strike off sudden moments of ' natural ', almost
colloquial truth, which were remembered by many people as the
high points of the performance – though these ' daring' devia-
tions were resented by other playgoers. (Such a moment – wildly
applauded – was his choked ejaculation of ' Liar and Slave!' in
the last act of Macbeth when the Messenger brings the news of
Birnam Wood.) He could be agile, energetic and rapid when he
thought it necessary – as Hotspur or Henry v, for instance;
although such occasions were, in his view, rare. Dignity came
first.

The aesthetic ideal which Kemble served may seem, today, a
false one, yet his achievements in its service should be recognized,
not only as manager but as actor. He created a ' classic ' style out
of nowhere, improvizing a tradition in a vacuum, trying to estab-

lish – almost single-handed – a ' Comédie Anglaise ' which would be honoured as a temple of the drama. To perfect himself as the high priest of that temple, he subjected himself throughout his acting career to a painstaking course of discipline and study. Handicapped by asthma, he nevertheless made the best of a weak voice, so that even Hunt admitted he had ' done wonders ' with it. Boaden records that he seemed ' always to consider the work as still *to do* . . . To the last of him, Hamlet and Macbeth had still, as he conceived, calls upon him for improvement.' He was never too famous or too successful to stop learning. At the end of his life, he lamented: ' I am only just beginning thoroughly to understand my art.' Hazlitt called him ' the only great and truly impressive actor I remember, who rose to his stately height by the interposition of art and gradations of merit.'

Kemble's success was not the result of luck or instinct: he was, as John Taylor said, ' a manufactured actor '. He was not afraid to think about his art, to analyse technique, to impose his style upon the public. This was no easy victory, but – as Herschel Baker says – ' he had brought to his art a preparation and a care that had at first bewildered and then enchanted his audiences. Without possessing his sister's genius, he had a talent which in its own kind has never been surpassed.' He *made* himself into a great actor.

❖❖❖ 3 ❖❖❖

Edmund Kean

On a foggy, snowy night in January, when the cobbled streets of Regency London were thick with slush, few playgoers could be expected to desert their firesides just to see the début of a man from Exeter at Drury Lane. Preliminary puffs in the press had, it is true, compared this Mr Kean with Garrick, but Londoners had seen the failure of too many provincial recruits, advertised in advance with equal extravagance, to put any faith in such inspired rumours. Despite its brand-new architecture (it had been rebuilt in 1812) both the business and prestige of Drury Lane were at a low ebb. Talent scouts had been sent out in all directions to unearth some new tragedian who could compete with Kemble at Covent Garden, and exhibiting this unknown from the West Country clearly seemed to be another bid by the committee in charge of the theatre to recoup its fortunes. So on the night of 26 January 1814, the vast, cold, ornate playhouse was barely a quarter full. Before the curtain rose on *The Merchant of Venice,* a wintry depression had settled over both auditorium and stage. Resigned to the prospect of another fiasco, for this shabby little provincial had behaved very oddly at the play's one rehearsal at noon, the company moved apathetically through the opening scene. Then it happened. ' There came on the stage a small man, with an Italian face and fatal eye, which struck all.'

He stopped, leaned on his stick, rested his eyes on Antonio. The pall lifted. The house stirred. Then he spoke: ' Three thousand ducats – well?' It must be Shylock, thought the puzzled audience. But why was he so clean and tidy, and where was Shylock's red wig? Even Macklin had not dared to discard that. The man from Exeter wore a black gaberdine, a black beard and a

72

black wig; yet it was his black eyes, piercing and mesmeric, which
riveted attention to the Jew. Here, it was quickly recognized, was
not only a new wig but a new Shylock. Smouldering with scorn,
chuckling with grim humour, he was also – as a critic said in later
years – ' a chapter of Genesis '.

> Hath a *dog* money? Is it possible
> A *cur* can lend three thousand ducats . . .

he asked with fierce emphasis, and the house was surprised into
clapping. Excitement grew as the play went on, and the actor's
range was revealed. The lines seemed to be his own. His face was
a language, and his body spoke, too. ' We do not know whether
he is ambi-dexter, but his left and right arm seem equally serviceable, and move with equal effect,' noted an admirer in the pit
that night. Nobody on the English stage in 1814 could use his
arms and hands like that; no living actor was so eloquent in
silence; nobody could act with such burning, kindling force.
Astonished by the transformation, the other players cringed under
the onslaught, backing away from the fury in his voice and eyes.
It was the Tubal scene which confirmed his success. ' No passage in the range of tragedy,' says Kean's biographer, H. N. Hillebrand, ' lay more securely in the fortress of his powers. The vol-
canic intensity of feeling, the broken utterances, the sudden
passages from grief to exultation as Shylock learns alternately of
Jessica's squandering ducats in Genoa and Antonio's ships lost at
sea, were Kean's histrionic speciality, in which, perhaps, he
excelled over any other English actor.'

As the temperature and the noise increased, actors came out
from dressing-rooms and green-rooms to see what was happening:
' How the devil so few of them kicked up such a row was something marvellous,' said one of the players backstage that night.
People came hurrying away from Covent Garden to see if the
rumours were true. In the trial scene, Kean rounded off his victory, before an audience now on its toes with excitement, with his
bitter gloating over:

> I cannot find it: 'tis not in the bond.

George Frederick Cooke, the outstanding Shylock of that time,
used to give this, so a critic noted, ' with a savage sneer; Mr Kean
gave it with a transported chuckle; his inmost heart seemed to

laugh that no obstacle now remained to the completion of his
murderous purpose . . .' And this Shylock was defiant to the
end, going off the stage with one last malignant glare at Gratiano,
while the theatre rang with shouts of acclamation. After so many
disastrously bad nights, Drury Lane had found a saviour; after
the statuesque grandeur of the Kemble school, this kind of acting
seemed a revelation. As Shylock came off, the manager and the
leading actors, who had hitherto snubbed him with cold civility,
waited to welcome him with open arms. He pushed past them into
the dressing-room which he shared with several others, changed
rapidly into his clothes, and hurried back to his lodgings on the
other side of the Strand. His long-suffering wife was waiting for
news, when – so the story goes – Kean burst in through the door.
'Mary,' he cried in triumph, 'you shall ride in your carriage
and Charley shall go to Eton.' Both promises came true.

While the Keans were celebrating over their supper, the
dramatic critic of the *Morning Chronicle,* in a room not far away,
was making notes on Kean's performance. 'For voice, eye, action
and expression,' wrote William Hazlitt, 'no actor has come out
for many years at all equal to him. The applause, from the first
scene to the last, was general, loud and uninterrupted. Indeed,
the very first scene . . . showed the master in his art, and at once
decided the opinion of the audience.' In the following week, when
Kean repeated his Shylock, Hazlitt went further: 'His style of
acting is, if we may use the expression, more significant, more
pregnant with meaning, more varied and alive in every part, than
any we have almost ever witnessed . . . It is not saying too much
of him, though it is saying a great deal, that he has all that Mr
Kemble *wants* of perfection. He reminds us of the descriptions
of the "far-darting eye" of Garrick.' This powerful support
helped to draw bigger audiences to Drury Lane, but Kean was
still ignored by many papers. Apart from Hazlitt, only one other
critic saw the first night. It was not until some two weeks later,
after his performance in *Richard III,* that Kean conquered the
town. On the night of 6 February, he was watched by a large
audience which included many of the 'taste-making' élite. They
were ready for anything, and they were not disappointed. 'I wish
that I had a talent for the drama,' Byron wrote in his diary that
month, 'I would write a tragedy now.'

In the words of H. N. Hillebrand, reconstructing the impact of

Kean's Crookback, 'the performance was from the first soliloquy
to the death, a triumph keyed to the pitch of trumpets and
hosannas. The little tragedian was in everything he did prodigious.
He was the master virtuoso who swept through the gamut of
moods, throwing his hearers, with each change, into new ecstasies
. . . here were the thunder and the lightning, here were storms
and bursts of sunlight, here were the colours of the rainbow and
the terrible shadows of crime and death, here in a word was
nature in all her enchanting variety.' Like Garrick, he was at his
best in the courtship of Anne and the death-scene. 'He fought
like one drunk with wounds,' Hazlitt noted, 'and the attitude
in which he stands with his hands stretched out, after his sword
is taken from him, had a preternatural and terrific grandeur, as
if his will could not be disarmed, and the very phantoms of his
despair had a withering power.' There he stood, looking at Richmond (so Leigh Hunt said), 'as if he was already a disembodied
spirit, searching him with the eyes of another world; or, as if he
silently cursed him with some new scorn, to which death and its
dreadful knowledge had given him a right.' He grasped blindly
at Richmond, with his bare hands, staggered backwards and fell;
writhing on the ground, he gnashed his teeth as he uttered his
last words, blinked and then expired, rolling on his back.

This performance, added to his Shylock, made Kean the talk
of the town. He followed it, in this same remarkable season of
1813-14, with his Hamlet, Othello and Iago. In each of them
he won homage, and open war broke out between his supporters
and the champions of John Philip Kemble. As we have seen,
Kean had, in Hazlitt's view, 'destroyed the Kemble "religion"'.

The immediate recognition of Edmund Kean at Drury Lane
in 1814, in triumphant opposition to the current school of acting, recalls the night at Goodman's Fields in 1741 when David
Garrick made his début. Both were twenty-four; both were unknown; both were small in stature; both were hailed for their
'natural' style. Yet their lives, both before and after these initial
victories, were sharply different, and the difference is reflected in
their art. Mystery surrounds the birth, parentage and childhood
of Edmund Kean, a mystery which his own love of tall stories
helped to thicken (he liked to suggest, variously, that he was
a duke's bastard, an Old Etonian, and an erstwhile cabin boy).
Was he born in 1787, 1789 or 1790? (We will settle, here, for the

middle date). Was he the son of Aaron, Edmund or Moses Kean or of the Duke of Norfolk? Was his mother Nancy Carey or Charlotte Tidswell? Who brought him up? Was he trained at Drury Lane? When did he start acting? Nobody can be certain: all that is certain is that Kean's childhood was wild, harsh and nomadic, marked by poverty, privation, and a precocious acquaintance with the more brutal facts of life in Georgian London. He never had a settled home for long. His education was scanty and irregular. It seems most likely, according to the evidence in Giles Playfair's biography, that he was born in 1790, the illegitimate child of Nancy Carey and Edmund Kean. His father was a drunkard, who went mad and committed suicide in his early twenties (when Edmund was three). Like his famous brother, Moses Kean, and his mistress's father, George Saville Carey, the elder Kean was an orator and a mimic, and enjoyed some popularity at concerts and recitals on the fringe of the professional theatre. Nancy Carey was an obscure and apparently disreputable actress, who scraped a living as a street hawker when she could find no work with strollers or in the London fairs and pleasure gardens. She seems to have had scant affection for Edmund, farming him out for long periods to other women, and he felt no love or respect for her. (Her grandfather, Henry Carey, best known as author of ' Sally in our Alley ', also committed suicide.) Although the boy took his mother's name, and probably spent a good deal of his childhood with her on the road, earning a few pence in barns, taverns and fairs, it was the Kean family which showed him most affection. He was looked after by the Keans' widowed sister, Mrs Price, who lived near Leicester Square, and by Moses Kean's mistress, Charlotte Tidswell, an obscure actress at Drury Lane, where she worked for nearly forty years. Perhaps, as many writers suppose, Miss Tidswell paid for his theatrical training; he may have been taught singing by Incledon and fencing by Angelo, the masters of their crafts; and he may have made occasional appearances on the Drury Lane stage, although there is no evidence that he was ever in the company or attracted any notice. (His name appears on no surviving bills, although these include the names of many other obscure infant troupers.) Yet, like most other children born into the theatre of the time, and unlike any other of our great actors, he was already an experienced performer before he was ten. Edmund Carey learned not only how to stand and deliver in the tragedian's style, but also how to sing, dance, do imitations, walk a rope, ride a horse, do somersaults and other acrobatic tricks. In 1801 he was billed at a minor theatre as 'the Celebrated Theatrical Child'; in 1802 – at the age of twelve – he appeared as 'the celebrated Master Carey' at Covent Garden in a short programme of recitations. Allowing for publicity puffing, he was clearly something of a success, and this no doubt made it all the harder for his proud, ambitious nature to endure waiting for recognition in manhood.

Kean's first recorded provincial engagement was in 1804, when he joined the stock company in Sheerness, 'still in boy's costume', and played a number of leading roles. From then onwards his course may intermittently be traced around the British Isles, from circuit to circuit, through a cloud of legend. He acted in Belfast, Maidstone, Canterbury, Tunbridge Wells, Rochester, Margate, Feversham and Deal; Gloucester and Stroud; Cheltenham (where he met and married Mary Chambers in 1808), Walsall, Lichfield and Birmingham; Swansea (where a son, Howard Anthony, was born in 1809), Carmarthen, Haverfordwest, and Waterford (where a second son, John Charles, was born in 1811); Edinburgh; York; Weymouth, Exeter, Totnes; Guernsey; Barnstaple and Dorchester, where he was engaged by Drury Lane (and where Howard died); and probably many other towns as well. He even appeared in London, in the Haymarket summer season of 1806, but his performances in such minor roles as Rosencrantz attracted no attention and he disappeared again. During these nine years in the provinces (which may well have been preceded by several more), Kean acted in tragedy, pantomime and farce, in melodrama, comedy and ballet; he sang, danced, gave recitations, helped with the stage management. He also made time to continue his self-education, writing out comments on Shakespeare, learning scraps of Latin, history and geography. In Shakespeare he played obscurely as Lennox, Gratiano and the rest, but the Works occupied a relatively small place in the large repertoire of these companies. Kean learned his trade in a host of long-buried dramas and after-pieces. His main 'serious' leading roles were Lord Hastings in Rowe's *Jane Shore* and Octavian in Colman's *The Mountaineers*. On the lighter side he was a popular Harlequin and Chimpanzee (a miming role in *La Pérouse* which gave the actor scope in a monkey skin for some crude humour, acrobatics, and pathos). It was not until he reached the Exeter circuit, probably at the age of twenty-two, that he began to tackle Shylock, Richard, and Macbeth. By that time his salary had advanced, in eight years, from fifteen shillings to twenty-five shillings a week.

Like all actors on the circuits, Kean suffered hunger, frustration and hardship, yet he felt them with special misery and resentment. Proud, lonely, vulnerable, envious and consumingly ambitious, he could not rest content with what, by provincial standards, was a moderate success. Many of his misfortunes were brought on by his own pride, in quarrelling with managers over pay or status. It was not the poverty that irked Kean: he was inured to it. It was the humiliation. Something of his fiery spirit is shown in the story of his return to Sheerness in 1807, when he opened in the title-role of *Alexander the Great*. An officer in one of the stage-boxes, in the way of Georgian gentlemen at the play, amused himself by continually interrupting the young actor. ' Alexander the little! Alexander the little! ' he called mockingly, until Kean could tolerate it no longer. Folding his arms, he walked over to the box, fixed the officer with a ferocious stare, and declaimed vehemently: ' Yes – with *a great soul*! ' Again, in Stroud the manager engaged Master Betty, the Infant Roscius, to play Norval and Hamlet; Kean was billed to play Glenalvon and Laertes; but Kean was not there on the night. When Betty had gone, he returned, limping and hungry, but still in a rage. ' I've had nothing to eat but turnips and cabbages, but I'll go hungry again, before I play such characters,' he told the company. ' I won't play second to any man – except John Kemble.' That is the story, and whether it is literally true or not, it is certainly in character. He despised most of the men and women he acted with. He believed implacably in his own genius. And when he seemed alone in that belief, he relieved his black melancholia by bouts of drinking. His marriage soon proved to be a failure, and his wife's life was made a misery. ' Could he have endured a little longer,' she wrote to a friend, ' Fortune might have rewarded his very great abilities. To forget sorrow he first took to Drinking – every dissipation follow'd of course. His Nights were spent with a Set of wretches a Disgrace to Human nature. One step led to another, till ruin, inevitable ruin, was the end.'

That was in September 1813, a few weeks before those ' very

great abilities ' were rewarded at the great age of twenty-four. Yet Kean's health and character were, indeed, already ruined by his debauchery, not so much because of his premature disappointment in his career but rather by the self-destructive fever raging in his blood, inflamed by his own blazing megalomania and his deep feeling of social inferiority. He could never come to terms with society, even in his own world of the theatre; and perhaps his greatest successes on the stage were as a public enemy defying the conventions, ' the man they loved to hate '.

While playing at Barnstaple, he agreed in despair – having now given up hope of being engaged by either of the 'patent houses ' – to join the company of the theatre in Wych Street, not far from Drury Lane, which was then run by R. W. Elliston. As this was a 'minor' theatre, where legitimate drama was forbidden, it seemed unlikely that he would now ever go to Drury Lane or Covent Garden. But a month later, while at Dorchester, he was suddenly offered a contract by Samuel Arnold, the manager of Drury Lane. Kean accepted, but did not disclose his prior commitment. When Elliston protested about such conduct and refused to surrender his rights in the actor, Kean was treated with cold disdain by the Lane's committee. They refused to let him act at Drury Lane or anywhere else until Elliston released him, and he was plunged once again into despair. Agreement was reached at last, however, and the committee – having taught the offender a lesson and exhausted other expedients – reluctantly allowed Kean to play.

On Kean's nights in that first triumphant season, described in the opening pages of this chapter, Drury Lane was packed to the doors, and people fought for a place. In March his salary was doubled, and after Hamlet it was raised to £20 a week; the committee gave him a cheque for £500, and other gifts were showered upon him by aristocratic admirers; his humble lodgings in Cecil Street became a place of pilgrimage; he was patronized, lionized, adored. By October he had earned over £4,000. Among his admirers was David Garrick's widow, who praised the resemblance of his Crookback to her husband's, and gave him some of the properties which Garrick had used (which Kean accepted) together with some good advice (which Kean could accept from nobody). To be publicly honoured as Garrick's heir gave Kean

especial pleasure. Yet unlike Garrick, he did not know how to
cope with this social triumph. He did his best for a time to live
up to the demands of his wife and the expectations of his noble
patrons, struggling with small talk and the genteel niceties, keeping up appearances. But he was too bitterly conscious of his lack
of 'family' and education, too uninterested in anything but the
stage, drink, and his own career, ever to be at ease in a salon or
at a fashionable dining-table. His very success whetted his sense
of isolation and resentment, his inability to tolerate competition
or criticism, and he suffered agonies of humiliation from the
Kemble-ites' personal attacks upon his lack of inches and graces,
his ignorance and vulgarity. Put on the defensive in this strange
new world, Kean soon gave up the fight to be, offstage, a second
Garrick. Unable to conform, compromise and flatter, he went to
the other extreme. Ostentatiously rebellious, he boasted of his pet
lion, his black horses, and his hard-drinking Wolf Club; he
fought boxing-matches in the parlour of his new house in Clarges
Street; but he found his pleasure, more often, in pot-houses.
Already in 1816 he missed a performance because, it was thought,
of a drunken orgy in Deptford: whatever the cause of that
absence, it was to be followed in later years by many, many more
for which the reasons were only too obvious. As Kean lost personal self-control he lost professional pride, and he more frequently appeared on the stage quite drunk.

In that first season of 1813-14, moreover, Kean was already –
at the age of twenty-four – marked by privations, excesses and
overwork. He embarked on his London career not, like Garrick,
in the fresh, full vigour of young manhood, but with a constitu-
tion already weakened. After each of the big Shakespearian roles,
it was noticed, he was utterly exhausted. He spat blood after his
first performance of Crookback at Drury Lane. Yet that fierce,
self-destructive will drove him on after the performance from
tavern to tavern, never resting or relaxing, burning up his energy,
his strength, his authority. Partly because of this way of life, he
lacked stamina. He showed London the best cards up his sleeve
in his first season. In his second season box-office receipts already
dropped well below the 1814 level, and within a few years he
often played to half-empty houses. In the provinces his popularity
was much more constant than in London, and it was in the
provinces that he made most of his money – for over sixteen years

he earned, it is estimated, at the rate of £10,000 a year (worth
perhaps seven or eight times as much today). Till the end of his
life, moreover, he kept his place as leader of the stage – or, at any
rate, as its first player. What he did, at his best, he did supremely
and uniquely well. But nevertheless, compared with Garrick or
with Kemble, he lost the audience's active allegiance in a remarkably short space of time.

If Kean had enjoyed, like Garrick, unrestricted power over
Drury Lane, would it all have been different? Perhaps. Certainly
the committee's rule was, while it lasted, deplorably weak and
inefficient (as is the way of committees in the arts), and a shrewd
manager with a free hand might have presented Kean with a
stronger company in better plays. Yet his word was, in effect, law
at the Lane for several years, and he had far more power than
Kemble ever enjoyed under Sheridan. He could get the committee, however much they disliked him as a man, to give him what
he wanted as an actor. But what he wanted was to shine alone. He
would not tolerate any talent of distracting magnitude beside him
on the stage, and his taste in choosing plays and actors was usually
bad. He seemed to have no clear idea of his own limits or powers,
for he failed in role after role of his own selection, yet he would
brook no interference or advice. Apparently devoid of self-
criticism and humility, he went his own road to perdition. When
he had a chance to take the lease of Drury Lane in 1819, with
the complete collapse of the committee's system, he ruined it by
his arrogance; the shareholders preferred to deal with Elliston,
a lesser actor but a better manager, endowed – for all his grandiose airs – with tact, common sense and capital. Kean at once
announced that he could never work for such a man. He would go
to America. But he soon had to reconcile himself to the painful
necessity of remaining at Drury Lane, for Elliston politely
threatened him with a possible claim of up to £10,000 in damages
if he broke his contract. This was, for Kean, yet another of Fate's
persistently unfair cuts. In the turbulent drama he made of his
own life, he was always the innocent hero, victim of injustice and
treachery.

Elliston allowed Kean to visit America in the following year.
At first he made a triumphal progress, until he arrived in Boston.
Enthusiasm here was tepid, and on the third night Kean refused
to play because there were not enough customers in the house.

The American press then fell upon him with hysterical savagery and his sudden unpopularity was exaggerated by the sneering tone of his 'apology' (Kean was never at his best in letters to the press, or indeed in his relations with the public). When he returned in disgrace to London in 1821, announcing to Elliston that he was 'full of health and ambition', he was given a spectacular welcome – but broke down after a few nights, and took several weeks to recuperate. It was a poor season, in which Kean failed with six new parts. For the season of 1822-3 Elliston shrewdly engaged Charles Mayne Young, a tragedian of the Kemble school, who had hitherto been the mainstay of Covent Garden. Kean protested fiercely that he would leave England rather than act with Young. 'The Throne is mine – no man, in this profession, can rob me of the character of the first English Actor.' Yet the contrast of styles, as Elliston foresaw, revived interest in the other tragedian and confirmed his supremacy. In the next season Macready replaced Young, and Kean's indignation deepened when Elliston planned to put them together on the stage. Once again he spoke of leaving England for America.

It was not Macready who was the danger now. In the spring of 1824 the press began to refer glancingly to incidents in Kean's private life which were within a few months to bring his world down in ruins. The storm burst in January 1825, when Robert Cox, a London alderman and member of the Drury Lane committee, sued his friend Edmund Kean for 'criminal conversation' with Mrs Cox. The defence pleaded the husband's complicity, in an affair of at least seven years' standing, and brought up enough evidence to strip Cox of public sympathy and cut his claim of £2,000 to an award of £800. But Kean was in the pillory, the laughing-stock of England; his love letters were read aloud and broadcast in the press; ballads and prints kept his disgrace alive; and *The Times*, which devoted half an issue to reporting the case, pursued him with particular virulence, virtually encouraging audiences to riot against 'that obscene little personage'. What exacerbated the public fury was that Kean acted at Drury Lane a few days after the trial. He had no thought of postponement. 'I am prepared for war,' he is reported to have told Elliston, and he stood his ground bravely in a battle royal which lasted for several nights of continuous uproar. He quickly reasserted his authority in London, on the stage at least, but angry demonstrations broke out again during his provincial tour that summer and also in America, to which he rashly returned in the winter. It was not so much the fact of adultery that shocked the two nations, nor was this by any means altogether a fit of hypocritical hysteria. Behind the outburst against Kean lay a long accumulation of resentments, among all classes. It is partly true, as Giles Playfair says, that ' they hated him – because he was not a gentleman and yet had refused to be humble. He had flaunted himself in the face of society. It was his real fault not to have outraged morality, but to have outraged caste.' (Sir Walter Scott called him 'a copper laced, twopenny tearmouth, rendered mad by conceit and success.') Yet he had also outraged the traditional codes of the audience, which were based on something more than mere snobbery, by his arrogance, his drunkenness, his breaches of faith.

On his return from America in January 1827, Kean played Shylock with all his old flair. ' A rush so fearful, an audience so packed, a reconciliation so complete, acting so faultless and a dramatic enjoyment so exquisite, I have never experienced,' wrote one reliable observer, Dr Doran. Yet the recovery was short-lived. Kean was now estranged from wife and son, ostracized outside the theatre by most of his former patrons, and almost completely surrendered to a life of debauchery. His genius slid into decline, with occasional flares of greatness to light the way. ' His self-respect was gone to the last shred,' says Hillebrand, ' and with it whatever authority he had over himself.' Soon Kean discovered, one agonizing evening at the Lane, that his memory had gone: he could learn no more new roles. But he went on acting, in London and the provinces, living on his past glories, frequently too ill or too drunk to play. Every now and then he would make his farewell to the stage, but in a month or two he was back, unsteadily, in harness. How else could he live? He had earned a fortune in his long career of dissipation, and had never learned how to keep it. In 1832, Dr Doran noted, ' Genius was not traceable in that bloated face; intellect was all but quenched in those once matchless eyes; and the power seemed gone, despite the will that would recall it.'

At his estate in Bute, he lived out his fantasies of power with a prostitute, Ophelia Benjamin, as his companion. Over the gate were four busts, of Shakespeare, Massinger, Garrick and himself;

the walls were papered with copies of his successes; and sometimes he patrolled the grounds dressed as Richard or Sir Giles.
Often he appeared, in the street or on the stage, in the costume
of the Huron Indians, which he had brought back from America
and of which – together with his Huron name, Alanienouidet –
he was grotesquely proud. Blotched face painted with streaks of
red and yellow, bloodshot eyes looking out from beneath a head-
dress of eagle's feathers, gold rings through his nose and ears,
and a tomahawk in his belt, Kean lived out his favourite role to
the end – as an enemy of society, ready to scalp all conspirators
against his genius. The end came at last in 1833, during a performance of *Othello* at Covent Garden. Ill and weak though he
was, Kean endured until 'Villain, be sure thou prove my love a
whore', but then he collapsed with his arm round Iago (played by
his son Charles), and was carried off the stage. He never came
back. Several weeks later, at his home in Richmond, on the
morning of 15 May, Edmund Kean died. He was, in all proba-
bility, only forty-three.

A few months after Kean's London début, Hazlitt made a sharp
attack on the Drury Lane management for its lack of enterprise.
'Why not bring him out at once in a variety of characters?' he
demanded. 'It seems, by all we can find, that versatility is, perhaps, Mr Kean's greatest excellence. Why, then, not give him his
range?' Far from being versatile, however, Kean worked within
narrow limits. The roll-call of his parts, old and new, is a long
list of failures. Fired by emulation, he tried continually to surpass
other actors in parts they had made their own. He failed in farce
and comedy, when he challenged the memory of Garrick (Kitely
and Drugger) and Cooke (Sir Pertinax MacSycophant). He failed
as a tragic victim (Orestes) and a romantic lover (Romeo). He
failed to match Macready as Virginius, or Kemble as Penruddock,
Coriolanus, King John and Wolsey. Although he attempted
scores of new roles after his first London season, he added only
four of any size to his permanent repertoire during the next
twenty-seven years. They were: Macbeth, in November 1814;
Sir Giles Overreach in January 1816 (it almost equalled Richard
in popularity); Brutus in December 1818 (not in Shakespeare's
Julius Caesar, but in *Brutus, or The Fall of Tarquin*, by John
Howard Payne, the author of *Home, Sweet Home*); and King

Lear, in April 1820. They were, in other words, all achieved within six years of his initial success. Unlike Garrick, whose reputation grew and whose range expanded during his thirty years of theatrical sovereignty, Kean never fully recaptured the glory of his first London season; and for the rest of his career he lived, in the main, upon his Richard, Shylock, Hamlet, Othello and Sir Giles. Other leading parts were such pasteboard devils as Bajazet, the bloodthirsty Tartar ('the fiery soul of barbarous revenge stung to madness') and Zanga, the avenging Moor ('the glowing energy of the untamed children of the sun'). Moreover, his Hamlet, Macbeth, and Richard II were all, it seems, strongly akin to his Crookback, for he was often irrelevantly violent, harsh and sardonic; 'we seldom entirely lose sight of his Richard.'

Few people admired him in comedy. Hazlitt was one of them. But he wrote, as early as 1815,

Mr Kean's imagination appears not to have the principles of joy, or hope, or love in it. He seems chiefly sensible to pain, or to the passions that spring from it, and to the terrible energies of mind or body, which are necessary to grapple with, or to avert it. Even over the world of passion he holds but a divided sway: he either does not feel, or seldom expresses, deep, sustained, internal sentiment – there is no repose in his mind: no feeling seems to take full possession of it, that is not linked to action, and that does not goad him on to the phrenzy of despair. Or if he ever conveys the sublimer pathos of thought and feelings, it is after the storm of passion, to which he has been worked up, had subsided.

Within his range, there were, moreover, many conspicuous faults. In its upper registers Kean's voice was, as both Genest and Hazlitt agree, 'very bad': he usually overstrained it, trying to fill the vast theatre, and frequently became inaudible. Even in 1814 it often sounded 'thick and hoarse, somewhat between an apoplexy and a cold', screeching and croaking when he forced it in the heat of passion. Like Garrick he was somewhat handicapped by his height – he was about five feet seven; but he lacked Garrick's fluent physical grace, being round-shouldered and heavily built. 'His figure was not only diminutive but insignificant,' as one observer put it, 'his natural appearance . . . was mean': so much so that offstage he seemed smaller than he really was, and his height has usually been put at five feet four. Deficient in dignity, he was unroyal, even in his best roles. His

kings and princes were unmistakably plebeian, and his Hamlet –
in particular – had also little touch of either gentleman or scholar.
More significant was his apparent disregard for the text, especially
in Shakespeare, for he misused even the traditionally corrupted
versions of the plays. At his best in the 'busy' scenes, when
there was something to *do,* he hurried over long speeches of des-
criptive and meditative verse, slurring the words and adding his
own emendations as he went along: 'He translated his characters
with great freedom and ingenuity into a language of his own,'
said the idolatrous Hazlitt. Sometimes, as in a performance of
Richard III in 1814, 'he gave the energy of action alone. He
merely gesticulated, or at best vociferated the part.' He bent all
his energies, through the burning glass of his genius, on a series
of particular 'points', careless of what happened to the rest of
the play, concentrating sometimes upon one single word. As Shylock, in the scene with Tubal, he hurried through the catalogue
of Antonio's misdeeds with a high-pitched, rapid delivery; and
then – in sudden transition to a gentle, suffering simplicity of
tone – said 'I am a Jew!' It always brought the house down.
Between the lightning flashes he did not always seem to be identified with the character he was playing: there was not, as in
Kemble's work, a consistent and thorough study of the role. In
Richard III, for instance, there appeared to be – said Hazlitt –
'a perpetual assumption of his part . . . The excellence of his
acting is in proportion to the number of hits, for he has not equal
truth and purity of style.' In the last act of *Macbeth,* to quote
Hazlitt again, he 'seemed to be studying the part, rather than
performing it – striving to make every word more emphatic than
the last.' This method was most conspicuously unsuccessful in his
Lear, for in spite of some 'single hits', it seems, he failed to comprehend the play. At his worst he made 'every sentence an alter-
nation of dead pauses and rapid transitions', with sudden drops
and jumps in the voice, and his vocal mannerisms became more
evident as he grew older. A Philadelphia critic in 1821 deplored
his 'sudden, mechanical depression and quick, violent vicissi-
tudes of tone – the precipitate strain and extreme volubility immediately preceding or following long pauses . . .' If Kemble was
too statuesque, Kean went to the other extreme in his physical
restlessness, which his detractors spoke of as St Vitus's dance.
'His hands,' said the Philadelphia critic, quoted in Mr Hille-

brand's biography, 'are kept in unremitting and the most rapid, convulsive movement; seeking, as it were, a resting place in some part of his upper dress, and occasionally pressed together on the crown of his head.' He was, Hazlitt wrote of his Othello, 'always on full stretch – never relaxed . . . He is too often in the highest key of passion, too uniformly on the verge of extravagance, too constantly on the rack,' or as the Philadelphia critic phrased it, 'his excellencies are perpetually passing into extremes, or degenerating into defects.' When he played Romeo, one hostile critic complained of 'a rotatory movement of the hand, as if describing the revolution of a spinning jenny; multiplied slaps upon his forehead, and manual elevation of his fell of hair; repeated knocking upon his own breast and occasional rapping at the chests of others . . .' Kean had his deliberate tricks, too. Like many other stars, he 'upstaged' his colleagues and always kept his face to the front; he was apt to prelude a sentence by 'a hesitation, or a sound as of a half-laugh like a cue for the applause of *claqueurs*'; and he had a way of 'going quickly off, then returning slowly but unexpectedly'. As he grew older, he grew trickier: in 1821 his Lear showed a resolve, said Hazlitt, 'to give the passages in a way which nobody else could give them, and in which nobody else would expect them to be given.'

Yet, to repeat the words of G. H. Lewes: 'The greatest artist is he who is greatest in the highest reaches of his art, even although he may lack the qualities necessary for the adequate execution of some minor details. It is not by his faults, but by his excellences, that we measure a great man . . . Thus estimated, Edmund Kean was incomparably the greatest actor I have seen . . .' At his best he transcended all limitations of face, body and voice, and he acted with his whole being: 'One might almost say "his body thought".' As Othello, he 'swelled up' till he looked almost as tall as Kemble, and all the deficiencies of his voice were forgotten in the 'farewell' speech. 'I could hardly keep from crying,' wrote Crabb Robinson in his diary, 'it was pure feeling.' Hazlitt said that this speech 'struck on the heart like the swelling notes of some divine music, like the sound of years of departed happiness.' It was, Leigh Hunt records, 'spoken in long, lingering tones, like the sound of a parting knell . . .' Keats, indeed, praised all Kean's speaking, 'the elegance, gracefulness and music of elocution . . . The sensual life of verse springs warm from the lips of Kean'; and there seems little doubt that some of the violence of the opposition to Kean's acting – like the violence of his partisans – came from his apparent association with a ' movement ' which roused fierce controversy in the world of literature and with which Keats himself was identified, together with Hazlitt, Hunt and other admirers of the actor. To many people Kean seemed the embodiment of Romanticism. Not everyone would go as far as Keats in finding the tragedian 'a relict of romance ' and ' a posthumous ray of chivalry ', but Coleridge's celebrated verdict that ' to see Kean was to read Shakespeare by flashes of lightning ' expresses not only one substantial reason for Kean's popularity, but also a significant aspect of the romantic approach to experience in the theatre.

At his best he transcended all physical and vocal limitations. Leigh Hunt said that ' his little person absolutely becomes tall, and rises to the height of moral grandeur in such characters as that of Othello '; Lewes explained that ' all defects were overlooked or disregarded, because it was impossible to watch Kean as Shylock, Othello, Richard or Sir Giles Overreach without being strangely shaken by the terror, and the pathos, and the passion of a stormy spirit uttering itself in tones of irresistible power.' Much of Kean's impact, however, depended on where you were sitting in the theatre. As Sir Edward Mortimer in *The Iron Chest*, leaving the stage, he had to say the famous line of warning: ' Wilford, remember! ' Lewes noted that ' Kean used to pause after " Wilford ", and during the pause his face underwent a rapid succession of expressions fluently melting into each other, and all tending to one climax of threat; and then the deep tones of " remember! " came like muttered thunder. Those spectators who were unable to catch these expressions considered the pause a mere trick; and sometimes the pauses were only tricks, but often they were subtle truths.' Again, Hazlitt noted: ' I have seen Mr Kean play Sir Giles Overreach one night from the front of the pit, and a few nights after from the front boxes, facing the stage. It was another being altogether. That which had been so lately nothing but flesh and blood, a living fibre, " instinct with fire " and spirit, was no better than a little fantoccini figure, darting backwards and forwards on the stage, starting, screaming and playing a number of fantastic tricks before the audience.' Those who saw Kean from the boxes, Hazlitt explained, ' have not seen him at all. The expression of his face is quite lost, and only the harsh and grating tones of his voice produce their full effect on the ear . . . All you discover is an abstraction of his defects, both of person, voice and manner. He appears to be a little man in a great passion.' If Kean was a victim of contemporary architecture (and the patent laws) it was because, again in Hazlitt's words, ' his face is the running comment on his acting, which reconciles the audience to it. Without that index to his mind, you are not prepared for the vehemence and suddenness of his gestures; his pauses are long, abrupt and unaccountable, if not filled up by the expression; it is in the working of his face that you see the writhing and coiling of his passions before they make their serpent-spring; the lightning of his eye precedes the hoarse burst of thunder from his voice.' When he appeared at the Lyceum, which was a good deal smaller than Covent Garden or Drury Lane, a critic commented: ' To see Kean at this house, is something like looking at a beautiful object through a microscope, all the brilliancy of which is enhanced, and minuter beauties invisible to the naked eye, are developed with a perfection that astonishes you . . .'

It was, above all, Kean's eyes that had to be seen near-at-hand: ' black, large, brilliant and penetrating, and remarkable for the shortness of their upper lid, which discovered a clearly defined line of white above the ball.' They contributed largely to the brilliance of his mime. After his Othello, one playgoer wrote: ' I saw those eyes all night.' With all his limitations of voice, it is not surprising that most of Kean's greatest ' points ' were scored in silence or when, instead of speaking the words, he choked over them in grief and rage. Such a scene was Macbeth's appearance after the murder: ' The hesitation, the bewildered look, the coming to himself when he sees his hands bloody; the manner in which his voice clung to his throat, and choked his utterance; his agony and tears, the force of nature overcome by passion, beggared description.' Hazlitt observed that as Othello, ' where he listens in dumb despair to the fiend-like insinuations of Iago, he presented the very face, the marble aspect of Dante's Count Ugolino. On his fixed eyelids " Horror sat plumed ".' As Romeo, two moments were remembered – when he gulped with tenderness over Juliet's name, and when he died.

Kean's death-scenes were justly famous, and have been distinguished by Leigh Hunt. As Richard III,

he falls from exhaustion – and as loss of blood may be presumed to cool his frame and restore his sanity, so does he grow calmer and calmer through the dying speech, till his mighty heart is hushed for ever. In *Othello*, death is occasioned by piercing himself to the heart with a poignard; can you not mark the frozen shudder, as the steel enters the frame, and the choking expression, with distended eyes and open mouth . . . Death by a *heart* wound is *instantaneous*. Thus does he portray it; he literally dies standing; it is the dead body only of Othello that falls, heavily and at once; there is no *rebound*, which speaks of vitality and of living muscles. It is the dull weight of clay seeking its kindred earth. But the scene that actors admire most . . . is his death in Hamlet. The Prince does not die of a sword-wound, but from the poison impregnated in that wound; of course, from its rapidity in doing the work of death, it must have been a powerful mineral. What are the effects of such a poison? Intense internal pain, wandering vision, swelling veins in the temple. All this Kean details with awful reality: his eyes dilate and then lose lustre: he gnaws his hand in the vain effort to repress emotion; the veins thicken in his forehead; his limbs shudder and quiver, and as life grows fainter, and his hand drops from between his stiffening lips, he utters a cry of expiring nature, so exquisite that I can only compare it to the stifled sob of a fainting woman, or the little wail of a suffering child.

If he sometimes failed to distinguish his characters in life, they won their differences in death. ' The very eye-lid dies,' said Keats. But the opposite testimony of the Philadelphia critic should be noted, that ' although these were wonders of ingenuity ' and ' stupendous achievements of mind and body ', yet ' no mortal, wounded and moribund, ever fell with the precision of pitch, the nicety of contour and straightness of prostration which mark Mr Kean's exits from the world.'

Kean's art was one of romantic chiaroscuro, with many sharp contrasts in light and shade, and he found perhaps his richest opportunities and his fullest range – if not his most characteristic success – in the third act of *Othello*.

Never were the workings of the human heart more successfully laid open than in the scene following that in which Iago first excites his jealousy. In every tone of the voice, in every movement of the face and body, it might be seen labouring under the accumulated agonies of unbounded love, struggling with and at length yielding to doubt. The depth of expression thrown into the words, ' I found not Cassio's

kisses on her lips ', has never been surpassed; then came the utter
heart-sinking and helplessness which inevitably succeeds to the pro-
tracted operation of powerful passion. The speech beginning ' Oh now
for ever, farewell,' etc., was given in a tone of quiet despair, which
evinced the most exquisite delicacy of conception, embodied in expression absolutely perfect. To this calm succeeded a storm of contend-
ing passions – rage, hatred, intervening doubt – until at length the
whole of his already excited energies were yielded up to revenge;
the look and action accompanying the word ' O, blood! Iago, blood!'
cast a chill over everyone's frame.

G. H. Lewes wrote, of a much later performance in the same
role: ' In the successive unfolding of these great scenes he
represented with incomparable effect the lion-like fury, the deep
and haggard pathos, the forlorn sense of desolation alternating
with gusts of stormy cries for vengeance, the misgivings and sudden reassurance, the calm and deadly resolution of one not easily
moved, but who, being moved, was stirred to the very depths.
One playgoer said: ' I never saw such acting. I am not sure
whether I like it; admire it I must – it is nature.' Dumas *père*
described him as ' a wild beast, half-man, half-tiger '. It was,
Hazlitt said, ' twenty times more powerful ' than Kean's Shylock
and ' the finest piece of acting in the world '. Yet Kean played
Othello with a complexion of ' tawny brick-dust ', in the costume
of an Albanian Greek, and struck at least one dissenter as ' a little
vixenish black girl in short petticoats '.

Compared with the patrician Kemble, he was – as Hazlitt said
– ' a *radical* performer ': this was Left-wing acting. Yet, compared with Garrick, he was often stagy: in Mrs Siddons's words,
' he is forever energetic and often natural, which Garrick was
always '. He made points where Garrick lived the role. Consciously, and at times ostentatiously, he switched from the grand
style to the intimate, and back again. He was ' all effort, all
violence, all extreme passion '. To many observers all this fire
and turbulence and fury was the outpouring of nature, unpre-
meditated and instinctive. Certainly the electricity and thunder
of Kean's storms upon the stage were charged by the energies of
his own unruly and disordered soul: that was the force which
gave the look of ' naturalism ', of inevitability, to so many of the
characters he played: that was why so many people found him
impossible to resist. ' He lifted you off your feet,' said Samuel

Phelps: he swept the audience with a tidal wave of passion. But, even at his most oceanic, Kean usually acted with systematic care and deliberation. To an inexperienced playgoer like Keats, it seemed that he 'delivered himself up to the instant feeling, without a shadow of a thought about anything else '. Yet G. H. Lewes assures us that he 'vigilantly and patiently rehearsed every detail, trying the tones until his ear was satisfied, practising looks and gestures until his artistic sense was satisfied . . . one who often acted with him informed me that when Kean was rehearsing on a new stage he accurately counted the number of steps he had to take before reaching a certain spot, or before uttering a certain word . . .' George Vandenhoff, who appeared with Kean, recorded that ' his delivery of Othello's " farewell " ran on the same tones and semitones, had the same rests and breaks, the same forte and piano, the same crescendo and diminuendo, night after night, as if he spoke it from a musical score. So, all his most striking attitudes – and he was the most picturesque of players – all his most effective *points*, and abrupt transitions of voice and manner, were reproduced in oft-repeated performances . . . so that his admirers were ready with their applause almost by anticipation . . .'

' Did this detract from his genius?' Vandenhoff asked, and he rightly answered: ' No; it proved that he was an *artist*; and there is no art without *method* and *design* ' – a truism that has sometimes been forgotten among romantic critics of the English stage. If English actors may be divided, according to the categories of Nietzsche, into ' Apollonian ' and ' Dionysian ' schools, there is no doubt where Kean should be placed. Yet it is as misleading to label him ' romantic ' as to call Kemble a ' classic ' actor. Both were empiricists, outside all schools, in the wider world of art: both were painstaking, self-conscious craftsmen, building their personal eccentricities and weaknesses into a highly individual style of acting. In many respects, Kean was the lesser artist of the two. He never shared the interest of Kemble and other great actors in production, in management, in the prestige or progress of the theatre: he seemed to be concerned with the stage only as a platform for himself alone – for the glory of *his* art and *his* personality. He could not tolerate competition: there was no future for rival talent under his management. What is more, he lost control of his daemon. Harnessed by his conscience as an artist, it made him famous; but, once off the leash, it helped to destroy him. Yet the fact is that Kean was a great actor. He became a great legend. And as long as there are theatres for living actors, his name will be remembered with awe, and homage, and compassion.

❖❖❖4❖❖❖

William Charles
Macready

'O God! You brute!' The despairing bellow echoed along the
corridors of Covent Garden. 'Beast of Hell!' A shriek of murderous fury came from the wings. The actors in the dressing-
rooms, preparing for the worst, merely exchanged glances over
their make-up trays. It was that insupportable, bad-tempered
snob Macready working himself up into a rage again. Some unlucky stage-hand or supernumerary had touched off one of his
blistering tempests of bullying. That night, however, much was
forgiven Macready back-stage at Covent Garden, for everyone
knew that the fate of the theatre might depend upon his performance. This arrogant young tragedian, who had made an unspec-
tacular London début two years before, was actually daring to
challenge Edmund Kean in his prize role of Richard III. The
town had risen to the bait, and Covent Garden was packed to the
doors for the first time in many months.

Within two years of John Philip Kemble's retirement, the
great green-and-gold theatre had run upon the rocks. By the
autumn of 1819 it was in danger of breaking up. Drury Lane had
Kean and Munden, Fanny Kelly and Eliza Vestris, but Covent
Garden had lost nearly all its stars. Charles Mayne Young had
seceded, Miss O'Neill had retired, Liston was ill, Kitty Stephens
was on leave, and Charles Kemble had walked out after quarrelling with the proprietor, Henry Harris. Persistently bad business
was made worse by accumulated building debts. The situation was
so desperate that the leading actors agreed to work without pay
until Christmas. 'I never knew in the morning,' said Harris later,
'whether I should not shoot myself before the night.' Macready
was his standby. Under pressure from the box office, Harris asked
'the great W.C.M.' – as Kean scornfully called him – to under-

take the role of Gloucester. Macready, deeply conscious of the
risk, refused. But Harris's requests became more urgent, then
more peremptory, until at last he forced the actor's hand by
announcing the performance on the bills, at six days' notice.
' There was now no escape! ' Macready wrote in his reminiscences.
' I was committed to the public, and must undergo the ordeal.'
The days were spent in concentrated study, with ' alternations of
hope and fear '. Only the stock costumes of the theatre's wardrobe were available, and Macready had to pay out of his own
pocket for their alteration, for there was not a penny to spare
in the treasury. Although he had played Crookback before during
his provincial apprenticeship (this was a role in the pack of every
leading actor), it was not one of his favourites, and he believed
that he could not look the part (' a hump-backed tall man is not
in nature '). Yet if he failed in it at Covent Garden, his promising
career might well be ruined. Much was in the balance on the night
of 25 October, 1819. For Macready it was ' a life-and-death
grapple, and I threw my whole soul into all I did '. As a critic
said the next morning, ' there was no middle point between
disgrace and glory.'

The house buzzed with excited anticipation. Partisans of Kean
and Kemble had come in force to watch this presumptuous young
man – known hitherto for his villains in melodrama – make an
exhibition of himself. When he came on, they saw an actor of
medium height (Macready was five feet nine), with large blue
eyes, square chin, high cheekbones, small mouth, massive forehead, and irregular nose, set in a flat, dark and somewhat ugly
face. He was very nervous, and showed it. In his early scenes he
was subdued and self-conscious. Behind the scenes there was
gloom and despondency: among the Kean-ites in front there was
high glee. Yet Macready rose with the play. His eyes flashed fire.
His voice filled the theatre. His new conception of the character,
owing little to Cooke or to Kean, gradually took command of the
audience. He showed, as Hunt said later, ' the gayer part ' of
Crookback. ' His very step, in the more sanguine scenes, had a
princely gaiety of self-possession, and seemed to walk off to the
music of its approaching triumph.' Compared with Kean, whose
strength was already waning, he maintained greater energy and
consistency, lighting up sections of the play which the older
tragedian hurried over between his famous ' points '. Hunt, a dis-

ciple of Kean, wrote that 'Mr Kean's is the more gloomy and reflective villain, rendered so by the united effect of his deformity and subtle-mindedness; Mr Macready's is the more ardent and bold-faced one, borne up by a temperament naturally high and sanguine, though pulled down by mortification.' Although this version followed the usual Cibber text, Macready had tried in his study of the character to 'carry the spirit of the great original' through what he contemptuously described as these 'sententious and stagey lines'. (A year later he restored more of the 'great original's' play to the stage.)

It was in giving Tyrrel orders for disposing of the Princes' bodies that Macready's triumph was assured. As Tyrrel hurried off, and Crookback triumphantly exclaimed. 'Why then my loudest fears are hushed!' the pit rose at him. People stood up, waving hats and handkerchiefs, and cheering for several minutes. In the tent scene, where Kean scored some of his greatest effects, there was another excited outburst of applause; and the pit rose again at Crookback's death, Kean's *pièce de resistance*. When, after the curtain fell, an actor appeared (according to custom) to 'give out' the play – that is, to announce its next performance – the audience would not give him a hearing. Stamping their feet and cheering wildly, they shouted for Macready. For the first time in the history of Covent Garden the star of the evening was called before the curtain to take his bow. Not even John Philip Kemble had been so honoured. Macready had not eclipsed Kean in the role, but he was now acknowledged in many quarters as his peer. 'His Richard was perfectly original,' as the *Morning Chronicle* said next day, 'yet there was no apparent struggle after originality, no laborious effort to mark a difference in passages of small importance . . . It was the natural unforced and unaffected effort of an intellect relying on its own powers . . .' With one performance he had put his elders, Charles Kemble and Charles Young, in the shade. 'The mark at which I had aimed so long was now attained. I was the undisputed head of the theatre.' And the theatre was saved.

A month later, on 29 November, Macready made – at Henry Harris's request – another audacious experiment. He appeared as Coriolanus. John Philip Kemble had appeared in what was probably his greatest role at the same theatre only two years before, at his farewell from the stage, and Macready – fully con-

scious of the risks of challenging ' the noblest Roman's memory
– went into training during November. In order ' to add dignity
and grace to my deportment ', he took lessons from the ballet-
master in ' the various attitudes from the antique ', practising
statuesque poses and a classic stride. Yet he had no intention of
appearing as a second-rate Kemble. Although he hoped to ' master
the patrician's outward bearing ', he aimed at ' giving full vent
to the unbridled passion of the man,' following a conception of
Caius Marcius in strong contrast to John Philip's remembered
marble grandeur. Instead of working up the one sentiment of
dignified contempt to an extraordinary pitch of intensity, in John
Forster's words, he brought to life a fierce, proud man fighting a
tumult of emotions. Macready could not inspire the awe with
which Kemble's Coriolanus filled the audience; but in place of
Kemble's relatively monotonous declamation, he gave a ranging
variety of speech, in what Leigh Hunt described as ' the finest
and most heroic ' voice on the stage. When the Covent Garden
curtain fell, the cheering audience once again demanded that
Macready himself should appear before it and ' give out ' the
play, repeating the honour they had paid to his Richard.

Macready had now, at the age of twenty-six, successfully challenged both Kean and Kemble in their best roles. He rounded
off this momentous season of 1819-20 with a triumphant performance in a play which owed nothing to either actor, for Macready
introduced it to the London stage. It was called *Virginius: or,
The Liberation of Rome,* and had recently been turned down by
Kean. At his first reading of the manuscript in April 1820,
Macready saw its rich opportunities. He persuaded Harris to
accept it, paid for his own costumes (' not one sixpence was
allowed for its *mise-en-scène*,' he says), and produced it himself,
putting the company through unprecedentedly painstaking rehearsals. Within a month of receiving the manuscript, Macready had
mounted *Virginius* at Covent Garden, and the first performance,
on 17 May, was a triumph both for him and for the Irish school-
teacher-author, James Sheridan Knowles. Several of Knowles's
plays had already been produced in the provinces, but it was with
Virginius in 1820 that he first made his mark in the London
theatre, where for a generation his work was highly honoured. To
the modern reader *Virginius* and its companion pieces may well
seem mortuary fare, with their pseudo-Elizabethan verse and

their cardboard psychology, yet Knowles was an ex-actor with the gift – surprisingly rare among aspiring dramatists, now as then – of writing actable rhetoric and arranging stage-worthy situations, and *Virginius* stood out above the contemporary fustian by virtue of its humanity and sentiment. For some thirty years it provided Macready with perhaps the most popular part in his repertoire – as a noble Roman father who stabs his own daughter to save her from the lust of a tyrant. It gave him scope for the terror and the pathos in which he excelled (he could command ' a tone of exquisite touchingness '); and it introduced, moreover, that kind of relative naturalism with which he had already coloured Coriolanus. The appeal of Virginius lay, as the critic R. H. Horne said, in its ' domestic feeling. The costume, the setting, the decorations are heroic. We have Roman tunics but a modern English heart – the scene is the Forum, but the sentiments those of the " Bedford Arms ".'

At the end of this successful season, Macready played Macbeth for the first time, on his benefit night. He was received with great enthusiasm. The performance became, in later years, one of the most popular in his repertoire. Yet the occasion was remarkable for another reason, too. By long-standing tradition, playgoers took the opportunity of a benefit night to give a present – usually in money – to the player concerned. But Macready broke the tradition by sending all the gifts back, and making it a rule ' not to accept more than the value of the tickets required '. Among the aristocratic patrons snubbed in this way were Lord Glengall and Colonel Berkeley, but they admitted – Macready says proudly in his reminiscences – that ' it was " impossible to be offended " with me '. That he was prepared to risk, for he was determined to be accepted as a gentleman. ' I could not consider myself sitting down to table on terms of social equality with a man to whom I had been obliged for the gift of five, ten or twenty pounds.' John Philip Kemble had no such scruples: here was an omen for the future.

Here, too, was a triple achievement – as Richard, Coriolanus and Virginius – which signified the highest promise for Macready's future. Yet, in spite of many successes in plays old and new, he marked time for years. It was not until after Kean's death, in 1833, that he was acknowledged as the first player of the English stage, and even today his claim to be ranked with

Kean and Kemble is often hotly contested. In death, as in life, Macready is still the subject of argument.

William Charles Macready was born in London, on 3 March 1793, the fifth child, and eldest surviving son, of an Irish actor and his English wife. The elder Macready (whose name was also spelt M'Cready and McCready) was the son of a Dublin upholsterer, who had come to England eight years before in search of theatrical glory. He soon found a wife in Christina Birch, a fellowmember of the Manchester company, and a job as 'walking gentleman' at Covent Garden; but there he remained, in serviceable obscurity, throughout the rest of his acting career. This ended, however, when Macready was five years old, for his father moved into a very different social sphere by taking over the full-time management of the Theatre Royal, Birmingham, with a circuit of satellite theatres in Leicester, Stafford and other towns. Macready's childhood, then, was steeped in theatrical lore; he was well acquainted with the backstage world of provincial players; but he had no inclination to join them – and his father had no intention, it seems, of putting him on the boards. The elder Macready was both ambitious and successful enough to send his son to Rugby, with an eye on Oxford and the Bar; but at the age of fifteen he was obliged to leave : his father had overreached himself by leasing a new theatre in Manchester, and was now unable to pay the Rugby fees. With deep reluctance, but a strong sense of duty, Macready prepared to make a career upon the stage. The circumstances of that decision affected his entire life, and probably warped his development as an artist.

Under the intermittent supervision of his father, who frequently went into hiding to avoid arrest, Macready began to train himself in Manchester for his new profession after the Christmas of 1808. He took lessons in fencing; learned by heart some suitable 'juvenile' roles; and listened to his father's lectures on the style of Charles Macklin and John Henderson, whom he set up as models in acting. (' In after life,' Macready wrote mournfully in his reminiscences, ' I had . . . the difficult task of unlearning much that was impressed on me in my boyish days.') Within a few months of leaving Rugby, this sixteen-year-old boy had to shoulder the responsibility of looking after a theatre on his own : he managed his father's company at Newcastle for two months in the summer. In the autumn he paid his first visit to London, in order to study the leading actors of the day and to take fencing lessons with Angelo. Macready saw Charles Kemble, Elliston, Munden, Cooke, Emery and Liston, but he was expressly forbidden by his father to watch John Philip Kemble, in case he should become a mere copyist of the great man's style. The day after he returned to Manchester, his father went to prison for debt, and Macready was left alone to look after his interests. It was a hard and sudden lesson, but he met the challenge well. He took charge of the company at Chester, where rent and salaries were in arrears, and both actors and proprietors were hostile. Having cleared off the debts, he managed to open the Newcastle theatre on Boxing Day (by pawning his watch) and to run a successful season there. Before it had ended, his resilient father was at liberty again and in full command.

Macready's brief experience of poverty and hardship was already over. From now onwards it was plain sailing. That summer his father reopened the Birmingham theatre, and arranged his son's début as an actor, anonymously, in the role of Romeo, on 7 June 1810. Lacking any sense of vocation, he assures us, Macready did his best to prepare for the dreaded event by hard labour, until he 'got by rote . . . every particular of place, gesture, feeling and intonation'. At first, he records in his reminiscences, he was like 'an automaton' in a 'kind of waking dream', but then he was wakened by the applause. 'I gained my self-possession, and really entered into the spirit of the character and, I may say, felt the passion I was to represent.' When, after the curtain fell, someone asked the young Macready how he felt, he answered exuberantly: 'I feel as if I should like to act it all over again.' Here is a key to the rest of his career. For all his hankerings after Church and Bar, he was born for the stage.

After Romeo, emerging under his own name, he played Norval, Zanga and George Barnwell with success in that inaugural season. Every night, on getting home, the young man conducted private rehearsals, polishing up and correcting his performance. Every Sunday he got the key to the theatre from his father, and after morning service he would lock himself in, take the stage, and practise exits, entrances, gestures and attitudes, acting over all his characters until he was tired out. For four years, Macready continued his apprenticeship – but as the leading man, and, often

enough, as director (though the job of 'getting up' and rehearsing a play was not then a specialized profession). He led his
father's companies in Newcastle, Leicester, Glasgow, Dumfries
and Carlisle, playing most of the main roles in the repertoire, both
comedy and tragedy, history and spectacle – Rolla, Oronooko,
Young Marlow, Falconbridge, Aladdin, Orestes, Mark Antony,
and Richard III and Hamlet (at eighteen) – in all, some eighty
parts. He played with Mrs Jordan, and was impressed by her
meticulous care in rehearsals and her advice to write out verse
as if it were prose and study the copy rather than the original,
to avoid declamatory monotony. He played with Charles Mayne
Young. 'Young gentleman,' he told Macready, 'you expend a
degree of power unnecessarily; half the energy and fire that you
employ would be more sufficient.' He played with Mrs Siddons,
and treasured her example of unity in performance. 'You are in
the right way,' she advised him, 'but remember what I say. Study,
study, study, and do not marry until you are thirty.' Macready
took all the advice to heart (he married at thirty-one) treasured
the experience, and learned to command himself and others.
Although he was under his father's thumb, a position of dependence from which he sometimes broke away in a fierce quarrel, he
was in authority at the theatre. At Bath, in 1814, he acted for
the first time outside the family circuit, with some success. Word
of his quality reached London, and John Fawcett, stage manager
of Covent Garden and an old friend of his father, was sent down
to investigate and negotiate. But Macready was in no hurry; his
place was secure, and he had much to learn; so he refused the
offer, and went off to Glasgow and Dublin. It was not until two
years later that he signed a contract with Covent Garden for the
long-term engagement that he wanted – for five years, with a
weekly salary rising from £16 to £18.

Macready made his début on 16 September 1816, in an
auburn wig and a pseudo-Greek tunic in a pseudo-Greek play. He
appeared as Orestes in *The Distrest Mother*, Ambrose Philips's
version of Racine's *Andromaque*, carefully chosen for the purpose
because it had not been revived for some years and would therefore not provoke comparisons with established actors of the day.
At rehearsals, Macready was secretly dismayed by the vastness
of the theatre, so alarmingly bigger than the provincial playhouses
to which he was accustomed; but at night, he overcame all his

difficulties and was given an enthusiastic reception, in which Kean – conspicuous in a box – ostentatiously shared. Not all the critics were so warm: *The Times* classified him condescendingly as ' a man of clear conception, of much energy, and some skill ', and the *News* observed that ' Mr Macready is the plainest and most awkwardly-made man that ever trod the stage '. But the *News* continued that it preferred him to Kean ' in some respects ', and Hazlitt wrote that he was unquestionably ' by far the best tragic actor that has come out in our rememberance, with the exception of Mr Kean '. At Covent Garden, however, scope for him was limited, while Charles Young and Charles Kemble led the company. Most of the leading roles were closed to him, and during the next three years he made a reputation as a stage villain, or – in his own dry words – as ' the undisputed representative of the disagreeable '. Gradually, he hammered out a style, taking the measure of the house, the audience and himself, unlearning the lessons of his father and absorbing those of Kean and others. By October 1817, his self-education was already in danger. Offended by the ' puerility ' of his parts and the manners of his fellow actors (he objected to the moral tone of the greenroom gossip) he contemplated entering the Church. But then another call upon his loyalties kept him on the stage: he found that he needed money to buy a commission for his favourite brother Edward, so he swallowed his scruples and continued reluctantly in his career. That, at least, is Macready's story. In March 1818, he made a success as Rob Roy, in the first dramatization (with music) of Scott's novel (published three months before); and after the triumph of the 1819-20 season (described at the opening of this chapter) he made no more plans to exchange the stage for the pulpit.

For the next sixteen years Macready held his place as a star, second only to Edmund Kean. When he was in London, he acted – from 1823 onwards – at Drury Lane; but he spent much of the time on tour in the provinces, with a small repertoire of his most popular roles, and he made a successful visit to America. Scores of new roles, in plays ancient and modern, were attempted. He triumphed in Byron's *Werner* (much amended by himself) and Sheridan Knowles's *William Tell;* he made one of his rare successes in comedy as Oakley in *The Jealous Wife;* he added Leontes, King John, Lear and Wolsey to his Shakespearian laurels; and all the while he continued to improve and strengthen his Macbeth, Hamlet, Iago and Virginius. Despising the company of actors, Macready made his friends outside the theatre among writers and artists such as Talfourd, Dickens, Bulwer Lytton, Stanfield. He occupied a special place in London society as a gentlemanly actor, at a time when Kean had intensified the odium of his profession, and he earned enough money – some £4,000 a year – to maintain it. He was, moreover, happily married, and became the devoted father of a large family. Yet, in spite of this success, he was frustrated and dissatisfied; and, indeed, he failed to grow to the size which critics had expected on the showing of his 1819-20 season. If he had died or retired from the stage in the winter of 1835-6, as William Archer says, ' it might have been said with apparent truth that he had for some time been losing ground, and had not fulfilled the promise of his early years.'

For this blockage in Macready's career there were, perhaps, two principal reasons – psychological and theatrical. As a man, he could not brook being under ' the single sway of an actor ': that was why he left Covent Garden in 1823, in a fury against Charles Kemble: he had to be in charge, unchallenged, at the top. In his life, as in his art, he was by nature ' a despot ', as he himself admitted. As long as Kean lived, he was under a cloud. But, what was more, he had to work – for sixteen years – under the instructions of a motley collection of managers whom he despised. He was a displaced actor, without a theatre. He had to act at one of the patent theatres, because they were the only ones licensed for legitimate drama, but he loathed the whole ramshackle system. Even in Garrick's time, neither Covent Garden nor Drury Lane could survive without their afterpieces, but by the 1830s both theatres, overwhelmed by debt and threatened by competition, were in desperate straits. The vast new urban audience preferred, increasingly, to take its light entertainment at the ' minor ' theatres which sprang up to meet the needs of a rapidly expanding London, and although a new tragedian might draw the crowds for a time to the Garden or the Lane the prestige and popularity of the old Shakespearian and pseudo-classic repertoire was in decline. These two enormous playhouses were doomed as temples of the drama, although a succession of managers tried to save them with circus, opera and other expedients, and the 'patent' system which had inflated them to such monstrous and unprofitable proportions was doomed as well.

For Macready the last straw was Alfred Bunn. This bouncy, vulgar showman took over both theatres in dual harness from 1833 to 1835, cutting salaries and making one company work a double shift, in the effort to make the 'patents' pay. This venture also failed, and in the season 1835-6 Bunn had only the Lane under his command, with Macready (whom he strongly disliked) as his leading actor. He had invited Macready back because of his drawing power in the legitimate drama, but when a new opera and melodrama caught the fancy of the town the great tragedian was virtually shelved for several months. What was worse, Bunn made him appear in an after-piece, *William Tell*. But the final indignity was the humiliating announcement that Macready must play in an abbreviated, three-act version of *Richard III*, to make room in the same bill for the popular melodramatic spectacle, *The Jewess,* and the 'grand chivalric entertainment' of *Chevy Chase*. After furious protests at this insult to himself and to his art, Macready obeyed Bunn's orders; but after the performance that night, passing the manager's office, all his rage boiled up again and exploded. He threw open the door, shouted: 'You damned scoundrel! How dare you use me in this manner?' and as the astonished Bunn rose to his feet Macready struck him hard across the face. A fierce scuffle began. Bunn's ankle was sprained and Macready's finger was bitten before the two panting men were pulled apart. The manager was carried off to bed, and the tragedian was banned from the theatre. Later Macready was sued for assault, and had to pay Bunn £150 damages. To the end of his life he repented that brawl, sometimes noting its anniversary in his diary as a day of shame, yet in a curious way it seems to have pushed him out of his rut and opened a new phase in his career.

Twelve days after the fight at Drury Lane Macready appeared as Macbeth at Covent Garden. He feared the worst: if outraged, the audience's sense of propriety could, as Kemble and Kean knew only too well, take strange and violent forms of protest. But as he entered, Macready saw the house rise to its feet in a warm and tumultuous welcome; and his public apology after the performance – 'I feel, and shall never cease to feel, the deepest and most poignant self-reproach and regret' – was greeted with fervent enthusiasm. Never before, perhaps, had Macready been quite so popular – as a man. His assault on Bunn won him, for a time at least, a place in the public's affections, and his prestige as an artist was enhanced by his discovery of a new role. Before the month was out, Macready achieved one of his greatest successes in *Ion*, a Greco-Victorian tragedy by his lawyer-friend Thomas Talfourd, who borrowed the theme from Euripides: Macready appeared as a noble youth of Argos, who sacrifices himself and his royal father to save the city. Another good augury was his appearance, early in 1836, in a new play by the fashionable novelist and politician Edward Bulwer (later Lord Lytton) who was to create two of Macready's most popular roles, although Bragelone, in *The Duchess de la Vallière*, was not one of them. Robert Browning, too, wrote a play for Macready, though *Strafford* unfortunately belongs to that bizarre theatrical category labelled 'study drama'. Browning and Bulwer were among the many writers and artists in Macready's circle. With their encouragement, he now took a decisive step forward. In the summer of 1837, not long after the accession of Queen Victoria, he decided that it was time to begin his own reign. At the age of forty-four, he at last resolved to assume the management of a theatre. Before the patent system was ended, he would take advantage of its privileges to restore the honour and glory of the stage. No other candidate was in the field; his hated enemy, Bunn, was still in power at Drury Lane; and so, in October 1837, he inaugurated his regime at Covent Garden. He engaged a strong company, including Helen Faucit, Priscilla Horton and Samuel Phelps, who later became in his turn the leader of the English stage; and including, of course, the usual establishment of pantomimists and singers, for like all the patent managers Macready could not afford – for all his high ideals – to live on the drama alone. With a commendable faith in good public relations, the new manager explained the purpose of his season to the press and asked celebrities in science, art and literature to his first nights (Carlyle and Faraday, invited in this way, became two of Macready's firm admirers). He also took steps to improve the moral tone of the theatre, by checking the pernicious system of puffery in the bills, and by excluding prostitutes from their accustomed hunting-grounds in the boxes. All went surprisingly well, and Covent Garden won back much of its old honour. Yet within two years Macready was exhausted and bored by the burdens of management. After a short gap he embarked on another theatrical command – this time at Drury Lane – but that, too, only lasted for two years, from 1841 to 1843. In the following year the ancient privileges of the patent houses were annulled by Act of Parliament, and an era of free trade in the theatre was launched. Macready never repeated the experiment in management. ' In his heart of hearts,' one historian says, ' he cared too little about the enterprise to give it any chance of permanency.' Yet at Covent Garden and at Drury Lane, in his four years of leadership, Macready wrote a new chapter in the history of the English stage.

To begin with, he set and kept his standards high. It would have been easy to avoid losses by maintaining his most successful productions in the repertoire until their popularity was exhausted, but he insisted upon frequent changes of programme, on the primacy of the legitimate drama, and, in particular, upon the supremacy of Shakespeare. Macready set his face against the ' long run ', which was soon to remould the shape of the English theatre. What is more, he showed an unprecedented respect for the Shakespearian text. He restored *The Tempest* to the stage (although the shipwreck was presented only as a spectacle, and Ariel was played by a girl, Priscilla Horton). He restored the Chorus to *Henry V* (although he introduced decorative tableaux to illustrate the speeches, with a Stanfield diorama). His *Macbeth* still included the singing witches, but *The Times* observed that it was ' almost a new play '. But perhaps the most striking of Macready's reforms was his rejection of the Nahum Tate *King Lear*, and his restoration of the greater part of the original (although he cast Miss Horton as the Fool).

Macready also did his conscientious best for the contemporary drama, presenting such plays as Westland Marston's *The Patrician's Daughter*, Sheridan Knowles's *Woman's Wit*, Byron's *Marino Faliero*, and Browning's *A Blot on the 'Scutcheon*. He created fifty new roles. Few of these were box-office successes, but two of Macready's new plays became public favourites throughout the century. Both were written for him by Lytton, and both were costume dramas. Feeling ' something of the Brotherhood of Art ', the author made a present to Macready of *The Lady of Lyons*, in which the tragedian appeared as a ' juvenile lead ' at the age of forty-nine, and played it until he was sixty. He took the role of Claude Melnotte, a young French peasant who masquerades as a prince, marries an heiress, but reveals himself in his true colours before the marriage is consummated. In spite of his deception, Pauline promises to wait for him, and he goes off to the wars to make his fortune, returning two years later covered in glory and gold. Even more popular was Lytton's *Richelieu*, in which Macready – moving into a more appropriate age-group – triumphed as the foxy old cardinal of seventeenth-century France, outwitting all his enemies, threatening ' the curse of Rome ', shamming death to win a last-minute victory at the final curtain. In print this may seem a stagy confection of romantic rhetoric – ' a mixture of bad Hugo with worse Dumas ', according to one disapproving French critic – but Macready was only the first of many great actors, on both sides of the Atlantic, to use it as a platform for some of his finest work. In the contemporary drama, generally, he exercised a freedom denied to him in Shakespeare, where he went only halfway in the realistic psychological reshaping of the great roles, faced by the continuing strength of the Kemble tradition.

Macready was, moreover, a pioneer in the producer's art. He persuaded the actors, at times, to play outside their ' line of business '; and he insisted on their complete attention in rehearsals, instead of tolerating the traditional perfunctory run-through. He resolved, as he put it, ' to rehearse with the same earnestness as I should act ', and this resulted – in the words of Dr Ernest Bradlee Watson – in ' the most influential and radical changes in the manner and tone of acting that had been known since, at least, the days of Garrick.' Macready rehearsals became notorious in the profession: long, squabbling, and often humiliating ordeals in which he appeared at his most despotic. ' I thought for and acted to myself every character and every supernumerary figure,' he noted, ' and taught them to act as I would have done had I been cast in their places.' Such martinet discipline is not in favour today, and it helped to create a ' Macready school ' in which – as in all such schools of acting – the mannerisms of the master were usually more noticeable than his talent. Yet one result was that, according to an eye-witness, ' London saw its literary drama carefully acted in all its parts ' for the first time. Macready was particularly successful with the production of crowd scenes in Shakespeare. ' The mob in *Coriolanus*,' said John Forster, ' were now for the first time shown upon the stage, on a level with the witches in *Macbeth,* as agents of the tragic catastrophe . . . a proper, massy crowd of dangerous, violent fellows ', instead of the half-dozen supernumeraries pitted against John Philip Kemble. In the same production, the Volscian army on the Appian Way, with battering-rams and moving-towers, seemed to spread over the stage in their thousands; and Macready contrived a memorable effect when the red-tunics of the Volscian ranks opened for a long file of Roman women dressed in black, ' one long dreary sable line of monotonous misery '. Here, indeed, as in other productions, he seems – as William Archer observed – to have anticipated many of the methods of the Meiningen company, which made such an impression upon the European theatre sixty years later. With painstaking concern for pictorial effect and accuracy of setting, he carried a good deal further the reforms of John Philip Kemble and Charles Kean. His Shakespearian staging was elaborate, picturesque, and, by the standards of the time, realistic. Alan Downer, in his excellent study *The Eminent Tragedian,* goes so far as to say that his experiments in stagecraft, in attempting to achieve unity of effect in production, ' made possible the advances which define and distinguish the modern theatre '. For the first time, ' audiences were made aware that a play was something to be experienced as a whole, as a work of art.'

After the Drury Lane season of 1842-3, however, Macready made no attempt to continue his reforms elsewhere. During the next eight years he spent a large part of the time on tour in the provinces and America, accumulating enough money to support his large family and to retire from the stage. The end of his acting career was unhappily overclouded by the events of his second American tour in 1848-9. The leading transatlantic tragedian, Edwin Forrest, whose monomania was probably surpassed only by Macready's and whose talents were certainly inferior, believed that Macready was responsible for the general lack of enthusiasm displayed by the British public for his own acting. The English actor had, so Forrest asserted, influenced the critics, the managers and the playgoers against him. Such fantasies had an unfortunate effect upon the inflammable national vanity of some of Forrest's compatriots. Throughout Macready's tour there were signs of organized opposition in the press and the audience, and when he appeared in May at the Astor Place Opera

House in New York this underground resentment bubbled to the surface. Violent riots broke out; the theatre was besieged; troops were called in; and a pitched battle was fought, in which many people were killed. Macready's own life was in danger, and he had to leave New York in disguise.

Two years later – on 26 February 1851 – he gave his farewell performance at Drury Lane, in the role of Macbeth. He noted in his diary: 'Not one feeling of regret intermingled with the placid satisfaction accompanying my performance of every act, needfully preparative to the coming event, as I said to myself, " I shall never have to do this again ".' The feeling of relief was profound: the good-bye was final. Never again was Macready seen upon the stage, although he lived for another twenty-two years, apparently enjoying the quiet retirement of a country life in the role of an English squire. When he died – on 27 April 1873 – Covent Garden had long been turned over to opera; the number of playhouses in London had trebled since he first entered the profession of acting; and the entire British theatre was being transformed.

In print, William Charles Macready is the most fascinating of our actors. His diaries ensure him a place in theatrical literature, not only because front-rank players are rarely so articulate, but because of the horrified candour with which he records the dramatic conflict in his own soul, the violent love-and-hate he cherished towards his own profession, the mixture of monstrous vanity and agonized humility. Understandably enough, he was one of the best loathed men in the annals of the English theatre. Like Kemble, Macready was born into the managerial purple, but he had none of Black Jack's experience of the ranks. Had he been obliged in his youth to tout for work, to go hungry, to sweat on the treadmill of the 'walking gentleman', he might have had more patience with his colleagues and subordinates, but he never knew the heartaches and hardships of the average player's life. From the moment of his début he was accustomed to power, and he found it insupportably difficult – after the long dominion of his father – to take orders from anybody else. Garrick, too, began at the top, without experience of the rank and file, but he had in a high degree the gifts of compromise and diplomacy. For Macready it was a personal humiliation to appear with inferior actors, to tolerate anything that detracted from his own glory and the virtue of the play. Extravagantly vain and ferociously proud, he was autocratic without dignity and self-analytical without charity: he had none of Kemble's good fellowship offstage, his love of a stag party. He treated most of his actors abominably, and they detested him. To 'Sergeant Macready' most of these 'miserable wretches' were 'Beasts'; all too often they were 'Beasts of Hell'. True, there were beasts in plenty, especially on the provincial stage: the leading lady who fell down dead drunk at her first speech, the prompter who gave Macready the word during his pauses, the stage manager who had to be put in a straitjacket, the actors who 'dried up', or came on holding up their breeches, or simply failed to appear. But the trouble was that Macready seemed pathologically ashamed, off the stage, of being an actor at all, and he took his revenge on his fellow galley-slaves. At his most choleric he dismissed them all: 'the members of this profession – I know of no exception – are either utter blackguards or most ignorant empirics . . . I had rather see one of my children dead than on the stage.' In cooler mood, before a committee of inquiry in 1832, he humbled his own craft: 'The profession of the actor appears at present to be the very worst that an intellectual man can select . . . no person who had the power of doing anything better would, unless deluded into it, take it up.'

Macready was not, of course, 'deluded' into it. He was, so he would have us believe, forced into it by filial piety, kept in it by brotherly love, and remained in it because of financial necessity. These were all virtuous excuses; but Macready would never admit, to the public or to himself, the fundamental reason why he suffered the indignity of the 'beasts' and 'brutes' who, for him, made up the acting profession, and why he allowed himself to be branded as a rogue and vagabond, why he maintained throughout his career a fierce defensive war against a largely imaginary barrage of insults and snubs. It was, quite simply, that he enjoyed being an actor – on the stage: he could not escape his nature. 'Whatever he might say,' as J. C. Trewin observes, 'William Charles Macready belonged to the theatre.' It was the knowledge that he belonged, that he was an actor in spite of himself, which convulsed him with violent rage and inner doubt, and which spurred him on to achieve that long, gentlemanly retire-

ment, undisturbed for over twenty years by any return to the art
he had practised with so much reluctance and so much honour.

As the first player of the English stage, Macready had many
obvious weaknesses. Physically, he lacked the grace of Garrick,
the dignity of Kemble, the lithe energy of Kean: 'he handled
a foil like a pitchfork.' His face was flat and seemed, in his
younger days, ugly and inexpressive. When Charles Kemble
prophesied that Macready would be a star, his brother John
'took a pinch of snuff, and with a significant smile rejoined:
" Oh Charles! With *that* face!"' His Othello was once notoriously described as looking like 'an elderly negress, of ill repute,
going to a fancy ball'. Among his many mannerisms was a kind
of premeditated stutter, catching his breath in an ' er-er ' before
certain syllables; he made (like Kean) swoops in tone and volume;
he broke up the rhythm of the verse, in making sudden changes
from the grand to the conversational; and he is still remembered
for the 'Macready pause', though Garrick and Kemble had
probably paused, it seems, with no less frequency and emphasis.
In part, Alan Downer explains, this was the slowing down of
speeches to give the impression of thinking aloud; but, even more,
it was a deliberate timing of effect, allowing for the time-lag in
the huge theatres of the day. Similarly, he used sudden contrasts
of voice – ' extraordinary sinkings and transitions ' – to sharpen
the meaning and the impact of a scene; moving abruptly, in
particular, from the declamatory to the near-colloquial. As he
grew older his mannerisms grew more conspicuous, not only in
voice but in attitude. Westland Marston, a warm admirer, records
that ' he had, in moments of repose, a monotonous proneness to
standing in the same posture – one knee, a little bent, before the
other.' More serious was his occasional lack of control over his
own emotions: Macduffs were overwhelmed by whispered oaths
at Dunsinane, and sometimes took a cut too many; Desdemonas
were terrified that he would leave them black and blue. In general,
he stayed close to the human character and sometimes missed the
poetic truth. Leigh Hunt noted that he seemed ' afraid of the
poetry of some of his greatest parts, as if it would hurt the effect
of his naturalness and his more familiar passages ', and G. H.
Lewes complained that ' he was irritable where he should have
been passionate, querulous where he should have been terrible '.
On his first nights, in particular, he rarely soared. He seldom

struck twelve at once in the big Shakespearian roles, but worked his way forwards, steadily polishing and perfecting.

' Mac ' was one of his own sharpest critics. He noted in his diary that ' the habit of scowling or looking from under my brow, especially when an audience is close upon me, as in a small theatre, is a direct prevention to good acting '; or that he was ' relapsing into my old habitual sin of striving for effect by dint of muscular exertion and not restraining my body, while my face and voice alone are allowed to act '; or that ' I fail, when I allow my tongue and action to anticipate my thought '. As late as 1843, Macready was complaining about himself: ' The great defect of my style is hurry and want of clear discrimination . . . *I see how much of my conception* I lose through precipitancy.' He had the ideas – that was one of his distinguishing marks as an actor – but he could not always find the right shape for them. He noted in 1835 that Othello ' ought to be one of my best characters if I could realize my own conceptions '; as Macbeth in the same year, ' *I cannot reach in execution the standard of my own conception* '; after playing Othello ' wretchedly ' in 1836, ' I am perpetually *tortured* by my inability to realize my intentions.'

As a result, Macready was often out of touch with the audience – or was this, rather, the cause? He could not conquer them, as Kemble did, by simply Appearing, or as Kean did, by frightening them. All too often, especially in the later years, he felt that he simply could not communicate with the beasts in front of him. Acting Hamlet in Charleston in 1844, ' I strove and fought up against what I thought the immobility of the audience; I would not be beaten cravenly, but such a performance is never satisfactory – at least to the actor . . .' As Lear, in Edinburgh, he observed: ' It is slaughterous work to act these characters to these audiences.' As Hamlet, in Manchester, he explained: ' the inspiration is lost, the perfect *abandon,* under which one goes out of one's self, is impossible unless you enjoy the perfect sympathy of an audience.' Approval of bad work was even worse than indifference to good: ' Acted Posthumus in a most discreditable manner, undigested, unstudied . . . I was ashamed of myself . . . The audience applauded, but they knew not what they did.' Too much should not be made of this barrier between actor and audience; Kemble and Kean despised the playgoers of their

DAVID GARRICK. This picture in the National Portrait Gallery (from the studio of Sir Joshua Reynolds) seems to offer a more intimate glimpse of the actor's private face in middle age than better-known, more formal portraits.

Garrick in tragedy and comedy. Left, as Hamlet: his 'start' of terror on seeing the Ghost was the most celebrated point of his performance. Right, as Abel Drugger, in his version of Jonson's *The Alchemist* (from a conversation-piece by Zoffany).

JOHN PHILIP KEMBLE. This engraving – from a miniature by Chinnery – is dated 1799, when he was 42 and the acknowledged head of the English stage.

Two views of Kemble. Right, caricatured by Dighton in 1799 as Rolla in *Pizarro*, one of his prime successes. Below, idealised by Lawrence as Coriolanus.

EDMUND KEAN. Top: this romantic study by Samuel Cousins was made at the beginning of his London career, probably in 1814, when he was 25.

Bottom left: as Shylock, from 'a picture painted in ivory from life in March 1814.' Right: as Sir Giles Overreach, about 1820: attributed to George Clint.

WILLIAM CHARLES MACREADY.
Top: in 1843, at 50, from a
miniature by Robert Thorburn.
Bottom left: as William Tell
(after a painting by Henry
Inman). Right: as Macbeth in
1851, the year of his retirement,
from a picture by I. H. Wilson.

SIR HENRY IRVING. Top: off-stage in the 1870s – already a star at the Lyceum but not yet its manager.
Bottom: as Matthias in *The Bells*, with which he made his name in 1871.

Opposite: Irving as Mephistopheles: not one of his great roles, but Phil May's cartoon catches less perishably than most photographs something of the great actor's power.

JOHNSTON FORBES-ROBERTSON. Top: caricatured by Spy (Sir Leslie Ward) in 1895, at 42. Bottom: as Hamlet at Drury Lane in 1913, when he made his farewell to the London stage.

time no less, and might well have made very similar entries in their diaries; yet Macready seems to have lacked their power of personal dominion.

Yet if Macready did not always command the audience, or please himself, it was partly because of his unorthodox and somewhat experimental style of acting. He introduced a brand of naturalism which went a good deal further towards the behaviour of ' real life ' than the ' natural ' bursts of Kean, and was in sharp contrast to the formal tradition of Kemble which still served as the groundwork of English playing and was still, in some respects, the basis of his own. For Hazlitt, in 1817, Macready was already ' too natural '. He struggled, for one thing, against the codes of traffic-signal gesture, trying to keep his body still and to act from the mind. Influenced by a line in Dante about the dignity of repose, and by the example of Talma, he ' adopted all the modes I could devise to acquire the power of exciting myself into the wildest emotions of passion, coercing my limbs to perfect stillness.' He would, he admitted years later, lie on the floor, or pinion his arms with a bandage, and repeat the most violent passages of Lear, Othello or Macbeth. He attempted to characterize Shakespearian verse rather than simply to declaim it – ' I want to consider every line, and test each by a natural standard,' he wrote in 1833 – and this brought him under heavy fire. R. H. Horne, for example, complained that ' he reads poetry very badly, as to rhythm – broken up – without melody – harsh – unmusical – shattered prose! ' Fanny Kemble grumbled that his '*natural* style of speaking . . . was simply chopping it up into prose'; and Leigh Hunt (writing about Macready's Macbeth) complained that he seemed ' afraid of the poetry of some of his greatest parts, as if it would hurt the effect of his naturalness and his more familiar passages '. Yet Horne admitted that ' he speaks with exquisite distinctness, and very impressively, because he is thoroughly in earnest '. An American who objected because ' the sense alone directed the elocution ' – a rare phenomenon, in those days – went on to say that ' no false note was ever struck, no shade of meaning was left undiscriminated, no measured or monotonous recitation ever wearied the ear '. Macready's enthusiasm for realism, however, was exercised in a theatre where the house-lights were still left on during the play, where much of the performance took place on an apron stage, and where the conventions of the old theatrical tradition were still powerful. His work reflected the difficulties of a time of transition, socially and artistically.

Macready was trying, moreover, to present not only impressive pieces of character – but to give the man as a whole. ' The prescriptive criticism of this country,' as he himself complained, ' looks for particular points instead of contemplating one entire character.' Instead of acting from ' point ' to ' point ', instead of reserving his energies for ' bursts ', lighting up lines or phrases and leaving the areas between in darkness, he continually attempted – unlike Kean – to fuse and kindle the whole text. He wanted to *be* the man he personated; and, like a good follower of Stanislavsky, he sought 'offered circumstances' to help him. Whenever he played Hamlet, he summoned up a long-remembered dream in which a dead friend had appeared to him. As Virginius, he drew on his personal grief at his daughter's death. Before going on as Shylock, it is said, he used to whip up his anger in the wings by cursing fiercely under his breath and violently shaking a ladder, and during the final fight in *Macbeth* he worked himself into a personal frenzy. ' I cannot act Macbeth,' he noted in his diary, ' without *being* Macbeth, which I must have time to prepare my mind for.' Quite often, this identification was complete enough to satisfy him (' I was good; I was the character; I felt it '). Then he felt ' free from effort, prompt and spontaneous in my passion, with complete absence of all muscular exertion . . . [with] that *certainty* of preserving the *tout ensemble*.' He was, as he said, ' possessed '. He could not, like more experienced actors, secure such feelings of certainty and relaxation by the exercise of technique alone; and he attributed this deficiency, and other weaknesses in his acting, to his comparatively late entry on the stage. ' In comparing my performances with my rehearsals, when I frequently speak and act with an abandonment and a reality that surprises me, I feel the great advantage which Kean, Miss O'Neil and Mrs Siddons enjoyed in passing their earliest years upon the stage, and thereby obtaining a power of identification only to be so acquired.'

One of the most conspicuous aspects of Macready's relative naturalism was his emphasis on the humanity and domesticity of his more sympathetic characters: he insisted that they, too, were happily married men and loving fathers, on the best pattern of the early Victorian middle class. ' No feature of this actor was more especially his own,' said Westland Marston, ' that the sudden yet natural infusion into his more heroic vein of some homely touch of truth which gave reality to the scene.' Sheridan Knowles gave him particular scope for such ' homely touches ', in *Virginius* and *William Tell*. To Leigh Hunt, writing of his King John in 1830, Macready seemed ' best where he approaches domestic passion and has to give way to soft or overwhelming emotions. His greatest deficiency is shown in passages where the ideal is required; where nature puts on the robe of art, and speaks her truths, as it were, in art.' Yet it is notable that this was the best King John in Hunt's experience: ' not that it was so kingly as John Kemble's (or what he thought kingly, for he was a King John of his own, in a way) but because his was more like the real historical King John . . . less poetical than petulant and a bully.'

Macready had, indeed, many virtues. Although he was not handsome, he could assume good looks; and as he grew older, it seemed easier for him to play juveniles – thus, he triumphed as Ion at forty-three, and as Melnotte at forty-nine. In the latter part, said a colleague, ' when playing to a good house, he did not look more than twenty-five '; and G. H. Lewes witnessed that: ' None of the young men whom I have seen play Claude Melnotte had the youthfulness of Macready in that part.' He excelled in both pathos and villainy, in the domestic and the supernatural, in physical and intellectual combat. Although he lacked Kean's skill in fencing, his duelling in *Hamlet* and *Macbeth* was famous in his day; and, as his Richelieu showed, ' he was at home in finesse and strategy, and in all that involved intellectual gladiatorship.' He suffered well. He was impressive in anger. He had wide emotional sympathies and acute human insight, inside his range of characters, and his range was wide – much wider than Kean's or Kemble's. This may be seen from a list of his most popular roles (in order of public favour), published in 1850 in the *Theatrical Journal*: Werner, Richelieu, Iago, Iachimo, William Tell, Virginius, King of the Commons (James v of Scotland, in a romantic drama of that name), King Lear, King John, Cassius, Kitely and Hamlet. Among other successful roles were Macbeth, Leontes, Wolsey, Henry iv and Benedick; Ion, Rob Roy, Oakly in *The Jealous Wife*, Melantius in *The Bridal* (adapted by Knowles from Beaumont and Fletcher) and Joseph

Surface in *The School for Scandal* (a part he later disliked so much that he made it a condition of his contract with Bunn in 1835 that he should not be obliged to play it). Although he could not equal Garrick's mastery of comedy, he was not – like Kean and Kemble – a single-track player. His choice of new roles was, moreover, generous and catholic. However Macready might enrage and insult the authors, he did more for the contemporary drama of his time than any starring actor before or since.

As Werner, Macready won fame by his command of pathos – 'almost as remarkable,' said Lewes, 'as the heroic agony of Kean's Othello.' There was a famous moment when his son Ulric, who has committed a murder, defends himself by accusing his father of leading him astray, with the line:

> *Who* proclaimed to me
> That *there were crimes made venial by the occasion?*

Macready had already indicated Werner's sense of guilt 'by the convulsions of the face, by the hands, that first sought to close the ears, and then to beat back the fatal sounds that would enter '. At Ulric's line he produced, says Westland Marston, ' one of those rare effects which become traditions of the theatre. With a shrill cry of agony, as if pierced mortally by a dart, he bounded from his seat, and then, as if all strength had failed him, wavered and fluttered forward, so to speak, till he sank on one knee in front of the stage.' The fact that he could breathe life into Byron's play, wrote William Archer, appeared to him ' one of the most convincing proofs that he was really a great actor '.

In Shakespeare, Macbeth – his own favourite role – was one of his prime triumphs. He was acclaimed, in particular, for the dagger-scene (no sudden start, but a mesmerised movement of attraction and repulsion towards the image in the air); for the vivid terrors at the sight of Banquo's ghost; for the final fight and defiant on-stage death. ' Nothing could be finer,' G. H. Lewes wrote, ' than the indications he gave of a conscience wavering under the influence of " fate and metaphysical aid ", superstitious, and weakly cherishing the suggestions of superstition; but nothing could have been less heroic than his presentation of the great criminal. He was fretful and impatient under the provocations of his wife; he was ignoble under the terrors of remorse; he stole into the sleeping-chamber of Duncan like a man going to purloin a purse, not like a warrior going to snatch a crown.' Is Macready's way, as described by Lewes, not a legitimate interpretation? Yes, but Macready was not trying to give it: he himself aimed at the portrait of 'one living to command', a strong, heroic man. For Hazlitt, his Macbeth 'came out a mere modern, agitated by common sense and intelligible motives'. Yet this exit was especially praised by a contemporary, Westland Marston, because in the contrast with 'the erect, martial figure that entered in the first act' was 'the moral of the play made visible'.

Macready aroused contradictory verdicts more than most actors of his time. His Lear was criticized on one side for 'a psychological nicety almost unparalleled' which obscured the 'ideal and purely poetic truth' of the character. Yet in this role Lewes acknowledged that Macready was, indeed, 'great'. Instead of being feeble and senile from the opening scene, this Lear was 'a hale and zealous hunter', who grew old as the play went on. He was, moreover, kingly, showing in his gait a 'primitive, half-savage royalty'. In Lear's madness Macready found, as Archer observed, 'ample scope for that subtlety of psychological suggestion which was one of his great qualities': 'the keen, over-eager attention, the sudden diversion to new excitements, the light garrulousness, the unmeaning smiles, or the abstracted silence, denoted by turns so many shifting moods of fantasy through which one torturing recollection, like a knell . . . broke ever and annon.' Even in the great curses he won the sympathy of the audience for a father's feelings – one of his most frequent domestic touches, as Alan Downer observes. When it came to the recognition of Cordelia and, for the first time, her death upon the stage, he stirred the whole house with emotion: 'Who can ever forget the storm of sighs and tears which shook the audience?' asked one witness.

It was in his voice that Macready had the advantage over Kean, Kemble and, indeed, most of England's great actors. In his early days it was, Hunt said, 'the finest and most heroical on the stage'. Hazlitt extolled it as 'magnificent . . . powerful and flexible, varying with the greatest facility from the lowest to the highest pitch . . .' Miss Mitford admired, in 1824, its 'very exquisite music (except when he rants)'. Although it may have deteriorated, as Macready grew older and amended his acting style, his voice still remained – in Lewes's words – 'powerful, extensive in compass, capable of delicate modulation in quiet passages (though with a tendency to scream in violent passages) and having tones that thrilled and tones that stirred tears'. Unlike Kean, who had to be seen in close-up to be fully understood, Macready was fully intelligible at a distance – 'you may gather how he must look by what you hear.' He was, moreover, 'a master in the gradation of passion. He knew well how to raise an emotion by degrees to its full height, and had the skill to fill the cup of anguish drop by drop till it overflowed'. He demonstrated this at the end of *Macbeth* without Garrick's interpolated bit of dying rhetoric, which both Kemble and Kean had retained.

Was he, indeed, a great actor? Against him is the evidence of Hazlitt, with his damning verdict: 'Macready has talents and a magnificent voice, but he is, I fear, too improving an actor to be a man of genius. That little ill-looking vagabond Kean never improved in anything.' But Macready like Kemble, has suffered from the literary excellence of Hazlitt and Hunt, who put their faith in Kean. It is by Hazlitt's testimony, in particular, that Macready has been judged. Yet it concerns only the early part of his career, and even here there are such witnesses in the other camp as Tieck, who thought Macready superior to both Kean and Kemble. Better evidence comes from G. H. Lewes, who saw Macready in his maturity. He was, Lewes decided, 'a man of talent, but of talent so marked and individual that it approaches very near to genius.' Comparisons with Kean are, of course, inevitable. Macready refused to play Sir Giles Overreach or Sir Edward Mortimer, yet he triumphed as Richard III, Iago was one of his most successful roles, and he may be said to have surpassed Kean in both Lear and Hamlet. Kean, on the other hand, failed dismally in Macready's successes, and persistently refused to appear with him on the stage. 'I don't mind Young,' he wrote to the manager of Drury Lane, 'but I will not act with Macready . . . Fabius Maximus conquered not by fighting a powerful enemy, but by avoiding him. He weakened his resources, and saved the city of Rome.' Not until the very end of his career did Kean agree to appear as Othello to Macready's Iago. He was, said Lewes, 'puny' beside Macready until the third act. Then he moved towards Iago with 'a gouty hobble, seized him by the throat, and in a well-known explosion, "Villain! be sure you prove," &c seemed to swell in to a stature which made Macready appear small.' That has been taken as a demonstration of Kean's superiority; yet can we measure the other man's greatness by one ' burst '? Kean himself was clearly well aware of the danger presented by Macready. Summing up their differences, Mr Trewin writes: ' Kean, in a small group of parts, might surpass him and any actor that ever lived. Macready had a wider range, the longer list of successes. He was always very close to the top. Kean's record was a fever-chart with impenetrable depths.' William Archer suggests, in addition, that ' Kean was a greater actor, but not so great an artist '. As Macready himself said, ' If I am to excel it must be by consistent labour . . . I wish to play what I have to do in an artist-like manner.' Sometimes the labour showed; yet it bore a rich harvest, for himself and the English stage. I agree with Lewes: ' Yes, Macready *was* a great actor. Though not a man of genius, he was a man of intellect, of culture, of representative talent, with decided physical advantages, capable of depicting a wide range of unheroic characters, with truth and power, an ornament to his profession, the pride of his friends, and the favourite of the public.' He was a great actor not only because of what he did to the audience, but because of what he did for the theatre. He was a great actor in spite of himself.

5

Sir Henry Irving

When the gaslights were first lowered, less than half the shabby red-and-gold theatre was filled with first-nighters. It was a cold Saturday evening, and the opening farce, *Is He Jealous?* deepened the gloom. By a quarter to eight, when the curtains rose on the main play in the programme, a few more people had arrived; but most of that scanty mid-Victorian audience was expecting the worst. The last two plays had flopped, and it looked as if the new piece, *The Bells,* was going to follow them into oblivion. It was adapted from a Parisian success, but only twelve nights earlier another version of the same play had failed dismally at another London playhouse; and here the leading role of a murderer was to be played by a young comedian. The critics believed they knew what was coming, and had their epitaphs ready. Yet another manager was going to be defeated by this ' unlucky ' theatre in the Strand – the old Lyceum. That is what many people thought, on this night of 25 November 1871, and their pessimism was shared by the manager and his company – until about eight o'clock.

The curtain rose on the burgomaster's inn in Alsace, a quiet domestic interior filled with local colour and small talk in what one first-nighter described as ' that strange language – English in translation '. It was Christmas Eve, and everyone was waiting for Mathias, the burgomaster. Outside it was snowing; there were gusts of wind and an undercurrent of atmospheric music; and the rising storm reminded the people at the inn of a wild Christmas Eve fifteen years before, when a Polish Jew had mysteriously disappeared nearby. They found only his bloodstained cloak, his cap, and his dead sleigh-horse. Neither the body nor the murderer, they said, had ever been discovered, but half the audience – having read the press's account of the Erckmann-Chatrian original – was already well acquainted with the secret. Fifteen minutes went by. The critics yawned and fidgeted. Then the ' hurry ' music whirled up into a crescendo. A door at the back was suddenly flung open. And out of the storm appeared a tall, thin, commanding figure in a fur cap and heavy, snow-covered coat, waving his whip in greeting. Simply, if superfluously, he announced in ringing tones: ' It is I!' or rather ' Tz I!' Mathias the burgomaster had come home. Throwing off his coat and otter-skin cap, he moved downstage to a chair and started to take off his gaiters. Without knowing why, the audience found that they could not keep their eyes away from him. Henry Irving had already begun to cast his spell.

As he took off his gaiters, the conversation turned to a ' clever Parisian ' in a neighbouring village who could send people to sleep. ' What is more,' said one of the men in the inn, ' when they are asleep they tell him everything that weighs upon their conscience.' At the word ' conscience ', Mathias was buckling up his shoe. Then, as Gordon Craig wrote later, 'we suddenly saw these fingers stop their work; the crown of the head suddenly seemed to glitter and become frozen – and then, at the pace of the slowest and most terrified snail, the two hands, still motionless and dead, were seen to be coming up the side of the leg . . . the whole torso of the man, almost seeming frozen, was gradually, and by an almost imperceptible movement, seen to be drawing up and back, as it would straighten a little, and to lean a little against the back of the chair . . .' Fear spread out across the audience. Then Mathias recovered; the spell was broken; and the domestic gossip was continued. But a few minues later it happened again. The burgomaster was sitting at the table when someone mentioned the disappearance of the Polish Jew. He was just raising a glass of wine to his lips. He stopped, lowered it, and pretended with great deliberation to pick out a piece of cork. At that moment, far away, there was the sound of jingling sleigh-bells. Gradually the sound grew louder. Only Mathias, it was plain, could hear it, and the audience saw his eyes fill with guilt and horror. This is how Gordon Craig described the scene, as Irving played it in later years.

He moves his head slowly from us – the eyes still somehow with us – and moves it to the right – taking as long as a long journey to discover the truth takes. He looks to the faces on the right – nothing. Slowly the head revolves back again, down, and along the tunnels of thought and sorrow, and at the end the face and eyes are bent upon those to the left of him . . . utter stillness . . . nothing there either – every one is concerned with his or her little doings – smoking or knitting or unravelling wool or scraping a plate slowly and silently. A long pause, endless, breaking our hearts, comes down over everything, and on and on go these bells.

Mathias rose to his feet – ' never has any one seen another rising figure which slid slowly up like that ' – and asked the others if they had not heard the sound of sleigh-bells. None of them knew what he was talking about, and he began to shiver, his jaws chattering, visibly ill with fright.

When Mathias was left alone, a few moments later, the bells went on jingling: the stage darkened; and then the sound suddenly stopped. There above him, through a gauze, was a vision of snow-covered country, with a lime-kiln burning, and the Polish Jew standing on a sleigh drawn by a horse with bells in its harness. Following the sleigh was a man in a brown blouse with an axe in his hand. Suddenly the apparition of the murdered man turned his face round and fixed his eyes upon the burgomaster. With a shriek of terror Mathias fell to the floor – and the Lyceum curtain thudded down on the first act. There was a burst of applause from the audience, yet Irving's success was not yet assured: they were mesmerised but mystified. In the second act Mathias could be seen putting a smiling face upon his secret torment, in the preparations for his daughter's wedding, and the actor displayed his talents for pathos, tenderness and subtlety in characterization. But it was in the third act that Irving triumphed. Mathias dreams that he is on trial, is put under hypnosis to reveal the truth, and re-lives in ghastly detail what happened on the night of the murder. In a masterly sequence of prolonged mime, Irving enacted the murderer's greed and fear, taking the audience with him as he walked, in imagination, over the snow-covered fields, heard the bells of the sleigh approaching, cut down the Jew with his hatchet, seized his belt of gold, and tipped the body into the lime-kiln. 'Go into the fire, Jew, go into the fire,' he shouted eerily, pushing feverishly at the body with a pole. Then he cried out, covering his face with his hands, and staggering down the stage: 'Those eyes, oh those eyes! How he glares at me!' Still in his dream, Mathias fell asleep, was woken by the mesmerist, and – in rage and agony – heard the court pronounce the death sentence. The stage darkened, and the lights went up again on the burgomaster's bedroom. It was his daughter's wedding day, and they were knocking at his door to awaken him. When he made no answer, they burst the door open; and out through the curtains round his bed staggered Mathias, his face chalk-white with fear, his fingers scrabbling at his throat. In a strangled voice he croaked, 'Take the rope from my neck, take the rope from my neck!' His eyes rolled upwards; his gaunt limbs stiffened; and he sank, with a choked scream, into the arms of his wife. The death sentence had been carried out: the play was over.

It was, as one first-nighter said, 'almost hideously painful'; at least one spectator fainted; but the audience loved it. They had been terrified into submission. 'We did not at first understand a word; we did not understand his walk; nor any of his movements; but he gripped us, he interested us, he excited us, and the excitement increased and increased, until, when the last curtain fell, we could only sit, gasping, stunned and silent. But after a moment we leapt to our feet, we leapt on to the benches, we shouted, we waved handkerchiefs, caps, anything that could be waved, and we then and there consecrated Irving the greatest actor of our time.' He had brought a public execution to the stage; and he was to re-enact it over eight hundred times during the next thirty years, throughout Britain and America.

The evening, however, was not yet over: there was still another piece on the programme, with another part for Henry Irving. The agonized murderer of *The Bells* now appeared, after a short interval, as the seedy rascal of *Pickwick*, Mr Alfred Jingle. With a black beaver tipped over one eye, his lanky figure dressed in shabby, tight-fitting, black clothes, his swaggering walk and staccato speech, Irving seemed to many people the very incarnation of that famous Cockney grotesque, with the 'indescribable air of jaunty impudence and perfect self-possession' that his creator described. 'One would have thought,' noted an admirer, 'that Dickens must have seen him first and then put him into *Pickwick Papers*.' Pickwick and the others faded into insignificance beside this sardonic silhouette. Irving had already appeared in the role, for a longer version of *Pickwick* had preceded *The Bells;* but he had upset the balance by the vividness of his acting, and the play had been as unsuccessful as most dramatizations of Dickens. Now, cut down from eleven to seven scenes, it gave him the opportunity to show that he could not only make the audience shiver but make it laugh as well.

When the final curtain fell, on the unmasking of Mr Jingle in Mr Nupkins's library, there was a great ovation for Irving. The Lyceum, it was plain, had been saved, and a new star was shining in the theatrical firmament. At a small supper party, arranged by some friends in his honour, Irving exulted in his victory. His wife Florence, who did not approve of his theatrical friends or sympathize with his theatrical ambitions, sat apart in cold detachment, but Irving – accustomed to such wifely glumness after only two years of marriage – did not notice. In the cab going home, still elated, he said: 'Well, my dear, we too shall soon have our own carriage and pair!' Mrs Irving, who had said so little all evening, now said too much. 'Are you going on making a fool of yourself like this all your life?' she asked, in a burst of anger. At once Irving told the driver to stop. Without a word to his wife, he got out of the cab. He did not go home that night, and he never spoke to her again. In this way, it may be said, his private life ended on the very night that his public life began, on that remarkable night of 25 November 1871, which made Henry Irving the leader of the English stage.

Henry Irving was born on 6 February 1838 in the Somersetshire village of Keinton Mandeville, and spent most of his childhood in an atmosphere of rural peace and rigid piety. His baptismal name was John Henry Brodribb. At his birth his father, Samuel Brodribb, was a travelling salesman for the village store, but business grew so bad that within a few years the Brodribbs decided to try their luck in Bristol. For the sake of their only child however, they left him behind in the country, until they could make a secure home for him in town. That, at least, seemed their intention, but the temporary separation became a permanent estrangement. At the age of four, John Henry was handed over to his mother's sister, Sarah Penberthy; and under her strict but loving supervision he grew up in the Cornish mining village of Halsetown, seeing his parents for a few days every year.

Educated at a dame school, he supplemented this scanty school-
ing by his own intense reading of the only three books in the
house – the Bible, *Don Quixote,* and a book of ballads. From an
early age, he cherished a secret love of ' play-acting ', although his
aunt – like his mother – was convinced that all theatres were
under the special charge of the Devil. This appetite for forbidden
fruit was encouraged, so he recalled in later life, by a glimpse
of the famous lion-tamer Van Amburgh driving a team of twenty-
four horses in royal state through the streets of Bristol. Not until
he was ten was he reunited with his father and mother, and then
it was only on the grounds of economic necessity; his uncle Isaac
died suddenly, leaving his family in some distress, and there was
no longer a home for Johnnie Brodribb in Halsetown. It was to
his aunt and not to his mother, however, that he looked for help
and sympathy during the struggles of adolescence and early manhood. Mother and son were kept apart, and finally separated, by
the son's growing interest in the stage. This early separation
and loneliness must have been a formative experience in the
remaking of Irving's personality and its projection on the stage,
hiding Brodribb under a mask of mystery and power.

At the age of ten, Brodribb was plunged from the Cornish
moors into the heart of London: his father had found rooms in
Broad Street, and work as a caretaker. This nervous, dreamy
child, with a serious impediment in his West Country speech,
found himself among strangers at home and at school. He was
lucky, however, in discovering a headmaster with a passion for
elocution, who helped him to defeat not only his stutter but his
mother. It was under pressure from Dr Pinches that Mrs Brodribb reluctantly agreed to let her son enter a house of Satan –
to see Samuel Phelps play Hamlet. The theatre was Sadler's
Wells, where Macready's disciple had set up as actor-manager in
1843 – it was one of the most immediate and important effects of
abolishing the old patents – and where during the next twenty
years he presented nearly all Shakespeare's plays, winning a
special place in the history of the English stage. Young Brodribb's
initiation into this world, coupled with his encouragement in
public reciting at school, inflamed his ambitions. Not long afterwards, at the age of twelve, he began to earn his living, in order
to supplement the family funds – first as a junior clerk in the
office of a Cheapside lawyer, and then with an East India mer-

chant – and spent any pennies he could scrape together on secret visits to Sadler's Wells. With the same determination that had overcome his stutter, the young clerk set out to train himself for the stage. He learned plays by heart. He practised, alone and at a school of elocution, which sometimes arranged semi-public performances to which it invited the press. He took fencing lessons in Chancery Lane. He schooled his body in tests of endurance, and tried to discipline its clumsiness into grace. Every morning before he went to the office he walked to the Islington home of William Hoskins, one of Phelps's leading actors at the Wells, who gave the boy private tuition in the ABC of the stage. In order to pay for all this, Brodribb went without food, and this deliberate semi-starvation told on him in later life. 'It is strange how one never entirely makes up for not having had quite enough to eat in one's youth,' he said many years afterwards, at the height of his fame. He also, it may be, never made up for not having had quite enough love: this self-education was continued in the face of bitter opposition from his mother.

When Hoskins decided to go to Australia, he gave his pupil the chance of coming with him; when Brodribb (then seventeen) refused this generous offer, he introduced the boy to Phelps, who offered him a job at the Wells; yet although this might have seemed a heaven-sent opportunity to most stage-struck youths, Brodribb did not accept. He knew, it seems, that he was not yet ready for such a company. Awkward and inexperienced, he needed the training that could be won only in the provinces; but how was he to get a foothold there, without even the money for his own wigs? The following year, in 1856, his opportunity came out of the blue, when a kindly uncle gave him £100. Brodribb invested most of it in wigs, swords and other indispensable accessories, and bought himself the part of Romeo in an amateur's production at the Soho Theatre (for a few guineas any aspiring novice could take this way of testing himself on the stage). Satisfied with the result, he wrote to E. D. Davis, an influential theatre manager in the north, enclosing a letter of recommendation which Hoskins had left behind; Davis offered him an engagement (unpaid) with his Sunderland stock company the following month; and Brodribb set off for his new career, with the remainder of his uncle's money in his pocket, and in his heart the knowledge that to his mother he was not only a bad son but a damned soul. Mrs Brodribb never forgave him; his success in such evil courses only made his sin the greater in her eyes; and his later career may well be interpreted, in some respects, as a sustained attempt to prove that his mother was wrong in setting up the Church against the stage, and in writing off actors as men without God.

The tall, solemn, lanky clerk began his new life with a new name: he took it, symbolically enough, both from a preacher and from an artist, whose sermons and stories had figured largely in his life in Halsetown – Edward Irving and Washington Irving. It was as Henry Irving that he made his professional début on the stage of the Theatre Royal, Sunderland, on 29 September 1856, in *Richelieu*. As the Duke of Orleans, he opened the play with the line: ' Here's to our enterprise! ', and in the oriental pantomime that followed he appeared as a cook. (He did not take the name of Irving officially, by royal licence, until his fiftieth birthday.) During those first weeks, he found out – in hard and humiliating labour – how very much he had to learn. He sang in opera, he danced in burlesque, he walked on in dozens of plays. Yet in spite of his clumsiness and inexperience, he was kept in the company, and by the end of his first season he was even being paid, at the rate of twenty-five shillings a week. In January 1857 Irving went to the Edinburgh Theatre Royal, as a first walking gentleman (here, too, he began as the Duke of Orleans in *Richelieu*), and was soon promoted to be a juvenile lead (at thirty shillings a week).

During the next ten years, Henry Irving worked in the stock companies of England, Scotland and Ireland, inching his way up the ladder, learning and developing all the while. Day and night, with scarcely a break during the season, the work went on: studying, rehearsing and playing, in a triple bill that was usually changed every evening. At Edinburgh he once had to learn seventeen new parts in thirty days (and he was always conscientious about make-up and costume), and in two and a half years there he played over four hundred roles, ranging the gamut of a stock company's repertoire, taking the measure of many visiting stars from London. He was fiercely in earnest, and ready for any drudgery. By the autumn of 1859 it seemed as if his provincial apprenticeship was already over: he was enlisted in Augustus Harris's company at the Princess's Theatre, London. Within a few weeks, however, Irving's high hopes were dashed. Realizing that he was only exchanging one treadmill for another, he asked Harris to release him from his contract. This was a big setback, but it taught him a painful lesson: he would not leave the provinces until the right offer came from London. He had to wait a long time before that offer arrived. Meanwhile, he practised, studied and, on occasion, suffered. The London fiasco was followed by a visit to Dublin, where Irving was shouted down every night by a section of the audience, apparently inspired by hooligans in the pay of his predecessor in the company. This ordeal lasted for three weeks, and left many scars. Thereafter he acted in Glasgow, Manchester, Edinburgh, Birmingham, Liverpool and other cities, rising to a salary of £3 a week. By 1866, his tenth year in the profession, he was disillusioned, frustrated and penniless.

Then, without warning, the tide turned. During one of his increasingly frequent periods of unemployment, Irving was asked by the well-known dramatist Dion Boucicault to appear in Manchester in his new play *The Two Loves of Mary Leigh*. As the villainous Rawdon Scudamore, Irving scored a hit, and it was largely on his account that the play was brought to London – to the St James's – with Irving as both leading man and stage manager. Under the new title of *Hunted Down* it was put into rehearsal in September, but when it became clear that it would not be ready in time for the theatre's opening Louisa Herbert, the actress who ran the St James's, decided to start the season with the eighteenth-century comedy of *The Belle's Stratagem*, in which Irving took the lead as Doricourt. He aroused no interest until the brief scene where this man-about-town feigns madness in order to avoid a marriage; but here the play was interrupted by a prolonged ovation, which was repeated every night of the run. In November came the first night of *Hunted Down*, on which Irving had set his hopes. When the curtain fell on the last scene, George Eliot said to her friend G. H. Lewes; ' Well, what do you think of him?' ' In twenty years he will be at the head of the English stage,' Lewes answered. 'He is there, I think, already,' she replied. But for some time to come the name of Irving meant, to the public at large, the light comedian Joseph Irving. It was another five years before Henry Irving justified the promise of Rawdon Scudamore. During those years his namesake Joseph died, removing a shadow from his career; but his private life was darkened by three other deaths – of his mother, still unreconciled; of Nellie Moore, a girl he had hoped to make his wife; and of his first and only marriage.

The very success of his Scudamore fixed Irving, for a time, in the rut of stage villainy; but with the help of his lifelong friend J. L. Toole, the leading comic actor of the day, he broke free and emerged in 1879 as a light comedian and character actor with two semi-Dickensian portraits. The first of these was the Dombey-like role of Mr Chevenix in H. J. Byron's *Uncle Dick's Darling;* and influenced by this performance (and, perhaps, by the memory of William Dorrit) an obscure young dramatist wrote a new play with a part for Irving. As Digby Grant in James Albery's *Two Roses,* one of the most popular and more distinguished plays of the late Victorian theatre, Irving scored a personal triumph. He appeared as a vain, selfish, snobbish man: in poverty, smugly trading on his friends' good nature; in wealth, paying off his obligations with a cheque-book. Long after Irving's death, he was remembered ' in the shabby old dressing-gown, his heart bursting with self-adulation, handing to each of his former friends, with superb condescension, " a little cheque " . . .' It was *Two Roses* which led Irving to his destiny at the Lyceum. His performance of Digby Grant – praised at the time for its modern subtlety and naturalism – may seem to be remote from the romantic melodrama of *The Bells;* but on Irving's benefit night, near the end of the play's ten-month run, the actor surprised the audience by appearing in evening dress and reciting Thomas Hood's well-known poem about a conscience-stricken murderer, *The Dream of Eugene Aram.* This sombre piece was one of Irving's favourites, and he delivered it with a power and intensity that roused the theatre to a storm of applause. Sitting in the audience that night was an American manager, ' Colonel ' Hezekiah Bateman, who was planning a new venture in London. He was leasing the Lyceum Theatre in order to launch his youngest daughter Isabel as an actress – her sisters Kate and Virginia were already established in the profession – and he was so impressed by Irving's two performances that he immediately offered him a three-year contract as leading man. Irving accepted, with his usual shrewdness, on condition that Bateman produced *The Bells.*

After Irving's triumph as Mathias and Jingle, parts were difficult to find. Living dramatists were, in the 1870s, more than usually scarce, and the greatest of the dead seemed out of bounds, for Shakespearian drama was in the doldrums. Yet Irving never faltered and seldom failed. First of all, he found a new stablemate for Mathias in the old farce of *Raising the Wind*: with Alfred Jingle and Robert Macaire, Jeremy Diddler formed one of a trinity of jaunty, stylish, seedy rogues whom Irving delighted to play. For the next season the new house-dramatist of the Lyceum, W. G. Wills, wrote a play – at Irving's suggestion – which exhibited him as a martyr king. Although *Charles I* was little more than a string of domestic scenes from the sentimentalized life of that unhappy Stuart, it gave the Lyceum's leading man an opportunity to demonstrate his range. Modelling his make-up on the Van Dyck portraits, he appeared with royal dignity, sweetness, pathos and saintliness, persecuted by a cardboard ruffian Cromwell; but his final curtain line of 'Remember!' as he went off to the scaffold, reduced many of the audience to tears – not only on the first night but for years to come. This great success was followed in the next season by a new version of the story of Eugene Aram, already familiar through Hood's poem and Lytton's novel. Under Irving's guidance, W. G. Wills created another portrait of a guilty and remorseful man, living – like Mathias – under the shadow of a murder he had committed many years before, and exposed just as he is on the verge of finding happiness in marriage. Once again, as in *The Bells*, nature forestalls the law, and Irving scored in Aram's death agonies: he died in the churchyard at daybreak, in the arms of his beloved, while a choir was heard off stage. As in *The Bells*, it was in showing the mind of a murderer that Irving excelled; but in spite of the similarities in *genre,* admirers noted that there was not a jot of Mathias in Aram. Next, in the season of 1873-4, Irving turned – at Bateman's insistence – to a 'classic' test-piece, by challenging the memory of Macready and Phelps in *Richelieu*. Breaking clean away from the tradition, he remade the character in his own individual way, with subtle humour and austere authority. 'Nature designed him for a prince of the church,' said William Archer in later life, and Richelieu was the first of his three triumphs in theatrical holy orders. Yet half the press violently attacked it. Throughout most of his career – especially in the early years – Irving raised fierce opposition by the modernism and individualism of his methods.

It was only now that Henry Irving dared to attempt the great Shakespearian roles, and then it was against the strong resistance of his manager. When he insisted on playing Hamlet, Bateman would allow him only £100 for the production. For Irving, at thirty-six, it was ' now or never '. If he was to fulfil his ambitions, he could not be content with applause in melodrama. To fail would be disastrous: he staked his all on victory. From his first appearance, on the night of 31 October 1874, this Prince of Denmark took the audience by surprise. Irving wore a black, fur-trimmed tunic, simple and elegant, relieved only by a gold chain round his neck, with no miniature or orders; underneath his raven-black hair, his handsome face was very pale but composed, not set in studied grief; and instead of framing his performance around the traditional ' points ', he behaved with highly unorthodox naturalism and understatement. Instead of being terrified by the ghost (like Betterton and Garrick) he questioned it with yearning confidence. Instead of jeering at Polonius, he mocked him with courteous humour. Here was a gentlemanly, thoughtful, *thinking* prince, who had not been seen before on the stage; and in the first two acts, indeed, he was ' so simple, so quiet, so free from the exhibition of actors' artifices ' (as Ellen Terry said) that the audience was puzzled and unresponsive. Where were the usual points? Not until the nunnery scene did Irving break down the barrier between stage and stalls with the overpowering intensity of his tirade against women, a rage marked by an underlying tenderness. The delayed applause helped to strengthen the actor's purpose, and his fate was settled at the end of the play-scene. As the King and Queen hurried off in confusion, Hamlet jumped up with a shout of triumph and threw himself in the King's chair. Leaping up again, and swaying in half-hysterical exultation, he clutched Ophelia's fan of peacock feathers and began to chant:

> For thou dost know, O Damon dear,
>   This realm dismantled was
> Of Jove himself, and now reigns here
>   A very, very . . .

Here he paused, looked at the fan, and then finishing the line with a shriek of ' pajock ' (or peacock), flinging away the fan as he spoke. It brought the house down on that first night, and on nearly every other night that Irving played the Prince of Denmark. ' However prepared you were for it,' said one admirer, many years later, ' though you knew it must come, its thrill was never lessened, the shock hit you and lifted you out of your seat.' From that moment the success of Irving's gamble was assured. It was reinforced by the pathos and poignancy of his bowdlerized scenes with the Queen: he knelt and laid his head in her lap, making a domestic scene of what had usually been an exercise in declamation. When the curtain fell at last, after midnight, the clapping and cheering was in homage to a great actor, who had climbed his Everest. It was a victory not only for Irving, but also for his profession and for Shakespeare.

Hamlet broke all records by running for two hundred performances (a total not yet eclipsed). During its run ' Colonel ' Bateman died, but his widow continued to manage the Lyceum and his daughters continued to act with Irving, who went on to tackle three more Shakespearian peaks. He did not master either his first Macbeth, a craven, Caledonian Aram who welcomed death as an escape from his conscience, or his first Othello, a bronzed, tenor-voiced Venetian general not to the taste of playgoers accustomed to turbaned basses in blackface. But his Richard of Gloucester, created in January 1877, was another triumph for Irving, unanimously acclaimed. Discarding the stock hump and the butcher's scowl, he emphasized that aura of royalty which he could wear so well. ' Where,' asked Tennyson, ' did he get that *Plantagenet* look?' The answer is: from the same place that he took his *Stuart* look in *Charles I* – from the make-up box of his mind. Here, noted one critic, was ' the prince, the statesman, the courtier', yet this ' gentleman-villain ' was nonetheless coldly and fearfully malignant, deeply enjoying his own villainy, a panther who in war changed into a lion. ' Weird, sinister, sardonic, all in turn and all together,' Irving was a ' splendidly satanic ' Crookback; and he was, moreover, Shakespeare's Crookback. For the first time most of the original text was restored, and Cibber's claptrap was jettisoned at last.

Irving now deserted Shakespeare for a while at the Lyceum, and revived two successes of Charles Kean, eclipsing him in both. In *The Lyons Mail*, adapted by Charles Reade from a

Parisian success, he achieved one of those doubles so dear to Victorian playgoers – as Lesurques, an innocent man who is wrongly accused of murder, and as Dubosc, the true culprit. Here was no genteel villain, but a cold-blooded, swaggering brute with a devilry all his own: Irving *lived* Dubosc, it seemed, just as he lived Richelieu. After rifling his victim's body, James Agate recalled, he would 'first wipe his hands wet with blood on the horse's flank, and then pat the animal's neck', humming a few bars of the *Marseillaise;* he prepared to watch the execution of Lesurques with every appearance of drunken, sardonic enjoyment; and, when he was discovered at the last moment, fought like a fury against the avenging mob. Although Dubosc became one of Irving's most popular roles, ('a masterpiece of riotous diablerie', Henry Arthur Jones called it) other artists – including Ellen Terry – thought it an easy victory. It was Lesurques, they said, which was the *tour de force*. To act good men on the stage is always difficult, and 'to play a good man sincerely, as he did here,' wrote Ellen Terry, 'to show that double thing, the look of guilt which an innocent man wears when accused of crime, requires great acting . . .'

After *The Lyons Mail,* Irving revived another of Charles Kean's Parisian imports – *Louis XI,* which gave him another opportunity for villainy on the grand scale, and for a demonstration of the death throes in which he excelled and delighted. His great achievement, indeed, was – according to one actor – 'to die slowly from the beginning of his performance to the end, and to give that death a spiritual significance.' Irving showed a despotic old king – cruel, hypocritical, cowardly, querulous and senile – on his way to the tomb, in what Laurence Irving describes as 'the most elaborate and subtle' of all his stage portraits. Here is one of the climaxes, described by H. M. Walbrook, at the end of the fourth act.

Seated in his chair in the gloomy room lit only by a single candle, and still mumbling his superstitions and his hates, he presently looked up and saw his enemy standing before him dim and ominous. He seemed to shrink into himself; and the following dialogue ensued:

> Louis: Ne-mours! Mer-ci-ful God!
> Nemours: Not a word!
> Louis: Si-lence! Si-lence! Mer-cy! Mer-cy!

The King breathed each syllable in a long whisper as in a paroxysm of fear . . . Followed as it was by the wretched man's shrieks, prayers, grovellings, and final collapse to the floor, the curtain used to fall amid a veritable thunder of applause.

In the fifth act, Louis's end came at last. Into the throne-room tottered the tall, ashen-faced old man, dressed in the blue velvet robes of state, with a huge golden crown on his head, grey hair streaming over his shoulders, clutching the royal sceptre. He staggered forward, using his sceptre as a staff, and then dropped it as he was helped on to a couch. Once there, Irving began perhaps the most remarkable of all his public deaths.

With extraordinary elaborated graduations of insensibility, violently interrupted by spasms of vigour, [noted Edward Russell] he gradually loses his consciousness. No physical detail is neglected that can help to realize a sinking of mind and body into annihilating death. The voice and articulation have the weird, half-drunken thickness of paralysis. Even the effect observable in age and sickness of drawing the retreating lips in over the sunken teeth is somewhat simulated . . . Perhaps the greatest success of all is the still and silent impassibility into which the king sinks so absolutely that the courtiers and his son suppose it to be death. The actual death is not placid. The king struggles on his feet, and falls forward on a cushion, with his head toward the audience, as the low murmur, ' The King is dead, long live the King ' proclaims the close . . .

It is worth noting that Irving's make-up was slight: ' except for a waxen pallor and two " blacked out " teeth he looked much as usual ' offstage, says Graham Robertson in *Time Was*. Louis was, moreover, ' a sort of holiday part to him ' (according to his manager); Ellen Terry declares that he could have played it ' on his head ' three times a day; and Graham Robertson records that ' at the fall of the curtain he would rise up perfectly fresh and slip at once out of the part as he would have put off a coat, while out of the death trance of Mathias he would come half dazed, cold, breathless and trembling.'

In spite of his triumphs in the early 1870s, Irving felt that his progress was being checked by conditions at the Lyceum under the Bateman regime, notably by the weakness of the company and, in particular, of his leading lady, Isabel Bateman. He wanted to manage his own theatre, yet he was bound to the Batemans by ties of grateful friendship. When Isabel fell in love with him, unrequited, his future changed. Partly to solve this awkward domestic problem, and partly because she felt that the time was ripe for a separation, Mrs Bateman generously offered Irving the lease of the Lyceum – in the summer of 1878. It was the chance of a lifetime, and he took it with both hands. He spent freely on his preparations, assembling a new company and redecorating the building, and by the time the theatre reopened under his management on 30 December 1878 – with a revival of *Hamlet* – he had an overdraft of £12,000. Yet from that moment the Lyceum was established as the leading playhouse of London, and under Irving's management it kept its supremacy as the centre of the English theatre for over twenty years. And by his side throughout that time was the Ophelia of 1878, that great actress Ellen Terry, who made an indispensable contribution to the success of the enterprise.

Outside, over the portico with its massive pillars (all that now remains of Irving's Lyceum) three torches flamed in the London sky every night of the season. Inside, the waiting audience sat before the curtain, while ' gas-lit candles in their wine-coloured shades glowed softly on the myrtle-green and cream and purple . . . the green baize in a diffused bluish mist; the music that did not start but insinuated itself upon you till the baize melted and you were in the picture, beholding yet part of it.' Composing the right kind of picture, and bringing the audience into the picture-frame, was one main factor in Irving's success: he set new standards of illusion, of unity in make-believe, and he brought stage design into line with the dominant trends in Victorian art. He had, moreover, a gift for administration (if not finance), reinforced by the power of inspiring loyalty in both staff and actors: the continuity of the theatre's organization, and the awe in which the ' Guv'nor ' or the ' Chief ' was held by most of his subordinates, played a sizable part in the Lyceum's long record of achievement. Irving's bizarre, single-minded, autocratic personality was stamped on the theatre, behind and in front of the stage. The Lyceum was dedicated to his art – and to his mission in restoring that art to honour in the national life; and this helped to give the theatre its special ' semi-sacred ' atmosphere, so that going to a first night there was – so wrote one admirer – ' something between a social duty and a religious rite '. According to another Lyceum-ite, ' there was a sacerdotal air about the entire building '. It was, in fact, a temple of dramatic art, of Irving's dramatic art. It had dignity, beauty and *permanence*, and from the early years of Irving's regime it was supported by the Victorian élite. Under his guidance, the Lyceum became nearly as fashionable as the opera.

When he took over the management in 1878, Irving had already established many of the main roles in his repertoire, and repeated them throughout his life on tour and in London: they were the foundation of his supremacy. But during the next twenty years the cares of management, at home and abroad, did not deter him from continually trying out new parts: the cares of management, indeed, demanded them. He revived Sir Edward Mortimer, and Charles Kean's dual role of Fabien and Louis dei Franchi in *The Corsican Brothers,* Dr Primrose (in W. G. Wills's version of *The Vicar of Wakefield*), and the Sidney Carton-like hero of *The Dead Heart*; he created Edgar in a stage version of *The Bride of Lammermoor;* Corporal Brewster (a Chelsea pensioner in Sir Arthur Conan Doyle's one-act *A Story of Waterloo*), and Mephistopheles (in the spectacular charade into which Irving turned *Faust*). Most of these parts were fustian and flimsy; but perhaps the most distinguished and the most successful was Becket in Tennyson's verse-drama, which he played in 1893 four months after the poet's death and twelve years after he had completed the play. There was almost unanimous acclaim for Irving, partly, William Archer suggested, because ' his cast of countenance, his expression, his manner, are all prelatical in the highest degree.' But partly, too, because – compared with his Lear or Wolsey – he spoke the verse so well. Tennyson, it seemed, suited his diction better than Shakespeare. Such was the impact that Irving made on the audience and on himself in this role that, according to Laurence Irving's admirable biography, ' he came . . . to regard the Augustinian habit which he assumed as the vestment of an officiating priest . . . having striven all his life to wring from the Church a benediction on his art, he persuaded himself that in the performance of Becket, spanning the gulf between Church and Stage, he and his audience united in an act of worship.'

Irving also added, of course, to his Shakespearian laurels during his reign at the Lyceum. He revived his Hamlet in 1879, and ran it for a hundred nights: not only had he improved on the earlier performance, said Tennyson, but he had 'lifted it to heaven'. In the same year he created Shylock, one of his prime achievements. It struck a new note by stressing the Jew's dignity, nobility, grim humour, pathos and pride in humiliation. The trial scene, says Laurence Irving, was 'the finest performance of his life'. He began with icy calm, cracked by increasing nervousness, changing into cruel impatience; but his best moment came, so many people thought, at the end, as Shylock left the court: 'the quiet shrug, the glance of ineffable, unfathomable contempt at the exultant booby, Gratiano . . . the expression of defeat in every limb and feature, the deep, gasping sigh, as he passes slowly out, and the crowd rush from the court to hoot and howl at him outside.' Henry Arthur Jones, one of Irving's more persistent critics, admitted that this was 'undoubtedly a great piece of acting. It was, however, quite ex-Shakespearian, if not anti-Shakespearian. It illustrates a frequent habit and method of Irving – that of getting his greatest effects not in, and by, the text and obvious meaning of his author, but in his own extraneous bits of business.' Yet it was those 'bits of business' that helped to keep him in dominion over the English stage.

He scored another triumph in 1881 as Iago, when he doubled this role and Othello with Edwin Booth. As the Moor he was blacker and more African than in 1876, but no better or more effective. Yet as Iago – cold, plausibly specious, Italianate, and delighting, 'almost genially', in the success of his schemes – he gave so effective though unorthodox a performance that for the first time, according to Laurence Irving, 'his most fanatical admirers, his sternest critics and his most mischievous enemies found themselves in complete, if uneasy agreement.' His second Benedick, which followed in 1882, was a hit in a different kind in spite of Irving's age (forty-four), praised for its chivalry and dry humour (though marred, according to Gordon Crosse, by 'undignified clowning'). Moreover, his second Macbeth, in 1888, succeeded where he had failed in 1875, although the interpretation remained unchanged – that of a moral coward, driven by terror. Henry James, who saw the 1875 version and approved of the conception, though not the execution, described him as 'a nature trembling and quaking to its innermost spiritual recesses'. At Banquo's appearance Irving achieved one of his special effects by grovelling in fear at the foot of the throne, with his head

E*

buried in his red cloak (though Shaw dismissed this as 'ludicrously beyond his powers'); and he kept the role from sagging
in the last act by nervous intensity and magnetic power, looking,
Ellen Terry says, like 'a great famished wolf'. It was, she
records, the performance in which Irving believed he had done
his best work. His valet thought so too: Sir Henry, he said,
sweated twice as much as in Hamlet. His other Shakespearian
successes at the Lyceum were Wolsey, Iachimo, and a revival of
Richard III. His failures were comparatively few: Romeo (which
he played at forty-four), Malvolio (he was booed on the first
night in 1884), Lear (this opening night, too, was a disaster in
1892) and his bearded Coriolanus of 1901 (on the last night,
Ellen Terry said, he took off the beard and transformed the performance). By the time he tackled Lear he was fifty-eight, and his
voice could not cope. On the first night of *Coriolanus* it gave out.
The long years of overwork and privation had taken their toll. Yet
it was his Lear, all the same, that remained among the most vivid
memories of those who saw him act in his later years.

Towards the end of his life Irving found it increasingly difficult
to discover good parts, or even satisfactory vehicles. He appeared
in a succession of curiously assorted historical disguises, as King
Arthur, Don Quixote, Napoleon, Peter the Great, Robespierre
and Dante – extraordinary people for his extraordinary personality
to inhabit – and the actor was, perhaps, undermined by the
manager and producer. Yet, although *The Bells* was the most
popular of all his plays until his death, he was never content to rest
on such triumphs of the past. As a director, moreover, he was
never content with less than the best – as he conceived it. He
imposed his own conception of the role on each member of his
company, coaching them in the details he had already planned
before the first rehearsal, insisting on their obedience with a
patience and discipline that had no precedent. 'Very often it
only ended,' said Ellen Terry, 'in his producing actors who gave
colourless, feeble and unintelligent imitations of him.' He did not
choose to surround himself with colourless docile talent, as other
actor-managers have been known to do. Strong-willed actors,
however, sometimes found it difficult to submit to such autocratic
methods: after five or six hours of the Chief's hectoring, said
George Alexander, he would go home nearly in tears. Yet these
methods helped to establish the unity, in conception and execu-

tion, that was the hallmark of Irving's productions. He paid even closer attention to the scenery and the music, bringing into the theatre such leading painters and musicians as Sir Edward Burne-Jones, Sir Laurence Alma-Tadema, Sir Edward German, and Sir Arthur Sullivan. It was established stage artists like Hawes Craven and William Telbin, however, who designed some of Irving's most successful settings: the church scene of *Much Ado About Nothing* was described by Irving himself as ' Telbin's masterpiece, with its real built-out round pillars thirty feet high, its canopied roof of crimson plush from which hung the golden lamps universally used in Italian cathedrals, its painted canopy overhanging the altar, its great ironwork gates, its altar with cases of flowers and flaming candles rising to a height of eighteen feet, its stained glass windows and statues of saints.' On such effects, Irving spent – even by modern standards – huge sums: *Faust* cost £8,000 and *Henry VIII* £12,000, corresponding to around £40,000 and £60,000 today. He carried to spectacular extremes the ' archaeological ' fuss of Macready and Charles Kean, in his concern for historical authenticity. Thus, for *Henry VIII,* a silk was specially woven to match a cardinal's robe of Wolsey's time, and was then sent to Rome to be dyed in the veritable red. For *Faust,* local colour was imported on the grand scale by buying crates full of costumes, furniture and properties in Nuremberg. Yet although the scenery sometimes overwhelmed the play, as in *Olivia,* and although Irving has often been accused of upholstering the drama, so that ' Lyceum Shakespeare ' became a synonym for over-elaborate pageantry at the expense of poetry, we have Ellen Terry's testimony that ' Henry would never accept anything that was not right *theatrically* as well as pictori-- ally beautiful '. Again, Gordon Craig says that ' all the correctness in the world was not worth a fig to Irving unless it *seemed* all right '; and, putting it at a somewhat lower estimate in Sir Max Beerbohm's words, ' Irving may sometimes have overdone it, but he always overdid it beautifully.' Much of his scenic success was due to his inventive artistry in lighting, using gas and limes (or calcium lights) with daring and imagination. ' Scenes lit by Irving had always the effect of oil-paintings, the boundaries lost in shade, highlights focusing the points of greatest interest.' That point was often Irving's own face, which was followed everywhere by ' a pin light of steel-blue '; but he was, it seems, the first to treat lighting as an essential strand in the director's art. 'The foundation of his method,' according to the theatrical historian, Muriel St Clare Byrne, 'was the consistent darkening of the auditorium throughout the performance – advocated by Ingegneri in 1598. Thanks to Irving, playhouse practice, after three centuries, caught up with Renaissance practice.' He secured greater flexibility of control and intensity of contrast; he experimented in the mixing of colour tones: he made a dramatic use of chiaroscuro in his romantic lighting, and all this was done with gas, which he insisted on retaining at the Lyceum long after electric light had been installed elsewhere in London.

Irving found his audience not only in the capital but throughout the country, touring the Lyceum productions from town to town for some four months in every year. Whereas Kean and Macready had travelled alone, appearing as 'guest stars' – in modern parlance – with the local stock companies, the development of the railways enabled Irving to tour the provinces with a company of over fifty in a special train. From the profits of these provincial journeys, and of the American tours organized in later years, he financed the rich and imaginative spectacle of his productions. For although his company, at home or on tour, made money on a bigger scale and for a longer time than any other enterprise in the history of the English drama, Irving's private income was much less than many of his less talented predecessors. With single-minded and far-sighted perfectionism, he put his money back in the theatre, maintaining the standards which helped to give the Lyceum its immense and justified reputation, which helped in turn to win new recognition for the actor, his art and his profession. Progress was swift. Within four years of taking over the Lyceum, Irving was elected to the Athenaeum under Rule 11 (an honour Macready had failed to secure); in the same year (1882) the Prince of Wales asked him to dinner, and later invited himself to one of the famous banquets on the Lyceum stage, which became a feature of late Victorian life in high society. In the following year, on the eve of his first American tour, a public banquet was given in Irving's honour attended by five hundred notables, with the Lord Chief Justice in the chair. Already Mr Gladstone thought of offering him a knighthood. Wisely, Irving let it be known that he felt he could not then accept; but twelve years later the theatre's moral and social redemption seemed to be confirmed when the actor-manager of the Lyceum left Windsor Castle as Sir Henry Irving. In giving him the accolade, and creating the first actor-knight of the English stage, Queen Victoria is reported to have broken her usual silence at such ceremonies and murmured: 'We are very, very pleased.'

This transformation from the outcast to the gentleman was not, of course, entirely due to the magic of Sir Henry Irving. Behind the new respectability of the stage lay the pressures of far-reaching social changes: the accumulation of a rapidly growing population in the towns, the spread of elementary education, the weakening of the Church's influence, the rise in living standards, the development of transport. From the 1870s onwards, playhouses sprang up in London and the provinces; the stage became an outlet for capital and a source of big profits; and the old theatrical system of mid-Victorian times disappeared under the impact of a new entertainment industry, with new values and new vogues. These changes, which helped Irving to win his campaign for social recognition, also helped to destroy him. By the turn of the century, his supremacy was over. The pioneer of the 1870s was attacked as a reactionary in the 1890s. For advocates of Ibsen and the 'drama of ideas', Irving (who ignored it) was the symbol of actor-worship, of the 'stagy' theatre they wished to destroy: Shaw was the most ferocious and unfair of Irving's enemies. Once supreme in the field, the Lyceum now had to face competition from other actor-managers with theatres of their own – Herbert Beerbohm Tree, Charles Wyndham, George Alexander, John Martin Harvey, and Johnston Forbes-Robertson (some of them Irving's pupils and all later knighted). Their talents were smaller, but so were their budgets. Irving's insistence on lavish staging, his refusal to stint his art or lower his standards in the face of rising costs and dwindling audiences, left the Lyceum without reserves. He had finally, moreover, exhausted his own physical reserves, prodigious as they were, by his arduous tours and his marathon performances of such roles as Hamlet and Macbeth seven and eight times a week for months on end. (He was the first leading actor to play such parts in a long run.)

At this time of his life came three crippling blows. First of all, his health collapsed. After the first night of a revived *Richard III* in December 1896, he fell ill for the first time in his life and never recovered his former strength. Then in February 1898 the Lyceum's entire store of scenery was destroyed by fire: 260 irreplaceable scenes for forty-four plays were wiped out in a night. Early in 1899, Irving made the mistake of handing over the theatre to a syndicate, which undertook to relieve him of financial responsibility: instead of being in command of the Lyceum, he was now the servant of a company, and the theatre slid towards its doom. This came in 1902, when the London County Council insisted on structural alterations which would cost £20,000. The Lyceum closed down, and with it closed a great era. Irving did not long survive. On a tour of the provinces, soon after playing Becket at the Bradford Theatre Royal, he collapsed in his hotel and died – on the night of 13 October 1905. He is buried in Westminster Abbey, next to David Garrick.

' There are only two ways of portraying a character on the stage,' Irving is reported to have said. ' Either you can try to turn yourself into that person – which is impossible – or, and this is the way to act, you can take that person and turn him into yourself. That is how I do it!' In his lifetime, one of the main charges of the vociferous anti-Irving camp was precisely this, that he was ' always Irving '; yet in an actor with so wide a range and so deep an understanding, the distinction between *acteur* and *comédien* seems of little value. ' He was always Irving, yes,' writes H. A. Saintsbury, ' but it was a different facet of Irving that he showed you in each character and they flashed blindingly as the light of his genius played on them.' Or, in the words of Sir Max Beerbohm's obituary, ' His voice, face, figure, port were not transformable. But so fine was the personality to which they belonged that none cried shame when this or that part had to submit to be crushed by it. Intransformable he was – multi-radiant though.' Ellen Terry tells us that ' he used to make his entrance in the *skin* of his part '; Violet Vanbrugh says that ' Irving didn't tell you things, he lived them on the stage '; but, as A. B. Walkley wrote, ' the finest thing . . . in any stage-character of Irving's was Irving himself.' ' His greatest triumphs,' said William Archer, ' are projections of himself, not reflections of the world around him . . . His physical advantages are all summed up in the one word intensity . . . The high forehead, the marked and overhanging but flexible eyebrows, the thin straight nose, the almost lipless, sensitive mouth, the hollow cheeks and marvellously mobile jaw combine to form an incomparable vehicle for the expression of a certain range of character and emotion.' His appearance lifted the spectator out of himself: he seemed 'a being of ultra-reality'. 'He was natural – like lightning,' said Gordon Craig. 'No one was ever as great as Irving looked,' said Sir John Pollock. Part of the secret, no doubt, was in his eyes – described by Ellen Terry as 'rather small dark eyes which can at a moment become immense, and hang like a bowl of dark liquid with light shining through.'

Most of his lives were at two extremes of human nature – saints and criminals; but sometimes he seemed to draw them together in a common intensity and extravagance, suffused with that strange, unearthly radiance that was part of his stage magic. Black turned into white, so that Shylock, for example, appeared – in Graham Robertson's words – as a 'dignified, heroic, intensely aristocratic martyr'. His comedy had a threat in it, a hint of evil, and his devilry was lit with grim humour. He excelled in what Henry James (one of his sharpest critics) described as 'the chord of the sinister-sardonic, flowered over as vividly as may be with the elegant-grotesque'; there was something Gothic in the villainy of his Richard, Iachimo, and Dubosc. He was a specialist in senility (Corporal Brewster, Richelieu, Louis XI; in priesthood (Becket, Dr Primrose, Wolsey); and in royalty (Hamlet, King Arthur, Charles I, Philip of Spain), though his grave dignity and authority sometimes gave an incongruous significance to his characters. As Doctor Primrose, 'one always had a lurking feeling that he should have been Archbishop of Canterbury and not a mere humble Vicar of Wakefield.' He was, moreover, a specialist in guilty consciences and public executions. Deeply melancholy in his own nature and passionately interested in crime (in Paris one of his main pleasures was to visit the morgue), his stage deaths gripped the mind of a generation. 'I do not believe,' wrote Maurice Baring, 'that so much anguish, suspense, terror and remorse have ever been administered to the public in so short a time, in such a powerful and compact dose, as when Irving played Mathias in *The Bells*.' As Mathias, says Ellen Terry, 'he really did almost die – he imagined death with such horrible intensity. His eyes would disappear upwards, his face grew grey, his limbs cold.' The 'mysticism' for which he was so often praised was, in part, the sense he gave to the audience of the imminent extinction of his own dominating personality. When he was murdered as Becket, wrote Baring, ' I felt that I had witnessed the martyrdom of a great saint.' And whatever Irving did, in whatever role he played, he radiated that mesmeric power, that mysterious magnetism, whose unaccountable, irresistible influence helps to make an actor great, and which he exerted more persistently and in larger measure, perhaps, than any other actor in our history. To this hypnosis, as Sir Max wrote at his death, ' rather than to the quality of his genius, which was a thing to be really appreciated only by the few, was due the unparalleled sway he had over the many.'

Yet this secret power did not blaze out upon the world when Irving first set foot upon the stage: it took many years to mature and apply, long years of painful self-improvement in the provinces; the magic needed a wide grounding in technique and experience before it could work its wonders. For a critic like Henry James, grounded in the Comédie Française, Irving's acceptance was, in one sense, an indictment of the British attitude to theatrical art. ' That an actor so handicapped . . . by nature and culture should have enjoyed so much prosperity is a striking proof of the absence of a standard, of the chaotic condition of taste.' Of Irving's ' handicaps ' there was certainly no doubt. ' Henry Irving at first had everything against him as an actor,' says Ellen Terry. ' He could not speak, he could not walk, he could not *look*. He wanted to do things in a part and he could not do them. His amazing power was imprisoned, and only after long and weary years did he succeed in setting it free.' Even in 1867, only four years before his triumph in *The Bells*, he was – she says – still ' stiff with self-consciousness; his eyes were dull and his face heavy.' He had a dragging leg, an eccentric walk, and a voice without music. His legs were too thin, his shoulders high, his body clumsy and untrained. Yet just as in youth Irving overcame his stutter, so he conquered such handicaps by will-power. He was, as Hazlitt said scornfully of Macready, an ' improving ' actor. Where he could not jettison his mannerisms, he made a virtue of them in his art by exaggerating them, and composing them into a highly personal idiom of self-expression. ' My father once told me,' the elder Laurence Irving is reported to have said, ' that when he resolved to play the great Shakespearian parts he realized that he had not the physical force to act them in the way they were usually represented, so he translated them into a language of his own.'

For some people, that language remained wilfully and sometimes ludicrously obscure. Henry James wrote in 1880, for example, that: ' Mr Irving's peculiarities and eccentricities of speech are so strange, so numerous, so personal to himself, his vices of pronunciation, of modulation, of elocution so highly developed, the tricks he plays with the divine mother tongue so audacious and fantastic, that the spectator who desires to be in sympathy with him finds himself confronted with a bristling hedge of difficulties.' Thus, he said ' naw ' for ' no ', ' Gud ' for ' God ', ' god ' for ' good ', ' rup ' for ' rope ', ' seyt ' for ' sight ', ' stod ' for ' stood ', and ' hond ' or ' hend ' for ' hand '; he spoke at times with almost painfully slow precision, with a curious nasal resonance, and like Kean and Macready indulged in swift transitions from high to low and back again; and he walked, in some roles, with a jerky and staccato gait, sometimes almost as if he were dancing, sometimes as if he were striding over a ploughed field, and sometimes stamping his feet in the old barnstorming style. Yet there was nothing accidental about these eccentricities. If he prolonged the vowels and lengthened the syllables it was, as Lena Ashwell said, ' to make up for the lack of depth in his voice '. If he re-scored (or merely ignored) the music of Shakespeare's verse, it was because he could not tune his own ' raven croak ' to the true melody. He gave the meaning, not the music, transforming the verse – all too often – into prose, cutting what he could not fit into his design. But that design was elaborately and meticulously planned. Nothing was left to chance: ' nothing real – all massively artificial – yet all flashing with the light and the pulse of nature,' wrote Gordon Craig. ' What he did was always and inevitably the right thing – the natural thing – the only thing, so it seemed, that was possible,' said one of his admirers, some twenty years after his death.

In his time, he was a realist. He broke with the old classic school, avoiding declamation and ' point-making '. He rethought all his parts, applying careful psychological study and using realistic technique (by the standards of the day). He had a command of pathos; a sense of humour and also a sense of horror; ' an incomparable power for eeriness, for stirring a dim sense of mystery ' (as Beerbohm said); a capacity for making faces – ' when he made one it was in granite,' said James Agate.

Partly influenced by what he described as Irving's ' extraordinary insensibility to literature ', Shaw dismissed him as having ' no brains – nothing but character and temperament '. Yet it was not only by magnetic power and personal merit that Irving triumphed, and that he is still remembered. He was a highly deliberate, resourceful, imaginative artist, who calculated his effects with masterly timing and self-knowledge, who continued to study and to learn throughout his working life. William Archer – one of Irving's most scathing critics – wrote: ' By intellect he makes us forget his negative failings and forgive his positive faults. By intellect he forces us to respect where we cannot admire. By intellect he dominates the stage.' Irving *thought* his way to greatness.

6

Sir Johnston
Forbes-Robertson

As the court of Denmark filed across the stage, excitement rose in the hushed and expectant theatre. The audience was waiting to greet Prince Hamlet, who had made his entrance in this royal procession since the time of John Philip Kemble. There, at the end of the file, came a tall, familiar figure. No wig surmounted one of the best-known faces in the English theatre, lean, clear-cut, fine-featured, though now deeply lined. He walked on without tragic pomp and circumstance, coming to Elsinore as if it were his home; and as he appeared the Lyceum filled with a storm of welcoming applause which even the theatre's overlord, Henry Irving, might have envied. It was the night of 11 September 1897, and Johnston Forbes-Roberston was playing Hamlet – for the first time. After twenty-three years on the stage, at the age of forty-four, he had begun to take the measure of the great roles in the English repertoire. At long last he was entering his inheritance.

Even more impressive than the applause, said a first-nighter, was ' the unbroken silence with which the whole house seemed to hang upon Hamlet's voice. Once or twice a cheer from the gallery broke upon the stillness, but it was promptly suppressed by a prolonged " sh " from all sides.' Here was a difference indeed from the rowdy, brawling crowds who watched Kean, Kemble and Macready; and the silence was due not only to the transformation in theatre manners but also to a change in acting style. Forbes-Robertson was not playing for ' points ', like his great predecessors. There were no ' audacious attempts at new readings ', no ' startling theatrical surprises,' whether of scenery or characterization. What seemed so extraordinary, indeed, was the very simplicity and humanity of this Prince of Denmark. After the romantic chiaroscuro of Irving's performance, Forbes-Robertson supplied a classical lucidity, consistency and harmony, with 'infinite and ever-changing phases and gradations of light and shade . . .' Instead of tailoring the text to his own intensities, he seemed to give all the words he used their proper value, as if he were thinking aloud, and as a result nearly all the character came to life (the cruelty and bawdiness disappeared with some of the cuts). Here was not merely an 'introspective philosopher' alternating with an 'impulsive avenger', but a Hamlet who matched 'in every particular' Ophelia's description:

> The courtier's, soldier's, scholar's eye, tongue, sword:
> The expectancy and rose of the fair state,
> The glass of fashion and the mould of form.

Here, said the critics, was Hamlet 'in his entirety', 'thoroughly natural', 'the most humanly natural of any impersonation known to the contemporary English stage', 'the most human, the most natural, and in temperament the most lovable'. Half-way through the evening a veteran critic was heard to exclaim: 'My dear sir, the man was born to play Hamlet!'

Instead of a gloomy and hysterical Dane, Forbes-Roberston presented a humorous, sweet-natured, gentlemanly prince, with a bubbling, impulsive *joie de vivre*, whose intellect – as Shaw put it – was 'the organ of his passion'. Other Hamlets, Shaw complained, treated the players, the gravedigger, Horatio, Rosencrantz and Guildenstern 'as if they were mutes at his own funeral.'

But go and watch Mr Forbes-Robertson's Hamlet seizing delightedly on every opportunity for a bit of philosophic discussion or artistic recreation to escape from the 'cursed spite' of revenge and love and other common troubles; see how he brightens up when the players come; how he tries to talk philosophy with Rosencrantz and Guildenstern the moment they come into the room; how he stops on his country walk with Horatio to lean over the churchyard wall and draw out the grave digger . . .; how even his fits of excitement find expression in declaiming scraps of poetry; how the shock of Ophelia's death relieves itself in the fiercest intellectual contempt for Laertes's ranting, whilst an hour afterwards, when Laertes stabs him, he bears no malice for that at all, but embraces him gallantly and comradely; and how he dies as we forgive everything to Charles II for dying, and makes 'the rest is silence' a touchingly humorous apology for not being able to finish his business. See all that; and you have seen a true classical Hamlet.

Earlier, Shaw had explained: 'What I mean by classical is that he can present a dramatic hero as a man whose passions are those which have produced the philosophy, the poetry, the art and the statecraft of the world, and not merely those which have produced its weddings, coroner's inquests, and executions.'

All Hamlets hitherto had brought down the curtain on 'the rest is silence', but Forbes-Robertson restored most of the original ending. Death-white, Hamlet staggered to the throne of Denmark, his face – as it seemed to one first-nighter – 'rapt and inspired with a vision of the higher mystery'. Groping with feeble fingers in the air, 'gazing on some unseen seraphic vision', he whispered 'The rest is silence' – and died, 'with an expiring flash, like a breeze passing unnoticed through the sultry air'. The court fell on their knees around the throne, Horatio placed the crown on Hamlet's knees between his hands, and then Fortinbras made his entrance – for the first time in nearly three hundred years. Horatio's speeches were cut down to a few lines, but when Fortinbras cried: 'Go, bid the soldiers shoot', four of his soldiers lifted Hamlet on to their shields, and carried him slowly off the stage, surrounded by torchbearers. Not everyone approved this restoration of the play's ending: to William Archer it seemed, astonishingly, 'of no literary value', and to J. T. Grein it was 'an anti-climax justified neither by a pretended respect for Shakespeare (for the text is none too gently treated in this performance) nor by the theatrical pageantry of which it was the occasion.' Yet to Shaw, and to posterity, it was one of Forbes-Robertson's most distinctive achievements.

How many generations of Hamlets, all thirsting to outshine their competitors in effect and originality, have regarded Fortinbras, and the clue he gives to this kingly death for Hamlet, as a wildly unpresentable blunder of the poor foolish old Swan, than whom they all knew so much better! How sweetly they have died in that faith to slow music, like Little Nell in *The Old Curiosity Shop*! And now how completely Mr Forbes-Robertson has bowled them all out by being clever enough to be simple.

With more justification, some critics complained about Forbes-Robertson's relative equability and restraint. Was he not, they

asked, overdoing the good manners? Was Hamlet quite so much
of an English gentleman? The ' consummate good breeding '
praised by one critic seemed paralysingly genteel to others. Many
Hamlets had triumphed in the ' mad ' scenes: Forbes-Robertson's
Prince was ' only mad when he would appear so, and not unmistakably mad even then '. And although, as Archer wrote so contemptuously, ' our forefathers took a delight in the contemplation
of insanity which we no longer feel, and it is evident that their
actors revelled in exhibitions of mopping, mowing, and gibbering,
such as would merely inspire us with disgust ', yet he could see no
reason for the ' exceeding tameness ' of Forbes-Robertson's acting after the Ghost's departure in the first act and in the nunnery
scene with Ophelia. He spoke to the Ghost ' in the cellarage ' with
' respectful melancholy '; he addressed Ophelia with almost
' paternal ' tenderness; he reproached his mother with gentle,
plaintive sorrow. He omitted, said Archer, ' a good many of the
wild and whirling words, and he puts no force or gusto into those
he utters . . . Artistic self-restraint is a very good thing but in this
case it verges on timidity.' Some of this ' timidity ' vanished after
the first night, but the quality of which critics complained was all
of a piece with the gentlemanly naturalism of this Hamlet's
character – with his friendly talk to the players, his kindly teasing
of Polonius, his gay banter with the gravedigger, which seemed
to some playgoers sadly deficient in true tragic solemnity.

Another complaint, from a generation brought up on Irving's
Hamlet, was that Forbes-Robertson spoke much too quickly.
Where were the pauses, the stresses, of the veteran Shakespearian
actor? Yet the fact was that the old method was, in this respect,
by then the wrong method. Now, for the first time in many years,
the text was given its full musical value by a star actor who not
only understood the verse but had the voice for all of it. Forbes-
Robertson's voice has probably never been equalled on the English stage. Deep, melodious and vibrant, it was his supreme asset.
He was not obliged to re-score the verse and invent new readings,
as Archer pointed out, ' in order to mask and excuse the breath-
ing-space required by deficient physical power, and lack of skill
in the management of the voice. He speaks his effects in Shakespeare's words, and not in his pauses . . .' Far from being too
rapid, said Archer, ' the bane of almost all recent Shakespearian
acting has been its torturing slowness . . .' Shaw also praised

Forbes-Robertson's handling of the verse. ' He does not utter half a line; then stop to act; then go on with another half line; and then stop to act again, with the clock running away with Shakespeare's chances all the time. He plays as Shakespeare should be played, on the line and to the line, with the utterance and acting simultaneous, inseparable, and in fact identical.' Hesketh Pearson records: ' He and Ellen Terry were the only two players in my experience who delivered the language of Shakespeare as if it were their natural idiom and whose beauty of diction matched the beauty of the words.'

For some people Forbes-Robertson was a reader, rather than an actor. He ' *recited* Hamlet, to perfection – Irving *felt* Hamlet ', as one unofficial critic put it. ' It would be impossible to imagine a more perfect reading than he gave: every line was spoken with a nicety so flawless that as it fell on the ear it satisfied by its perfect modulation as the rhythm of lapping waves. But there was never a spark, never a thrill – never a note of exultation, or the crash of passion.' Yet whatever the reservations of the minority, on that first September evening in 1897 at the old Lyceum there was no doubt about the triumph of Forbes-Robertson. On the next morning, he found Irving sitting at a table with the papers in front of him. Banging them with his hand, Forbes-Robertson recalled, Irving said to him: ' Well, you've done it.' ' I was very much played out, and had sunk into a chair on the other side of the table, but his cheering words, uttered while that wonderful smile played over his face, put new life into me. " Yes," he repeated, " you've done it, and now you must go and play Hamlet all over the world." ' For the next nineteen years, until his retirement at the age of sixty-three, ' Forbie ' followed Sir Henry's advice, and never lost command of his audience. ' Over and over again both in England and America,' he wrote in his autobiography, *A Player Under Three Reigns*, ' when the production of a new play had spelt failure, a revival of *Hamlet* had always set me on my feet again.' He was, indeed, at once recognized as ' the Hamlet of a generation of Hamlets ', and it is as the Prince of Denmark that he won his place among the great English actors.

It seems all the stranger that Forbes-Robertson delayed so long in attempting the role, and then, according to his own account, it was only under pressure from Irving. When planning a season at the Lyceum in 1897 (while Irving was on tour), he was at a loss for a play. With the whole range of the classic repertoire before him, after only two years of management, Forbes-Robertson did not know what to put on the stage. Sir Henry solved the problem, by telling him: 'Play *Hamlet*,' and offering to lend him the scenery and properties. The younger man, who regarded the role itself as Irving's property, was much impressed by this generosity; yet even then he was undecided. To Ellen Terry, he said: 'Everybody plays *Hamlet*; it has been played to death; people are sick of *Hamlet*.' Crushingly, Miss Terry asked him if he wanted violinists to stop playing some of Beethoven's best works because other violinists had also played them in the past. And so Forbes-Roberston was persuaded into greatness. It was an oddly sidelong approach to the summit, compared with the assault made by Irving and others upon the peaks of their art.

Johnston Forbes-Robertson was born in London on 16 January 1853, the eldest child of a Scottish art-critic and journalist. In notable contrast with most of his great predecessors, he enjoyed a peaceful, happy and comfortable childhood, in a home visited by many leading artists. Educated at Charterhouse, he spent most of his summer holidays in France. Under the guidance of his father (part-author of a biography of Samuel Phelps), he knew all the plays of Shakespeare before he was thirteen, learning by heart 'very many of the great passages'. At home, in the Christmas holidays, he attempted Macbeth (at fourteen) Hamlet (at fifteen) and Othello (at sixteen) with the support of his sister and brothers, before audiences which included such friends of his father as Alma-Tadema, Ford Madox Brown and Swinburne. He also began to train his voice, on a system recommended by another family acquaintance, the historian Dr Brewer. Forbes-Robertson had been ' reading a scene or two from *King Lear* to some friends in my mother's drawing-room', when the historian took him aside. ' He led me to the piano, and striking a very low note, said, "Now speak a line of six or seven words on that note, *don't sing* them, speak them. For instance, let's try the words, 'Angels and ministers of grace, defend us.'" This I did, and then he took me from note to note as high as it was possible for me to speak on the note he struck. Said he, "You must practise to extend your speaking register just as a singer does his notes, that you may get flexibility and variety of tone and thereby free your voice from monotony of delivery," ' The boy followed Dr. Brewer's advice and continued the exercise ' for many years '; it was his only training for the stage.

Amateur theatricals, however, were only one of young Forbes-Robertson's hobbies. He was also a keen painter, and the climate of his home encouraged his experiments in self-expression. A frequent visitor to the house was Dante Gabriel Rossetti, for whom he modelled Eros in the picture of ' Dante's Dream '. Impressed by some of the boy's oils, Rossetti urged Mr Forbes-Robertson to let Johnston take up painting, and as soon as he was old enough he was sent to Heatherley's, a famous art-school, to ' draw from the antique '. Within a year he was admitted to the Royal Academy, where he remained until he was nearly twenty-one. But although his father had put no obstacles in his way, and had indeed given all the help and encouragement he could wish for, Mr Forbes-Robertson was not a rich man. ' I was the eldest of a large family, and it was time for me to get out of the nest and make my own living.' He had to find a job, and he found it – by accident – on the stage. W. G. Wills, the dramatist, was dissatisfied with the ' juvenile lead ' in his new play, *Mary Queen of Scots*, and he asked Forbes-Robertson to take over the part. There is some mystery about how this happened. Wills's biographer says that the dramatist saw the young art student in the street, realized that he was ' cast by nature ' for the role of Chastelard, the poet-lover, and asked him ' on the spot.' Others report that Mr Forbes-Robertson, hearing of Wills's predicament, recommended Johnston – ' Why don't you try my eldest?' The actor himself says that it was because Wills had seen him perform as a boy in drawing-room Shakespeare. But whatever the explanation, Forbes-Robertson made his professional début on 12 March 1874, at the Princess's Theatre in Oxford Street – billed on the programme as ' Forbes-Robinson.' It was in this way, at two days' notice, that he entered the theatre, although, he assured the readers of his autobiography, ' it was no wish of mine to become an actor.' *Mary Queen of Scots* soon disappeared from the stage, but Forbes-Robertson remained on it for forty years. From then onwards he was never out of work for long, and within two years he had emerged as one of the white hopes of the younger generation of English players.

Untrained and inexperienced as he was, lacking in any rooted sense of vocation, Forbes-Robertson began his new career with two great advantages, his musical voice and his beauty. Ellen Terry, with whom he appeared on tour that year in his second part, recalled that he was 'wonderful – a dreamy, poetic-looking creature'. In the time of Kemble and Kean, such assets would not have been sufficient to win, at first go, a leading role for so green a novice; but the late Victorian theatre already offered rich opportunities to the new generation of gentlemanly amateurs, of whom Forbes-Robertson may be taken as a leader. With the expansion of the industry in London and the provinces, many managers were in search of handsome, personable young men; and the contemporary repertoire, under the long-run system, offered far less exacting avenues to success than the old 'patent' programmes. The general reduction in the size of playhouses (compared with the white elephants – so far as 'straight' drama was concerned – of Covent Garden and Drury Lane); the replacement of gas by electricity; the abolition of the pit and the introduction of the stalls (at twice the price); the establishment of picture-frame staging; the popularity of realistic scenery and furniture; the break-up of the stock companies with their stratified types and hierarchies; and, above all, the recruitment of a new middle-class audience – all these changes helped to shape English acting in the last twenty years of the century. Gentlemen were in demand, and already in 1880 Henry James noted the advent of young men from the middle classes who entered the theatre 'after being educated for something very different'. He observed that 'the art of acting as little as possible has . . . taken the place of the art of acting as much.' Bluster and rant were succeeded by self-restraint and good manners. Gentility all too often became a substitute for skill, 'personality' could triumph without technique, and acting gave way to *behaviour*.

Forbes-Robertson has sometimes been described as the last of the old school, in the Kemble-Macready-Irving tradition; he might with equal justice be labelled as the first of the new school; yet, as he himself said, 'There is the good old school, and the bad old school, and the former is the best school for any time.' He had the advantage in his first year of working with Samuel Phelps, perhaps the best survivor of the good old school. It happened at Manchester, where Forbes-Robertson was engaged for a few months in Charles Calvert's stock company (with which

Irving had spent two profitable years). In the traditional way –
a way soon to be destroyed – Phelps came to Manchester to play
Bottom in *A Midsummer Night's Dream* and to double the King
and Shallow in *Henry IV Part II*. Forbes-Robertson took the
part of Prince Hal.

During the first rehearsal of the impressive scene between the King
and the Prince, Phelps suddenly grunted out, ' Young man, you know
nothing about this part; come to my dressing-room tonight at seven
o'clock.' I knocked at his door in fear and trembling that night . . .
He went through my part with me, and my eyes were opened to many
things, the main one being that though I had worked much at the
part, I knew precious little about it . . . He bade me to his lodging
the next day for further study, and this was the beginning of an
interest he took in all my doings almost to the day of his death, and
from that time on he seldom played an engagement without me.

In December, when Phelps came to the Gaiety in London,
Forbes-Robertson came with him to play Fenton in *The Merry
Wives of Windsor;* and the old actor gave the handsome young
novice a thorough grounding in the classic repertoire and its
traditions, casting him in such parts as Joseph Surface, Cromwell,
Orsino and Antonio in *The Merchant of Venice*. In 1878, a few
months before Phelps died, Forbes-Robertson painted him as
Wolsey: it was in that role that Phelps made his last appearance,
collapsing in the arms of Forbes-Robertson's brother Norman.
' To be taken up so early in my career by one of the best of the
old school,' as Forbes-Robertson says, 'was my supreme good
fortune. He had been Macready's favourite actor, Macready had
played with Mrs Siddons, and she had played with Garrick, so
that I may boast of a good histrionic pedigree, and I confess to
pride at being a link with the great past in my calling . . . Samuel
Phelps's dignity of mind, his high ideals, his pride in his calling,
his contempt for wire-pullers, left a lasting impression which
remained with me through all my stage career. The attainments
of that career, such as they have been, are due to his influence
and teaching.'
During the next twenty years, however, although Forbes-
Robertson acted scores of parts in many theatres on both sides
of the Atlantic, he had few opportunities to show that he could
be considered as the heir of Phelps or as ' a link with the great
past '. The plays in which he appeared were, for the most part,

ephemeral romantic melodramas and comedies; and in none of them did he seize the public's imagination and command its allegiance as a great actor, although he enjoyed a steady success in the middle range. He showed, moreover, no desire to be his own master and choose his own roles, although the English stage now offered wider freedoms to the player who wanted to set up in business for himself. Actors and actresses leased London playhouses for long reigns with semi-permanent companies, which toured the provinces during the summer. It was with Buckstone's company at the Haymarket, in 1876, that Forbes-Robertson first came into the public eye (he appeared as a young sailor in W. S. Gilbert's Civil War drama, *Dan'l Druce, Blacksmith*). Later, after two seasons at the Olympic, he joined the Bancrofts, who were the pioneers of so many changes on both sides of the footlights. At the Prince of Wales Theatre, off the Tottenham Court Road, they introduced the domestic comedies of Tom Robertson, revolutionary in their ' naturalism '; they improved the comfort and appearance of the auditorium; they used real doors and windows and other ' practical ' scenery; they increased both the pay and prestige of actors; and they attracted a new section of society to the theatre, by making it ' respectable ' once more. Forbes-Robertson appeared in their last production at the old Prince of Wales's (as a comic Cockney sergeant in Robertson's *Ours*), and in their first venture at the Haymarket in 1880 (as Lord Glossmore in a revival of Lytton's *Money*). He was thus an eyewitness of the last of those riots which had marked the history of the English theatre.

When Forbes-Robertson played at the Haymarket under Buckstone, it had ' two rows of meagre stalls, into which ladies did not go '. The dress circle was then the fashionable part of the house. But Bancroft remodelled the theatre, turned the pit into stalls, and relegated the pittites to the gallery – a transformation which symbolized the social and economic changes in the English theatre as a whole. On the first night – 31 January 1880 – the gallery showed its disapproval by kicking up a storm of protest as soon as the curtain rose and Forbes-Robertson came on the stage. It was impossible to begin the play, and the barrackers would not listen to Bancroft's explanations. ' Give us back our pit! ' they shouted in chorus. Yet when Bancroft said, 'Well, if you won't listen to me, will you listen to the play?' they all answered, ' Yes ', and – according to Forbes-Robertson – ' the rest of the play was listened to with great attention.' That was the sum of the ' riot ', and although controversy about ' the pit question ' continued for some weeks, there were no more violent demonstrations at the theatre. Such docility, in contrast with the ferocity of the audiences who howled down Kean and Kemble, was a sign of the times.

Another sign was the fact that, between his work with Phelps and his Hamlet, Forbes-Robertson appeared in only five Shake-spearian roles. Two of these, Romeo and Orlando, came within his range as a *jeune premier*. He played Romeo to the Juliets of Helena Modjeska, the famous Polish actress, and Mary Anderson, the American star. With Modjeska he also appeared as Maurice de Saxe in *Adrienne Lecouvreur*, Leicester in *Mary Stuart*, and Armand Duval in *Lady of the Camelias;* and with Mary Anderson he toured the USA, playing Orlando, Claude Melnotte, and other parts. Later he played Leontes to her Hermione-Perdita in *The Winter's Tale*, for which he designed all the dresses. He worked with the Bancrofts until their retirement in 1885, and then joined John Hare's company at the Garrick, where he remained for six years. Two of his most notable successes here were as villains – Duncan Renishaw in Pinero's *The Profligate*, and Scarpia in Sardou's *La Tosca*. But his best work of all, it seems, was done for Irving at the Lyceum, where he worked in three productions: as Claudio in *Much Ado About Nothing* (1882), Buckingham in *Henry VIII* (1892) and Lancelot in *King Arthur* (1895). It was here that, once again, he made contact with the ' old school '.

Working with him in 1882, Ellen Terry noted a ' marvellous ' improvement in the past eight years. ' I had once said to him that he had far better stick to his painting and become an artist instead of an actor. His Claudio makes me " take it back ". It was beautiful . . . Forbes-Robertson put a touch of Leontes into it, a part which some years later he was to play magnificently . . .' Even now, one critic complained, Forbes-Robertson was ' too apt to throw his head back, and gesticulate too freely, and to wave arms and legs in an eccentric manner ', with what was des-cribed as ' an irrepressible gaucherie '. His Buckingham, how-ever, was a triumph. Because of the noble eloquence, pathos and dignity of the farewell speech, this performance has been classed with his Hamlet by many of Forbes-Robertson's admirers: ' like a medieval saint whose beautiful face above his black death robe recalled an exquisite early Italian carving in ivory, whose grand voice, ringing out between the strokes of the passing bell, drew all hearts towards him.' As Lancelot his main effect was pictorial. 'He has a beautiful costume,' noted Shaw dryly, 'most of plate-armour of Burne-Jonesian design; and he wears it beautifully, like a fifteenth-century St George . . . He was more than applauded on his entrance, he was positively adored.' Archer confirmed that 'his figure is absolutely beautiful', but complained that he suggested an 'affable archangel' from the paintings of Gozzoli or Carpaccio rather than a knight of the Round Table; 'or if indeed a knight, then the stainless Galahad rather than the superbly human Lancelot of the Lake.' Graham Robertson also observed that he 'played and looked Galahad to perfection'. During the run of *King Arthur* Forbes-Robertson left the Lyceum to play in Pinero's *The Notorious Mrs Ebbsmith,* in the somewhat less saintly character of Lucas Cleeve; but he wrote to Irving: 'My three engagements at the Lyceum have been the bright sunny spots in my stage life. I do not think you can have any idea what a pleasure it has been to me to act with you, to take up the tone and movement of the scene with you, to play into your hands as best I might. All this has been a labour of love.'

When Forbes-Robertson at last entered management, some months later, it was at the Lyceum, and he resolved to do his best to uphold the Irving tradition. Yet, he wrote in his autobiography, 'I would gladly have remained an actor pure and simple . . . I had acted with all the leading people of that time, though at periods being very hard worked, I had comparatively no anxieties. The very speculative and gambling nature of theatrical management was distasteful to me; and I knew that my own personal efforts as an actor would be considerably handicapped by all the extra labour and anxiety which management entails.' But if he was to 'maintain his place', he realized that he would have to shoulder the burden. He shared it, frequently, with Mrs Patrick Campbell, often subordinating himself as an actor, and with Gertrude Elliott, whom he married in 1900. Even when in control of his own destiny, Forbes-Robertson seemed to lack the appetite for supreme power which had marked most great actors. Unlike Irving and the Bancrofts, or such contemporaries as

George Alexander and Herbert Beerbohm Tree, Forbes-Robertson never had a theatre of his own and a consistent policy, nor did he maintain a large repertoire. He staged *The School for Scandal*, *Othello*, *Macbeth* and *Hamlet*. He presented Maeterlinck's *Pelléas and Mélisande* and Sudermann's *Magda*. He commissioned John Davidson's *For the Crown* (adapted from François Coppée) and Henry James's *The High Bid* (which came to grief in the provinces). He introduced *Caesar and Cleopatra*, written expressly for him by Shaw. But Forbes-Robertson's biggest successes were in more perishable stuff. In Madeleine Ryley's *Mice and Men*, he appeared as Mark Ambury, an eighteenth-century pedagogue who adopts a child in order to turn her into a model wife, but leaves love out of his scientific curriculum. In George Fleming's *The Light That Failed*, adapted from Kipling's novel, he took the role of Dick Helder, a disillusioned war correspondent and painter who loses his sight and his sweetheart (who is restored at the last curtain). And in Jerome K. Jerome's *The Passing of the Third Floor Back* – first staged at the St James's in 1908 – he scored the triumph of his career as a mysterious Christ-like stranger who visits a Bloomsbury lodging-house and remoulds the lives of the tenants. It was in this shoddy piece – ' vilely stupid . . . twaddle and vulgarity ', Max Beerbohm called it – that Forbes-Robertson established his popular ascendancy in the Edwardian theatre, and it dominated the last phase of his acting life. Five years later, he made his farewell to the London stage at Drury Lane, in a three-month season which included *Hamlet*, *Caesar and Cleopatra*, *The Merchant of Venice*, *Othello*, *The Light that Failed*, *Mice and Men* and *The Passing of the Third Floor Back*, and was knighted in the last week. His final appearance was as Hamlet, on 3 June 1913. Then he set out on a prolonged farewell tour of the USA.

It was not until April 1916 that Forbes-Robertson bade his last official good-bye to the stage. He appeared as Hamlet at Harvard, where the Sheldon Lecture Theatre had been turned for the occasion into a reconstructed version of Shakespeare's own playhouse. After the play was over, after all the presentations and speeches had been made, the old actor went down to his dressing-room with a light heart. He took off his Hamlet costume for the last time ' with no sort of regret, but rather with a great sense of relief '. For, looking back on his life, Sir Johnston Forbes-

Robertson decided that he was never really fitted to be an actor. ' Never at any time have I gone on the stage without longing for the moment when the curtain would come down on the last act. Rarely, very rarely have I enjoyed myself in acting. This cannot be the proper mental attitude for an actor, and I am persuaded . . . that I was not temperamentally suited to my calling.' It seems, in one sense, an appropriate abdication by the Hamlet of his generation. Except for one or two brief wartime appearances, Forbes-Robertson remained in retirement for over twenty years, publishing his autobiography in 1923. He died peacefully on 3 November 1937, at the age of eighty-four.

Was Forbes-Robertson really a great actor? There is evidence against the claim. He lacked the quicksilver versatility of Garrick, the lightning-flash intensity of Kean, the mesmeric power of Irving. Compared with Kemble and Macready, he lacked stamina, self-confidence and leadership. He entered his calling without enthusiasm, maintained it without ambition, and left it without regret – if we are to believe his own testimony. Unlike even Charles Kean and Samuel Phelps, he left small impression upon the theatre of his time. His range, moreover, was small – smaller than Kemble's or Kean's. Although he occasionally appeared in ' character ' comedy and achieved some success as a stage cad or even a villain, Forbes-Robertson's fame was built upon his prowess as a romantic hero and established by his authority as a Christian gentleman. A paragon of virtue and a prince of chivalry, he seemed – in his best roles – to radiate a special and authentic kind of suffering goodness inseparable from his personal beauty. Sometimes he was an Arthurian knight (Archer called his Lancelot a ' stained glass hero '), or a Balkan martyr (as Constantin Brancomir of *For the Crown* he seemed a ' young Charlemagne' who turned into 'a mixture of Ignatius Loyola and Savonarola '). More frequently, in his later years, he was in holy orders – as a Pastor Heffterdingk in *Magda* (resisting temptation), as Michael Feversham in *Michael and His Lost Angel* (yielding to temptation), as Sotheby in *Mrs Grundy* and Jacques Bernez in *The Sacrament of Judas*. And, with the consummation of *The Third Floor Back*, he appeared to be a visitor from the other world – if not Christ Himself. In the words of his obituary in *The Times,* the role of The Stranger ' brought out the sweetness and goodness that formed the basis of Forbes-Robertson's character ', the character which seemed to infuse his Hamlet with such personal grace, charity, and the quality so often described as ' spirituality '. When Forbes-Robertson is remembered today, it is most frequently perhaps as a tall, lean, and kindly man whose noble features were lit up by an other-worldly smile. Such was the pervasive sweetness of his personality, and the weakness of his craft, that it sometimes haloed other characters – quite incongruously – with the same nobility. Othello was refined into Christian virtue: ' I have seen no actor,' said one observer, Gordon Crosse, ' who could make the true nobility of Othello's soul shine out so convincingly.' As Macbeth, said J. T. Grein, he suggested ' a philosopher, a leader of men, a creature of mythical powers '. After taking the crown this Macbeth was distinguished by ' mournful, ironical self-pity '; with Banquo's assassins he was ' as slyly humorous and as unctuously courteous as Hamlet in his attitude towards Polonius '; he was ' demure ' in battle; and, until he revised his make-up, he reminded people forcibly – said Grein – of a well-known picture of Jesus. For many people the gentility of his voice clashed with the barbarism of his appearance: it carried the ' preachiness ' of a Victorian gentleman making the best of an awkward situation.

Yet both the Othello and the Macbeth were highly praised by such critics as Max Beerbohm for being so uncommonly ' human ' and ' natural ', the very epithets which marked off his Hamlet from all the others. To explain that impression in such great roles it is not enough to give the credit to Forbes-Robertson's ' personality ', to say that he was being ' natural ' to himself: he was being true to Shakespeare – and in a way that was unprecedented on the stage since Betterton. Not only did he pay a greater respect to the Shakespearian text than any of his predecessors in this book; not only did he shake off a few more of the encumbering traditions of stagy speech and behaviour; but he brought to the speaking of the verse and prose a keen intelligence, an artist's sensibility, and a splendid voice. Although his powers of characterization were limited, and his range of facial and physical expression was small, he knew – at his best – how to let the words do their work, how to speak a role ' not a line here or there in splendid isolation, not one soliloquy or five ' bursts ', but the entirety, both verse and prose. His lack of egotism, elsewhere

a disadvantage, was here a rare asset; he put Shakespeare before
Forbes-Robertson. Even if Forbes-Robertson's personality refused
obstinately to turn into a jealous Moor, a murdering Scot or a
vengeful Jew, his voice allowed you to hear the text in action.
'Forbie couldn't make faces,' as one old actor put it, 'but he
could make wonderful music.' His voice reminded some people of
Phelps (whom, when speaking at the reopening of Sadler's Wells
in January 1931, he described as 'my master'). Yet although he
was indebted to Phelps for his mastery of control, phrasing and
modulation, he did not imitate the pomps and pauses of the
Macready school. Forbes-Robertson's voice has been variously
compared with an organ and a cello. Shaw described it 'a
clarionet in A, played only in the chalumeau register'; but he
added that 'the chalumeau, sympathetically sounded, has a richly
melancholy and noble effect', and declared on another occasion
that Forbes-Robertson was 'the only actor I know who can find
out the feeling of a speech from its cadence. His art meets the
dramatist's art directly . . .'

For in Forbes-Robertson's 'naturalness' and 'humanity'
there was none of the everyday casualness and throw-away inco-
herence that is today sometimes confounded with truth in acting.
It was carefully practised, slowly perfected, premeditated. In his
movement, as in his speech, he was a classic actor.

That you will see Forbes-Robertson walk down and, especially,
across the stage is a sufficient reason for going to a theatre. [wrote
C. E. Montague] His use of the arms in rhetoric has the severe beauty
that some of the great orators must have had . . . The beauty of each
gesture and tone is almost abstract in its purity; the raised arm, did it
mean nothing, is still a lovely line; the cadences have the independent,
absolute values of music; they would please though you did not know
English. His is the acting that mainly relies for its charm on measure,
a comely order, 'discretion', 'smoothness', 'temperance', the
'modesty' of nature, all the set of qualities that Hamlet praised to
the players . . . He never tries, as naturalistic actors do, by some
sudden turn of queer, incontestable veracity, to shake you into a
troubling and importunate consciousness of the presence of life. It is
not in his art to trouble; rather to tranquillize; it soothes you like
some Augustan architecture, with its just proportions, the ranged
masses of its declamation, its expression of dependence on sound
reason, lucidity, intellectual balance. Romantic acting, like other
romantic art, is adventure, almost gambling; it comes off and it seems

to have found new worlds, or lit on the door of magic, or it fails and flops into grotesqueness. Classical acting like Forbes-Robertson's runs lesser risks; it may not take your breath away, or elicit whatever your special bodily signal may be of your mind's amazed and sudden surrender to some stroke of passionate genius. But there is one glory of the sun and another glory of the moon.

To that one may add the tribute of Professor Odell: 'To have been the Hamlet of one's time is a great glory; and such glory belongs to Forbes-Robertson.'

That is one answer to the question: was Forbes-Robertson really a great actor? He probably did less than any of the others in this gallery, but he was unequalled in what he could do. Although he worked in a theatre where – for a variety of reasons – it became more difficult to acquire the experience and training needed to reach the summits, he achieved his own perfection, unique in his time, of self-made classicism. Whatever Forbes-Robertson might say, in his humility, about his ' temperamental ' unsuitability for the stage; however he might seek to avoid the burdens of leadership and management; however he might deplore the rareness of that 'impersonal exaltation' which he thought he should have attained much more frequently; yet he was a patient, dedicated, self-improving actor who made his way to the heights and carried with him the conscience and the ideals of an artist. 'Now that you have left the stage,' Shaw wrote to him in 1925, after the publication of his autobiography, 'there is only the printed word to show . . . that to reach the highest rank it is not necessary to be an egotist or a monster . . .'

Part Two

Panorama: 1900–30

By the turn of the nineteenth century, tragedy had gone out of fashion; the domestic had replaced the heroic style; the dominant mode of acting – quicker, subtler, quieter, more realistic – had its roots in comedy. Versatility in impersonation and disguise was no longer a priority in training – the training-grounds, indeed, had disappeared, except in a few touring companies which kept the old repertoire alive. Instead of specializing in stock lines, actors attempted to develop one of their own. Many made a career by, in effect, playing themselves, through a long succession of type-cast roles; personality acting of this kind was not, of course, unknown in previous years, but with the advent of the long-run system it became much more common. Vocal and facial emphasis were muted in the new, more intimate playhouses under electric light. There was less need to shout or to strain. Extravagance in gesture and emotional display became increasingly out of favour in the neo-naturalist drama under the eye of the new middle-class public, brought up to dislike people who make a scene. Behind the picture-frame of the proscenium British actors aspired, from run to longer run, to live on the arts of understatement.

The grand manner was still demonstrated on the stage after it had disappeared from private and public life. It was visible at the beginning of the twentieth century – especially outside London – in melodrama, romantic costume drama and the classics; but the opportunities for displaying it continued to contract rapidly. The ' drama of ideas ', identified with Ibsen and Shaw, discouraged the romantic bravura of star acting in favour of thoughtful team-work under a director's control. Although Shaw himself was an eloquent advocate of the importance of acting verse correctly,

The Player Kings

and wrote rhetorical speeches ' like operatic solos ', champions of that chimera known as the ' writer's theatre ' applauded the reduction of acting opportunities – ' Drama has cast out the foreign elements of lyricism and rhetoric and become a pure art of interpretation through imitation,' wrote William Archer jubilantly when English acting was in one of its most depressed phases. (It is noticeable that the three contemporary actors outlined in the following chapters have largely ignored Ibsen and Shaw in their repertoire of roles.)

London theatres increasingly demanded what Charles Mathews called ' the drawing-room quietness of well-bred acting ', a kind of gentlemanly behaviour before a gentlemanly audience. As early as 1870 G. H. Lewes had described the ideal of this school:

It is a rare assemblage of qualities that enables an actor to be sufficiently good looking without being insufferably conceited, to be quiet without being absurdly insignificant, to be lively without being vulgar, to look like a gentleman, to speak and move like a gentleman, and yet to be interesting as if this quietness were only the restraint of power, not the absence of individuality.

This development was influenced by the changing social composition of the profession, now that the theatre had become safe for the middle classes. The sons and daughters of doctors, dons and clergymen who entered the theatre in increasing numbers brought their manners with them. One result was, in Shaw's words, that ' the art of acting is half strangled by the fashionable tailor'. By 1892 the veteran London critic Clement Scott protested that ' not one tenth of our leading actors and actresses have ever studied to speak blank verse or to render Shakespeare intelligible '. As the old traditions faded and the actor-managers died, retired or were pushed out of business, even the attempt ' to render Shakespeare intelligible ' was given up, in the major part of the theatre. The take-over by speculators of most London theatres during the First World War helped to accelerate the disappearance of the Shakespearian repertoire. (In the provinces it was kept alive mainly by the touring company of Sir Frank Benson. The thirty-year continuity of the Benson tradition and training was a prime factor in the rebirth of English acting in the 1930s.)

There was no place for the Works in the long-run system which governed both London and the provincial stage. An actor could

168

choose in the 1920s to be 'classical' or 'modern', and the vast majority were 'modern', because there was otherwise little hope of getting work in the theatre, and even less hope in films). It is significant that although Godfrey Tearle – an actor schooled in the old tradition – displayed great acting as Othello in 1921 (according to the reliable testimony of W. A. Darlington) it was not until eleven years later that any manager so much as suggested that he should act in Shakespeare again. As Mr Darlington puts it, Tearle's 'streak of genius was denied outlet by an accident of fashion' – and he was not the only victim.

In the general diminution of histrionics during the first half of this century, many British actors felt obliged, in meeting the new demand for diluted verisimilitude, to mirror the behaviour of their middle-class audience, not only in plays actually about the middle-class audience but in the rest of the parts they had the chance of acting (which were rather restricted in range). Attempting to follow the deceptively casual artistry of du Maurier or, later, Coward – masters of the throw-away and experts in timing – run-of-the-mill actors (deprived of the groundwork ensured by the old stock-company system) often dwindled into inaudibility. There was an overshadowing fear – rooted in their social training – that to raise, or even to project, one's voice was not only old-fashioned but vulgar: it was rude to point, and only foreigners used their hands in talking. The cast no longer had to be segregated to give them room to gesticulate, and the novice's pockets were no longer sewn up to teach him what to do with his hands – now he put them in his pockets with impunity, poured another drink or lit another cigarette. Instead of holding the stage with the conscious grace and deliberation that was once expected of the older school, such actors froze in their tracks or shambled about with a proper sense of British sincerity. In emotional crises they betrayed no unseemly feeling, but bit their lips, clenched their fists or stirred their tea cups with more than usual vigour.

With the disappearance of the stock companies vanished the opportunity of learning by acting a wide range of roles. Their successors, the provincial 'repertories', were still few in number and low in achievement, mostly concerned with reproducing West End successes. Barely half a dozen could approach the audacity of Birmingham or the prosperity of Liverpool. There was no state or civic aid. Irving played over four hundred roles in three years;

Gielgud played nearly forty in his first three years: Richard
Burton played seven in the same period. Few players learned how
to live in period costume, how to use a fan, a cane or a rapier,
how to deliver a Shakespearian soliloquy or a set-piece of Restoration prose, how to mime, sing or dance in the appropriate context. There was no commercial demand for that kind of context.
Anything markedly beyond the limits of Shaftesbury Avenue
theatricalism was likely to be dismissed as ham, especially in
London, and it was on London that everything depended. The
long tradition of light-comedy playing which runs from Charles
Mathews to Rex Harrison was amended and perfected by a series
of masterly soloists, working within the convention of understatement; while the even longer tradition of tragic, melodramatic and,
in general, 'serious' acting was neglected and ignored. This may
be explained not only by aesthetic, commercial and social reasons:
twentieth-century politics and psychology had a puncturing effect
upon the rhetorical, outsize and heroic view of life associated with
the classic tradition.

Yet the tradition persisted, stubbornly and seminally, in the
printed and oral evidence of the past, both recent and remote.
The three actors discussed in the following chapters have apparently studied closely the records of their six predecessors in the
book. Like many others, they have not only been influenced by
stories of Kean, Macready, Irving, Tree and Benson; but by the
propaganda of William Poel, Gordon Craig, and Harley Granville-
Barker, advocating, among other things, scenic simplicity, textual
fidelity and a return to Elizabethan staging; by the challenge of
Chekhov; by the example of the Compagnie des Quinze, the
French group of players who demonstrated to the 1930s what
ensemble acting means; by the ideals of the National Theatre.
But they have been governed, above all, by Shakespeare. It is
through the texts that the tradition of great acting has been maintained, renewed, and transformed. And this process went on,
more significantly than anywhere else, in one particular London
theatre . . .

In the eighteenth and nineteenth centuries, as we have seen,
Covent Garden and Drury Lane were the main homes of great
acting. Towards the end of the Victorian era the Lyceum, briefly,
succeeded them. But in the history of twentieth-century acting

to date another London theatre takes pride of place: a shabby old playhouse outside the industry and the West End, not far from the Elizabethan theatre quarter, in a working-class area south of the Thames. It was known successively as the Royal Coburg, the Royal Victoria, the Royal Victoria Coffee Music Hall and (conclusively) the Old Vic. When it was built in 1818, a year after Waterloo Bridge was opened, its surroundings were still semi-rural; but as London oozed southwards across the fields, slums grew thick around the theatre. The demands of audience participation changed it from a semi-legitimate house (Kean played there) to a music hall where brawling, boozing and prostitution thrived. Out of this 'hotbed of crime' in the Waterloo Road, denounced in Victorian times as 'the focus of every form of vice', grew a university college, two theatre schools, one of Britain's leading provincial repertories, a national ballet, a national opera, a national theatre – and most of the century's top stage actors.

A decisive chapter in the Old Vic's extraordinary story opened in 1880 when it was taken over by a committee of do-gooders headed by a social reformer, Emma Cons, whose prime concern was the betterment of the lower orders in underprivileged districts of London. Having begun by attempting to improve their housing in Lambeth she aspired, in due course, to clean up their amusements, which seemed at the Old Vic to be closely dependent upon gin, followed by assault and battery. The first step towards the 'purified entertainment' of her heart's desire was to stop the sale of intoxicating drink: the second was to smuggle into the variety bill one night a week for popular concerts and then, after a time, another night for lectures on science and other improving subjects. These lectures led not only to financial crises but to classes in the dressing-rooms and paint-room, and, in time, to the foundation of Morley College. The operatic extracts – introduced in 1889 – resulted years later in the establishment of the Royal Opera and the Royal Ballet.

It was not until 1914, after a brief experiment with films (whose moral standards failed to satisfy the management), that the Old Vic also became a home for Shakespeare under the sponsorship of Emma Cons's successor and niece, Lilian Baylis, who had been the theatre's acting manager since 1898. Miss Baylis, who came to believe that the theatre is 'our greatest power for good or evil' and 'a crying need for working men and women', cared nothing for the traditional glamour of the stage or for the demands of West End audiences; but she ran the Old Vic with a missionary zeal, a shrewd fervour and an inspiring if eccentric leadership that helped to make it one of the most important theatres in the world. It was helped, too, by the timing of its experiment with Shakespeare: the advent of the First World War, which proved so disastrous for the London theatre as a whole, was the making of the Old Vic. Actors who might otherwise have shunned the Waterloo Road were tempted, in the wartime confusion of the West End, by the relative security and continuity of the Baylis regime, the Shakespearian repertory and the popular audience. The Old Vic was rapidly established as a theatre with a distinctive, continuous purpose, atmosphere and public, using young actors and new directors in a great dramatic literature that was neglected on the other side of the Thames.

The Vic could not hold actors, as a rule, for more than two seasons: it was run cheese-paringly on the cheap, and paid far below the West End level. Rigid economy in administration combined with the aesthetic ideals of Miss Baylis's directors – notably Robert Atkins and Harcourt Williams (themselves influenced by Poel, Craig and Granville-Barker) – to set a new standard in *mise en scène*. Plays were presented with stock costumes, humdrum lighting and much-repainted flats; but the extravagant scenic splendours of a Tree or an Irving seemed, in time, not only to be financially impossible but aesthetically unnecessary. At their best the sets had an imaginative simplicity which allowed the actors to demonstrate that the play was the thing; and the text was treated with a completeness, a concern for verse-speaking and a stern rejection of the bad traditions of the past (including the exaltation of scenery and star personality) that influenced a new era of acting, when Shakespeare was once again tolerated by the unholy trade.

Sir John Gielgud

When Miss Lilian Baylis, ' C.H., M.A. Oxon (Hon.), Lessee and Manager ' – as she was styled on the three-penny programme – opened the Old Vic in September 1929 for her sixteenth season of Shakespeare and thirty-second season of opera in English, everything seemed to be much the same as usual at the shabby old playhouse in the Waterloo Road. There was, not for the first time, a threat of demolition. There was, as usual, a financial crisis. The bills outside were, as usual, austerely anonymous: no star names were listed – that was against ' the Lady's ' principles. Not many critics attended the opening play, *Romeo and Juliet* – this was not yet a fashionable theatre – and few of those who did were enthusiastic. That, too, was not unusual. Yet this was, in fact, an historic season; for the Vic's new Romeo, John Gielgud, went on to play a dozen leading Shakespearian roles on this stage, to be acclaimed as Britain's leading actor, and to help in changing the course of theatrical history.

This was not the first time that John Gielgud had acted here. While still a drama student, nine years earlier, he had walked on in *Henry V*, and was given his first speaking line on any professional stage, ' Here is the number of the slaughter'd French.' Far from making a good impression, he inspired several members of the company with a keen desire to warn him against becoming an actor: they resisted the temptation, but Gielgud was given no more lines, although he was allowed to walk on in *King Lear, Wat Tyler* and *Peer Gynt*. Now twenty-five, he had nearly sixty parts under his belt – many of them at special single performances for play-producing societies and clubs; he had worked on tour, in rep and in two long runs; since the beginning of his career his voice, intelligence and stage presence had attracted the attention of discerning critics; yet he felt strongly that he was not stretching his talent or using himself to the full, theatrically, and he welcomed the invitation to the Vic of Harcourt Williams, who had just taken over as its resident director, although the roles he was to play would not be settled until later in the season. (Like the opportunity to walk on, unpaid, this open-ended casting is unthinkable in the London theatre today.)

Gielgud now plunged into a succession of big parts, with little time for detailed preparation, rehearsal or development. Each play was staged four times a week, between performances of the opera, for some fourteen performances only. After the disappointments of *Romeo* (in which the new company was unused to working with each other and to the methods of the director: Williams, an Old Bensonian and a disciple of Granville-Barker, was attempting to establish a quicker pace of delivery which was then still unfamiliar to the actors as well as to the audience but which rapidly became accepted at the Vic), Gielgud appeared as Antonio in *The Merchant of Venice* and Cléante in an English version of *Le Malade Imaginaire*. But it was not until *Richard II*, two months after the season opened, that he found his feet – and made his mark. Although Macready had attempted, unsuccessfully, to establish the role in the repertory, it was generally out of favour among actors until Sir Frank Benson inaugurated a long line of twentieth-century Richards. Gielgud made the part his own. What he describes as 'the strange mixture of weakness and beauty' in Richard made an intimate appeal to him; and it is as this character – one in which (as newly conceived by a contemporary author) he was later to make a decisive West End hit, and to which (in Shakespeare's text) he was to return in 1937 – that many people of that generation identify him; they see him as (to quote Harcourt Williams) 'a tall, willowy figure in black velvet, surmounted by a fair head, the pale agonized face set beneath a glittering crown'. Looking back in 1961 Gielgud said (with characteristic candour) that this was the part into which he had put most of himself at the Old Vic – 'he was a shallow, spoiled young man, vain of his looks, with lovely things to say. I fancied myself no end in the part, but even that seemed to help my acting of it.' But although he might have been a little too pleased by the sound of his own voice, he demonstrated more fully than ever before, to himself as well as to the audience, the range and impact of this remarkable instrument, which he was to develop and perfect in the coming years.

Next came Oberon: ' It gave me a wonderful sense of power to feel that I was beginning to control the lovely language which at rehearsals moved me so much that tears would spring to my eyes.' As Mark Antony, Orlando and the Emperor in *Androcles and the Lion* Gielgud made no especial impact; but in mid-March he boldly tackled Macbeth, without much time to think about the audacity of the attempt. ' I simply imagined it, and acted it for the main development and broad lines of the character, without worrying about the technical, intellectual and psychological diffi-culties.' Perhaps it was just as well. Visually, he based his Mac-beth on Irving's, as drawn by Bernard Partridge and described by Ellen Terry. Although in appearing unconvincing as ' Bellona's bridegroom ' he failed to solve one of the perennial problems of acting the role, Gielgud won high praise – notably from James Agate. The influential critic of the *Sunday Times* described how Gielgud gave him that treasurable feeling – ' the fresh shock at something one knows so well that one takes it for granted ' – when he reappeared after the murder, carrying the daggers; and he also said that for the first time in his experience Macbeth retained his hold on the play till the end, partly because when he said he had supped full with horrors in the interval, he made you believe him. Vocally, Agate observed, Gielgud was ' superb ', and the production was in many respects the best he had seen.

Almost as soon as *Macbeth* opened, Gielgud began rehearsing *Hamlet,* which was launched at the end of April in an uncut ver-sion, played in Elizabethan costume, that ran from 6.30 to 11. This performance crowned the success of his first Old Vic season, and was soon to establish him at the top of his profession. Its magnificence, said Ivor Brown, had put him ' in the front rank '; J. T. Grein, praising it as a ' great ' performance, hailed ' a new histrionic force in our midst '; Agate called it ' the high water mark of English Shakespearian acting of our time '. An American manager was so impressed that at the end of the season the pro-duction – cut to standard length – was transferred to the Queen's in Shaftesbury Avenue. Its run there was short – strangely enough two other Hamlets were on view (Henry Ainley and Alexander Moissi, in German) – but its presentation was an augury of change.

Gielgud found his second Old Vic season less successful and more exhausting, largely because the company had to shuttle backwards and forwards between the Vic and the newly opened Sadler's Wells, where the acoustics proved to be peculiarly intractable, and because they were obliged to act eight times a week instead of four. But in addition to reviving his Richard II, he embarked on another wide range of parts, including three to which he has frequently returned. He played Hotspur, not too sympathetically; Prospero, weary and aristocratic, looking like a turbaned Eastern magician; Shaw's Sergius Saranoff; Lord Trinket, a fop in Colman's *The Jealous Wife* (played with ' an exquisite levity '); Antony, as a grizzled Elizabethan with a Drake beard and padded doublet – ' very miscast,' says Gielgud; a stiff Malvolio – ' as he was meant to be, a tragic figure,' said *Punch;* Benedick (extolled by W. A. Darlington as ' the personification of virility and spontaneous gaiety '); and, to round off the season, Lear. Although he seemed, patently, too young for the octogenarian king, and had neither the voice nor the physique for the storm scenes, he won golden words for valour – and rather more, in his scenes with the Fool and at the end. Ivor Brown said that he ' sweeps to a fullness of voice and a declamatory power which he has hardly touched before'. Agate, in cooler vein, wrote: ' In the manifest intelligence displayed throughout, and in the speaking of the verse, it is fine: time only can do the rest.'

Asked by a journalist at the end of his first Old Vic season what was the most important lesson he had learned, Gielgud had answered, ' The value of teamwork.' Supplemented by later experience and other influences, it was a lesson which he never forgot, and which he has taught many actors in the past forty years by his inspiring example.

Arthur John Gielgud (knighted 1953) is of medium height, halfway between Laurence Olivier and Michael Redgrave, although like all fine actors he seems to add inches at will on the stage if he needs them. As a young man he had light brown hair: by his mid-thirties his spreading tonsure called for a frequent use of wigs, but he has not otherwise – unlike Olivier – shown a great attachment to disguise. Gielgud has a spare, clear-cut, finely modelled face – ' His profile cuts through space,' said Rosamond Gilder in 1936, and its edge has been rarely honed since then –

with deep furrows between his eyebrows, a dome-like forehead, a big beaky nose, thin lips, a chin held aloofly up, and hooded blue eyes, often screwed up in intensities of different kinds, holding what Kenneth Tynan has identified as ' the secure, lamp-lit blaze . . . which is the mark of the high priest '. His patrician air of nervy hauteur and cold authority can relent at times into a smile which has been variously described as Gioconda, Royal Family and 'a benevolent wince'. He moves with a kind of eccentric grace: his shoulders are expressive, but his back is uncommonly straight, and his body is generally uneloquent.

He was born in London on 14 April 1904, into a conventional middle-class Kensington household, with unconventional stage connections. The family tree of his father, a stockbroker of Lithuanian descent, included soldiers, lawyers and a leading actress. As the daughter of Kate Terry, eldest of the famous Victorian acting clan, his mother was niece of Ellen, Marion and Fred; and the glamorous aura of his grandmother, great-uncle, great-aunts and his second cousin Gordon Craig gave an especial dynastic stimulus, first to the toy theatre game which the Gielgud children played for years and afterwards to his own ambitions. He has said, indeed, that the consciousness of belonging to the Terry family – and of having inherited ' a certain facility ' – stood him in very bad stead ' for many years '. Gielgud embarked on the traditional Edwardian education of prep school and public school, with university in view, but he soon resolved to take another course. At first he thought of trying to become a designer like Craig, but while still at Westminster he decided that he wanted to be an actor; and his parents agreed that, instead of going to Oxford, he should be allowed to train for the stage on the understanding that if he did not achieve success by the time he was twenty-five, he would give it up for architecture.

First of all, Gielgud won a scholarship at seventeen to a theatre school in Kensington run by Lady Benson, wife of the actor-manager Sir Frank. He was one of four boys among the thirty students. The first lesson in his three terms was given, accidentally, a few days after his arrival when Lady Benson suddenly burst out laughing in the middle of a rehearsal, pointed at him, and exclaimed, ' Good heavens, you walk exactly like a cat with rickets!' He realized, for the first time, that he was ' handicapped by a strange way of standing and a still stranger way of walking ': he moved from the knees instead of from the hips, and bent his legs when standing, instead of keeping them straight. This discovery depressed Gielgud extremely, and made him acutely self-conscious, though he apparently did not attempt to do anything about it. As a boy he had always dodged organized games and physical exercise: even as a student, he avoided fencing classes. After leaving Lady Benson's he got his first job – ' entirely through influence ', as he says in his entertaining auto-biography, *Early Stages*: his second cousin Phyllis Neilson Terry suddenly offered him work with her in a provincial tour of a melodrama, *The Wheel*. For £4 a week he understudied, spoke a few lines and served as assistant stage manager, learning the nightly routine of prompting and dogsbodying and the weekly chores of seeing the production in and out of provincial theatres.

When the tour ended after three months Gielgud decided that, instead of looking for another job, he would continue his training at the Royal Academy of Dramatic Art and he won a scholarship there in 1923. During his year at the Academy, Nigel Playfair – impressed by his performance in Barrie's *Admirable Crichton* – engaged him for two short-lived productions at a theatre opposite St Pancras Station, the Regent, where Gielgud first caught the attention of the critics – but not altogether favourably. At nine-teen his formal training was over: brief though it was, it was more than any of his predecessors in this book had ever received, for, in the days before drama schools were established, they learned by practical experience. But, as he would be the first to admit, he still had a great deal to learn himself. ' The imaginative part of my playing came too easily,' Gielgud wrote later, ' and the technical side was non-existent.'

His education continued at Oxford – not at the university, but at the Playhouse, a gimcrack, draughty hall run precariously as a weekly repertory theatre by J. B. Fagan (author of *The Wheel*) who had spotted Gielgud at the Regent. This actor-author-director was another ardent disciple of Granville-Barker – who was to become a prime inspiration of Gielgud's work – with one foot firmly planted in the commercial theatre, and the other in high-flying plans (soon to be grounded) for the regeneration of the drama in university towns. For two eight-week seasons Gielgud appeared here in a wide range of plays – Maeterlinck, Sierra, Ibsen, Benavente, Goldsmith, Shaw and Pirandello. His second role was Valentine in *Love for Love,* with which he was to score one of his greatest successes twenty years later; and Fagan introduced him to Chekhov, who was to become, after Shakespeare, perhaps the most important dramatist in influencing his career. Wearing a black beard and steel spectacles (modelling his make-up on his brother Val) he played Trofimov in *The Cherry Orchard* ('we were all absolutely bewildered by the play'), and learned the liberating effects of a character make-up and the first possibilities of relaxation in acting a role. Between Oxford seasons Gielgud was given his first big Shakespearian chance in London: he played Romeo for Barry Jackson at the Regent, to Gwen Ffrangcon-Davies's Juliet, but he was received without enthusiasm by most of the critics, who complained of 'niminy-piminy' effeminacy, mediocrity, fatigue and physical clumsiness. 'Mr Gielgud from the waist downwards means absolutely nothing,' said Ivor Brown with uncommon asperity. 'He has the most meaningless legs imaginable.' Yet even in this failure – 'I enjoyed indulging in my own emotions, and imagined that was acting' – Gielgud already had a few admirers. The *Daily Telegraph* singled him out as 'an exceptionally well-graced actor; he has a beautiful voice, which he knows how to use; a clear enunciation – rare merit in these days on our stage; and he moves well.' He had, from the start, something of the Terry charm, panache, presence and a voice which, for many people, compensated for his physical and vocal mannerisms and basic inexperience.

So, before he was twenty-one, Gielgud's provincial apprenticeship was over, and in England from now on he worked mostly in London – though he was often to tour for a few weeks before a West End opening, sometimes for many weeks at the end of a successful London run, and, during the war, visiting provincial cities and giving special performances to the troops. Compared with the long purgatory on the provincial treadmill of Kean or Irving it was a notably short initiation. It was all the more fortunate that although, during the next five years, he won many critical plaudits, he was prevented by a series of accidents from achieving the kind of spectacular personal success in a long run or a film which might well (as we have seen in so many cases during the last thirty years) have paralysed his development as an artist. He needed the time to grow, learning as he went along.

Gielgud picked up a good deal of miscellaneous experience

from short runs and special matinees, then common in the London theatre – appearing as Trotsky, Rosencrantz (in modern dress), Oswald in *Ghosts,* the Good Angel in *Dr Faustus,* Armand Duval in *The Lady of the Camelias,* and many more. He played in three West End flops – a farce, a thriller and a poetic melo-drama. He made his New York début, as the Tsarevich in another flop, *The Patriot.* He understudied Noël Coward, absorbed some of his mannerisms and took over from him in *The Vortex* and *The Constant Nymph,* in which he had his first long run: it gave him the opportunity to try out timing, study details of tone and inflection, control his own boredom, develop the capacity for give and take, learn how to produce effects without their original spontaneous impulse. He acted in Chekhov – 'perfection itself', Agate said of his Trofimov in 1925. In the same year Naomi Royde-Smith acclaimed him as 'unequalled as an English inter-preter of Russian drama', although it was not until after these notices that he worked with the Russian director, Komisarjevsky, who, he says taught him how to work from inside rather than outside.

By 1929, having escaped the perils of success as a leading juvenile, Gielgud felt that he was in danger of being pigeon-holed by managers for intense, neurotic roles. Harcourt Williams's invi-tation to the Old Vic seemed to come, by another of those happy accidents, at the right moment: the two seasons there were the cornerstone of his education, the turning-point in his career. But did they arrive too early? It might be said that the pattern of Gielgud's future had prematurely set by the time he left the Old Vic, already hailed at twenty-six as 'the great Shakespearian actor of our time'. He had played many of the big roles once: in the next forty years he was to develop and perfect some of them, and to explore other minor summits of the classic repertoire. But, in a sense, perhaps success came too quickly. 'The theatre has given me all I ever asked for, but too soon,' he said in 1961. 'At the beginning of the war I made a list of all the things I had wanted to do, and I found I had done them all.'

It seemed at first, after leaving the Old Vic in 1931, that Gielgud – secure in his new-flown stardom – would have no diffi-culty in finding new plays to direct and to act in. From the Waterloo Road he went straight into *The Good Companions,* a stage version of J. B. Priestley's best-selling picaresque novel, in the undemanding near-juvenile part of a stage-struck schoolmaster, Inigo Jollifant (he later played it in the film). The run turned out to be a long and prosperous one, and while it continued Gielgud received through the post at his dressing-room in His Majesty's two new manuscripts which were to prove his first successes outside the classic repertoire. Both were directly linked with his successes inside it.

In what had become a standard contractual deal for London actors, Gielgud signed a three-play agreement with Bronson Albery, a member of the theatrical dynasty which owned the New, Criterion and Wyndhams and, for many years, a producing manager associated with many of the West End's most distinguished ventures. The first of his plays for Albery was one of these postal surprises, *Musical Chairs,* the first work of an unknown author, Ronald Mackenzie. Set near his father's homeland, it gave him a long run in perhaps his best modern-dress role, one to which Gielgud has often looked nostalgically back: the 'successor to a long line of plain-clothes Hamlets', as Ivor Brown called it. As Joseph Schindler, he played a consumptive, self-torturing, neurotically intense, Anglo-Polish ex-airman, hiding with sardonic wit and occasional bursts of Beethoven a set of wounds too deep for tears – the main one being that he had bombed a German city and that his fiancée had died in the raid. A month after *Musical Chairs* came off he opened in his own production of the other play he had received during *The Good Companions,* much revised on Gielgud's advice: *Richard of Bordeaux,* by Gordon Daviot (Elizabeth Mackintosh). In this romantic historical pastiche of the character with which he had made his first mark at the Vic, Gielgud scored his biggest success yet, commercially and critically, reaching a far bigger public in its thirteen-month run than the handful who had seen his thirty performances in the Waterloo Road. Seizing the chance to infuse comedy into the Shakespearian character, and transcending a prose that seems somewhat threadbare on the printed page, he showed a deeper pathos and a richer authority than hitherto. He was, said *The Times,* 'acquiring the marks of a great actor'. To Desmond MacCarthy, he was already the First Player. Although it was far from being an age of great acting, said MacCarthy, ' the range of his emotional scope, and the intelligence with which he conceives his parts, put him right at the top of his profession.

Now his temptations will begin. He has the power to charm large audiences. Will he choose only plays which delight them?' To that Gielgud might well have answered, 'Why not?' But in fact, choosing the right kind of new plays became a major problem of his career, as of all the leading classic actors of the past forty years. For an earlier generation there was no dilemma: they would have revived and toured *Richard of Bordeaux* for many years, as Macready revived *Virginius* or as Gielgud's own great-uncle Fred Terry toured *Sweet Nell of Old Drury* and *The Scarlet Pimpernel*. But that era had gone forever: new successes had to be found to interest the London public, once the first long run had finished, and the old-style annual provincial tours of old favourites seemed unthinkable to the post-1918 London stars, even if they had been practical economically. Although Gielgud has seen more of the provinces than probably any other leading actor of the last three decades (Donald Wolfit excepted), the theatre outside London has played very little part in his career, compared with his great predecessors.

After touring in *Richard of Bordeaux* Gielgud next appeared in London in another modern role – as an agonized, self-sacrificing schoolmaster in Ronald Mackenzie's posthumous *The Maitlands* (the author died in a car crash during the run of *Musical Chairs*); but the part gave him scant opportunity and the play was not a success. Ten days after it closed, Gielgud opened at the New under Albery's management in his own production of *Hamlet*, broke all box-office records since Irving (with 155 performances), and sealed his supremacy in the role. Thereafter he acted predominantly in the classics. During the next thirty-five years, indeed, he appeared in London in barely a dozen new plays, and five of these were costume parts. He was, said Agate of *The Maitlands*, 'much too fine and romantic an actor to be happy away from rhetoric and robes'. Rightly or wrongly, he has worn modern dress relatively little ever since. It is odd to reflect that Garrick wore modern dress virtually all the time.

After *Hamlet* came *Noah* by André Obey in 1935 (see page 188). Then Gielgud produced *Romeo and Juliet,* in which he played Romeo and Mercutio turn about with Laurence Olivier. He took *Hamlet* to the States, where he again set up box-office records. Returning to London he directed and co-managed a new costume play, Emlyn Williams's *Spring 1600,* which rapidly expired. Then Gielgud made a historic venture into management, of a kind which no actor has since achieved inside the commercial system. He presented at the Queen's in 1937–8 a 'permanent' company in a nine-month 'repertory' season of four plays – *Richard II, The School for Scandal, The Three Sisters* and *The Merchant of Venice* – each of which was to be given the unprecedented luxury of eight weeks' rehearsal and a fixed run of eight to ten weeks. Gielgud was deeply influenced by the example of the Compagnie des Quinze, the celebrated French troupe inspired by Jacques Copeau and led by his nephew Michel St Denis, which on its visits to England had offered actors as well as audiences a new kind of theatrical experience in the unity of its acting, the simplicity of its design, the totality of its effect and the rightness of its style. With the help of St Denis, who had directed *Noah* and now took *The Three Sisters,* John Gielgud aimed at the creation of an acting ensemble outside the long-run system, and he achieved some remarkable and influential results. His company, which gave some of the key talents of later decades a taste of what seemed a golden oasis in the West End desert, included Peggy Ashcroft, Angela Baddeley, Harcourt Williams, Alec Guinness, Glen Byam Shaw, George Devine, Anthony Quayle, Leon Quartermaine and Michael Redgrave. The Queen's experiment worked not only theatrically but financially, without a penny of public money. Gielgud and a friend, John Perry, put up the capital themselves and actually made a small profit – an unthinkable miracle in the commercial conditions of today's West End. Yet when the nine months were over the company was dispersed, never to be reassembled, leaving the vision of an English Compagnie des Quinze to haunt a generation of playgoers and performers. Gielgud then took an undemanding role in Dodie Smith's family play, *Dear Octopus* – which turned out to be the smash-hit of the last West End season before war broke out – under the banner of the H. M. Tennent management, with which he has been associated ever since. He has never ventured personally into management again.

In the nineteenth century an actor who had risen so quickly to the front rank would expect to run his own theatre; but Shaftesbury Avenue economics after 1939 made such a consummation virtually impossible, and Gielgud had no enthusiasm for the administrative burdens of bricks-and-mortar business.

Although he had hoped, before the outbreak of war, to launch another season on the model of his Queen's experiment (he was, he told an interviewer in 1939, ' torn between being impresario-producer and actor-manager ') his later seasons at the Haymarket in 1944–6 and the Lyric, Hammersmith in 1953 were presented not by him but by the Tennent organization. Since 1939 Gielgud has, in fact, been content to work for a producing management, without aspiring to the autonomous power of the old actor-managers and their long London leases. He has enjoyed many of their advantages, without risking their managerial responsibilities, by working for the same management, especially as it was for years the most powerful and prosperous management in Britain, having dominated the ' straight ' theatre for a quarter-century. Under the leadership of a close friend, Hugh Beaumont – whose right-hand man, John Perry, was for many years Gielgud's personal manager – Tennent's have given Gielgud not only financial and administrative but technical support, with a permanent team of lighting, wardrobe, design and stage management staff. These rare benefits of continuity (so far as it is feasible inside the long-run system) have been reinforced for Gielgud by his belief in Beaumont's flair for both the art and business of the theatre – a flair which, together with his firm's greater generosity (or, said its rivals, extravagance) attracted the virtually undivided allegiance of many other leading British players for a West End generation.

Gielgud returned to the Old Vic for two months in 1940, playing Prospero and Lear: but otherwise after 1930 he stayed exclusively in the ' commercial ' theatre until 1950, when his career took a new turning at Stratford. In playing Angelo in *Measure for Measure,* Cassius, Benedick and Lear he showed a deeper authority and a wider range, and this was confirmed in the following year in London in his Leontes. The experience of acting in repertoire – instead of attempting the same role night after night – appeared to be a liberating one; and although Gielgud has not again tackled so full a programme as in 1950, he returned to Stratford in 1952 (Benedick); 1955 (Benedick and Lear); and 1957 (Prospero). His later visits to the non-commercial theatre were less rewarding. In 1958 he went back to the Old Vic after eighteen years, as Wolsey in *Henry VIII;* in 1961 he played Othello at Stratford, in a disastrous production by Franco

Zeffirelli; and in 1968 he joined the National Theatre Company
for what materialized as a disappointing season for him, playing
Orgon in *Tartuffe* and Oedipus in Peter Brook's dazzlingly
inventive version of Seneca. (Wearing the rehearsal uniform of
the rest of the cast, in dark jersey and slacks, Sir John subordinated himself to the *ensemble* patterns of sound and movement
with a discipline and humility that have characterized his later
career). The rest of Gielgud's roles in the past forty years have
been played under commercial auspices in the West End and on
Broadway, on tour in Britain and North America.

Although he did not again attempt the immense stretch of his
first Old Vic seasons; although he never recaptured at the Haymarket or the Lyric, Hammersmith the especial glory of his own
Queen's season; yet the record of performances and productions
through four decades is one of massive achievement. Who can
say if it could have been better or worse if a Bristol Old Vic, a
Royal Shakespeare Company and a National Theatre had been
open to him in the 1930s with all the subsidies of the 1970s?
One fact does seem clear: acting the classics is no longer economically feasible under commercial sponsorship, and the Gielguds
of tomorrow must find their Beamonts – if they exist – in the
offices of the national, state-supported theatres.

It also seems unlikely that future classical actors will be able
to concentrate as single-mindedly upon the stage as Gielgud has
done: for trends since 1950 have shown that acting in the theatre
is, increasingly, a part-time occupation for professional players.
Gielgud, too, has, of course, worked in other media. He has
broadcast frequently on sound radio, especially in the Third
Programme, which gave him the opportunity of playing roles
which he had given up or never attempted on the stage: his
Hamlet was heard on the BBC years after his last performance in
the theatre. He has also made many recordings: his Shakespearian long-playing records (notably the recording of his solo
stage anthology, *The Ages of Man*) have brought his voice to a
huge international public which has never had the chance of tun-
ing into the Third or watching him on the stage. But Gielgud
has, in general, ignored television: he did not make his TV début
until 1958 (in *A Day by the Sea*, his West End hit of 1953) and,
although this was also something of a triumph, he has seldom
appeared since then on the box. He shares this reluctance to work

in the TV studios with other stars of his generation, who find the financial and artistic temptations of the medium eminently resistible. Yet he has also, throughout most of his career, ignored – or been ignored by – the film industry, and here (as in so many other respects) he is an exceptional figure. He made his first film as long ago as 1924, while still at the Oxford Playhouse, but in the next twenty-five years he appeared in fewer than half-a-dozen more. He lacked the kind of good looks which would have tempted producers to snap him up for romantic juvenile leads; his brand of character acting seemed, perhaps, too stagy for the cinema; he was ill at ease in conventional modern dress roles; he distrusted and disliked the medium; and, in any case, he established his position in the theatre so quickly that he did not feel the pressure to divide his working life between the studios and the stage. It was not until 1952, when he translated his brilliant Stratford Cassius into Mankiewicz's *Julius Caesar,* that the cinema and Gielgud became aware of the mutual advantages to be gained by their collaboration. During the next decade he became a relatively busy film actor, notably successful in *Becket* (the King of France), *The Charge of the Light Brigade* (Raglan), and, above all, as Clarence in Olivier's *Richard III*. But Gielgud remains, more consistently than other leading actors of his own or later generations, a theatre actor – of the theatre, about the theatre, for the theatre.

Although Gielgud has no vocation for management, he loves to keep in his own hands another function of the old actor-managers – directing. He prefers it, so he has sometimes said, to acting. Whereas his predecessors, such as Kemble or Irving, directed only their own plays in their own theatres, Gielgud has worked throughout his life not only on his own productions but on those of other actors – most frequently, again, under the aegis of the Tennent organization. He started this side of his career soon after leaving the Old Vic, stirred by the very different influences of Komisarjevsky, Harcourt Williams, Gordon Craig and Granville-Barker. Gielgud's first production was amateur: *Romeo and Juliet* in 1932 for the Oxford University Dramatic Society with the Society's President, George Devine, as Mercutio, but also with Peggy Ashcroft as Juliet and Edith Evans as the Nurse, while the costumes were designed by the new firm of Motley.

186

All were to become closely linked with Gielgud's later work. Since then he has directed some forty productions, in many of which he has acted himself – a calculated dualism for which he has often been criticized and which has seemed at times to be responsible for the notorious flatness of his first nights as an actor.

It is one obvious measure of the difference in attitude towards acting, *per se*, between Gielgud and his great forerunners that he should so often subordinate his own opportunities as a virtuoso to his conscience as a director; and that he should have spent so much of his career in the development of other people's performances and the advancement of their technique and understanding. Most leading players of our time have appeared under Gielgud's direction; and, unlike most actor-directors of past eras, he has tried to avoid drawing attention to his directing style, leaving none of the phosphorescent fingerprints of 'producer's theatre' (as it was once dubbed). Although, like all directors, he has met occasional disasters (such as Ralph Richardson's Stratford *Macbeth*); although, at times, he has been so indecisively quicksilver in his drive for perfection through rehearsals that (on the first night, at least) the parts have obscured the whole; yet he has demonstrably devoted himself to unity of effect and *ensemble* playing, as far as it may be achieved within the limits of the picture-frame stage and the long-run system. With a unique responsiveness to the values of the spoken word, he joins an alert sensibility to pictorial effect and a meticulous regard for detail. He is a custodian of theatrical tradition, yet is ready to experiment, to change, and – too often, perhaps – to compromise. This is not the place to discuss Gielgud's work as a director in closer detail: except to say that, as in his acting, the rare brand of professional humility and perfectionism that lies behind his mask of patrician aloofness has sometimes proved, one suspects, to be the enemy of complete success, and certainly of instant success. Part of the reason for the impact of his early roles at Oxford and the Old Vic was, perhaps, the very speed and dash with which they were executed, with so little time for planning, reflection and re-examination, following the text under somebody else's direction.

In forty-eight years Gielgud has played 125 roles in the theatre (by comparison, Irving played three times as many in two years). Of these 125, two-thirds were tackled in the first decade of his career. Some have already been touched on in this survey, and any summary of such a mass of work must risk the tedium of an inventory. Yet before looking at Gielgud's main contribution to the theatre, which is in classic roles, his parts in new drama to date – since *The Maitlands* – may usefully be listed here. First his heaviest make-up outside Shakespeare – a ruddy-faced, gap-toothed, bewhiskered Noah in André Obey's play of that name, fired by the original Compagnie des Quinze production; a half-mad, doomed French princeling (the lost Louis XVII) in *He Was Born Gay* – an equally doomed play written for Gielgud by Emlyn Williams; Nicholas Randolph, the son on a silver cord in *Dear Octopus;* Raskolnikov in Rodney Ackland's version of *Crime and Punishment* ('the best thing after Hamlet he has ever given us,' declared Agate); Julian Anson, an icily comic portrait of a prim diplomat in mourning for his life, in N. C. Hunter's crypto-Chekhovian *A Day by the Sea;* a rascally comic valet in Coward's flimsy *Nude with Violin* (Gielgud wore the character as lightly and deftly as a carnival disguise); an ageing Caesar, just before his assassination, in *The Ides of March,* with a toga over his grey suit and a laurel-wreath; a suffering Nottingham journalist – 'transfixingly imposing', in spite of his attempts to look insignificant in mufti – who explores domestic and religious mysteries in Graham Greene's *The Potting Shed*; an eccentric, be-fezzed Rumanian prince in Enid Bagnold's ill-fated theatrical curiosity, *The Last Joke;* a blimpish, buffoonish but touching headmaster (mocking the part and the past but weeping for it, too) in Alan Bennett's *Forty Years On*; a Bertrand Russell-like sage, toppled off his pedestal, in Peter Shaffer's *The Battle of Shrivings*. Most have enjoyed some box-office success. Of them all perhaps the most theatrically rewarding since *Musical Chairs* and *Richard of Bordeaux* was Thomas Mendip, the neo-medieval soldier with a death wish in Christopher Fry's *The Lady's Not for Burning,* in Gielgud's own production. Safely out of trousers and into verse, Gielgud here fed on a rare feast of language; and, like a more garrulous Benedick, caught in 'the unholy mantrap of love', he advanced reluctantly towards happiness, still aloof. Even in this spring-time play of celebration he kept a mask of melancholy; indeed, if there is one factor common to his roles outside the classic repertoire it is that in most of them he has been presented in fairly continuous misery. His expertise in suffering has been exploited far more often than his mastery of comedy. Gielgud's reputation as a great actor was not exemplified by any one of these characters, however accomplished of their kind, and whatever their box-office success – or failure, which some people take perennially as a sign of supreme artistic merit. Yet if we judged Garrick, Kean and Irving only by their work in *new* plays, what would be left of their legendary greatness?

In classic parts, ancient and modern, Gielgud's main successes have been in Chekhov; in the high comedy of Congreve and Wilde; and, of course, in Shakespeare. First, let us take Chekhov, in whom a generation of actors, led by Gielgud and influenced (partly through him) by Komisarjevsky and Michel St Denis, found a kind of spiritual home and theatrical gymnasium, crammed with excellent parts in which they exercised and grew as artists. Like other actors, Gielgud here enjoyed the freedoms of poetic naturalism – the use of tirades, the musical orchestration of form, the un-English articulateness and self-revelation, the subtle half-tones, the mixture of pathos and comedy, the concentrated truth to life in both the particular and the general, the avoidance of black-and-white simplifications and stagy formulas. For Gielgud there was, perhaps, something particularly satisfying about the lack of dominant star parts, the re-creation *as a group* of the look, sound and atmosphere of that lost, yet curiously contemporary world. Chekhov's plays are meant for *ensemble* acting, and this proved hard to achieve in a long-run theatre with no permanent company where every production starts from scratch; but they also yield inexhaustibly rich opportunities for solo effects in characterization and charm, together with the standing temptations – which English actors find peculiarly hard to resist – to sprinkle Chekhov's people with excessive romantic sentiment or distort them into isolated eccentrics.

After making his mark as an interpreter of Chekhov in the 1920s, as Trofimov and Konstantin, Gielgud initiated in the late 1930s two definitive productions. When he played Trigorin in Komisarjevsky's *The Seagull* (1936) with Edith Evans and Peggy Ashcroft, admirers complained that he did not shine out as a star ought to do; and the same complaint was made about his Vershinin in Michel St Denis's *The Three Sisters,* at the Queen's in 1938. Yet here, as elsewhere, Gielgud was concerned with the total effect of the play, rather than with the primacy of his own performance; and he helped to establish the production of *The Three Sisters* as one of the most memorable in recent theatre history (for its actors as well as its audience), not only by the casting and the conditions of rehearsal and performance, but also by the controlled truth of his own acting, as part of the dramatic pattern.

This production was one of the highlights of Gielgud's career: yet thereafter he did not return to Chekhov, as an actor, for over twenty years. He came oddly late – perhaps too late – to *Ivanov,* Chekhov's early portrait of a Russian Hamlet, and failed to achieve a signal success in his own production. In *The Cherry Orchard* (1961), however, Gielgud added to his gallery of Chekhov triumphs with a brilliantly realized cameo of the feckless, billiards-playing, backward-looking Gaev, subtly blending sympathy and self-parody, lighting up the character both from inside and outside, and integrating it as best he could with the rest of the characters, although in this production not all appeared to be sharing the same Russia (or London). He seemed to call up not only Gaev's past, but his future, too: comic, elegant, wistful, futile and conscious of his futility. ' See it again and again, search it, analyse it, and I defy anyone to fault it,' wrote John Whiting. 'It is impudent to write about acting such as this. It must be seen to be believed.'

In English classic comedy Gielgud's achievement – as actor and director – has been the incarnation of style: not as an ornamental polish applied to the surface of a play through the proper conduct of canes, swords and handkerchiefs or the elaboration of conscious graces in gait and gesture, but as the expression of its inner life through the understanding of the text. With a meticulous care for period detail in setting, costume and manners, Gielgud has – at his best – improvised precisely as much of the social context of Congreve, Sheridan and Wilde as the production needs, and no more, without superfluous antiquarianism or modern theatrical camp. Perfection in this kind of revivalism is peculiarly difficult to achieve – it is perhaps the most elusive success of all, outside a permanent company – but Gielgud's own performance has usually been keyed into the pattern with a model felicity in phrasing, timing, modulation, elegance and intelligence, rooted in his unique responsiveness to the spoken word, respect for team-work and sensitivity to theatrical tradition.

It was as a director, rather than as an actor, that Gielgud distinguished himself in *The Way of the World*, (1953) where his Mirabell seemed somewhat too self-effacing and subdued, 'sacrificing the fun to the technique', as Brooks Atkinson put it, and sacrificing something of his own part to the whole. In *Love for Love*, which he first played at Oxford, directed for a long run at the Phoenix in 1943, and to which he returned at the Hay-market in 1944-5, he transformed Valentine, an unrewarding role in print, into one of his most discreetly stylish successes. What lifted the part out of its elegant rut was the mock-mad scene, in which Gielgud parodied his own Hamlet with controlled relish and skill: 'He extended the intense raptness, the silent inner lightnings, which he shares with Irving, until they reached delicious absurdity,' wrote Kenneth Tynan (who was then seventeen). In *The School for Scandal* he scored his biggest personal success at the Queen's in 1937, presenting Joseph Surface as a cool ironist savouring his own hypocrisy in action with the zest of an actor enjoying his own performance. When he played the role briefly again thirty years later, in his own production at the Haymarket before taking it to New York, T. C. Worsley singled out his 'instinctive feeling for the kind of civilized sharpness which lies not so much in the wit as in the shape of Sheridan's lines . . . Sir John makes every sentence seem to carry twice its weight by phrasing it so perfectly. It is the very model of how this language should be spoken; and yet the control is so perfect that the artificiality can be broken at will to make a human point.'

Another successful role which may be ranked in the domain of classic comedy, in spite of its relative modernity, was Arnold Champion-Cheney in Maugham's *The Circle*, presented at the Haymarket in 1944-5. One of Gielgud's own favourite parts, this frosty, tense, self-righteous husband was played with a stiff-backed humourlessness that was impeccably, elegantly funny, without ever slipping off the tightrope of style into caricature. Undoubtedly the peak of Gielgud's high comedy, however, was John Worthing in *The Importance of Being Earnest*, which he played in 1930, 1939-40, 1942, 1946 and (in Canada and the USA) 1947, perfecting it into a minor masterpiece. With one

dissenting voice, James Agate, who pronounced him 'totally unfitted for the part' (and who always questioned his compatibility
with comedy), Gielgud was hailed from the start by the critics.
W. A. Darlington praised the way in which 'he exaggerates ever
so slightly that admirable seriousness of his, and with it makes
point after comic point', combining 'a very exact feeling for
Wilde's language with a capacity for imitation grief which he
might have learned from the Mock Turtle himself'. Charles
Morgan described Gielgud and his first Lady Bracknell, his aunt
Mabel Terry-Lewis, as 'models for the true interpretation of
Wilde', commending the 'exquisite precision' of their diction.
In 1939, when Gielgud returned to the role with a new and
definitive Lady Bracknell in Edith Evans, his performance may
still have been flawed – as Desmond MacCarthy suggested – by
a little too much genuine emotion. But by 1946, it seemed beyond
improvement in its effortless elegance, unruffled gravity, feathery
lightness, and disconnection from any taint of real feeling or
common sense: it was also immensely funny. As MacCarthy said
in 1939, 'the secret of performing in artificial comedy is to im-
personate people who are already impersonating themselves and
revelling in acting their own characters.' Gielgud has often acted
acting, but never more consummately than in Wilde's 'trivial
comedy for serious people', and he achieved – against all the
familiar obstacles of casting and rehearsal – a remarkable degree
of harmony, balance and uniformity of style.

Outside Shakespeare, Gielgud has, surprisingly, not ventured
far into English classic tragedy or melodrama: the two exceptions to date are Ferdinand in *The Duchess of Malfi* (in his
Haymarket season) and Jaffier in *Venice Preserv'd* (in his Hammersmith season). Some critics found his Ferdinand too hysterical
and 'petulant'; others, with Ivor Brown, thought it 'overwhelming'. Gielgud was great in the first half, said Agate: if he
dwindled in the second half, it was because Burbage, Betterton
and Kean could not have done more with the character. As
Jaffier – 'a Jacobite Hamlet', as Philip Hope-Wallace called him
– he made up for the lachrymose absurdities of the man by the
dazzling sensibility and skill of his performance. 'All through,
the rare quality of a great actor was continually felt,' said Hope-
Wallace; and T. C. Worsley noted 'a new level of lyric power'
in Gielgud's voice.

In Shakespeare on the stage, since his Old Vic seasons of 1929-31, Gielgud's range has been comparatively small, limited by his tenor voice, his physique and his lack of impersonative power. He has never returned to Hotspur, Antony or Malvolio; he has curiously ignored Coriolanus and Timon; such characters as Jacques, Parolles, Iago, Pandarus, Thersites or Ulysses have seemingly never tempted him; he has avoided Kings John, Richard III, Henry V; not until he was over forty-five did he tackle Angelo, Cassius and Leontes; and only ten years later did he essay Othello. This was, perhaps, Gielgud's most complete failure (although, in spite of everything, such veteran judges as Harold Hobson and Alan Dent ranked it, in some ways, as their best Othello). He had dodged the role because he felt unfitted in temperament and in voice; and at Stratford in 1961 the incompatibilities were stressed while the virtues were muffled by the glaring incongruities of casting, lighting, scenery and general production. A Venetian, never a Moor (he seemed unchallengeably white beneath his bronze make-up), Gielgud spoke with incomparable intelligence, lucidity and music. But the voice was not incarnated in a character: the technique was practised in a vacuum; we were given much of the music but little of the man.

Gielgud's partial successes include his Shylock (1938), a less dominating and more squalid figure than is usual: this cringing creature of the ghetto was under-played as a nuisance rather than as a menace or a victim (the actor was influenced by Granville-Barker's interpretation of the Jew as a witch in a fairy-tale). He ranked it later as ' a failure, because I find it practically impossible to be disliked on stage '. In his Romeos Gielgud matured strikingly, it appears, from 1924 through 1929 to 1935. Yet in spite of his vocal command of the role he was not fully in control of the character: he seemed to be in love with the verse rather than with Juliet (the reverse of Olivier, his rival Romeo in 1935). As he wrote in 1939, four years after his last stage performance of the character, ' I have always felt I knew exactly how the part should be played; but I have neither the looks, the dash nor the virility to make a real success of it, however well I may speak the verse and feel the emotion . . . I love the language, and revel in it all too obviously.' His Macbeths (1930 and 1942) failed – like most Macbeths – to be convincing not only as a poet and neurotic but as a soldier and a murderer; although Agate (here, as often, in a minority of one) thought his 1942 performance ' much finer ' if ' less successful ' than his Hamlet, to date. The mastery and intelligence of his verse-speaking was largely un-questioned, as it was in his two Oberons (1929 and 1945); but in his later version the sinister earthiness of his fairy king, with neo-Roman costume and greenish make-up (' like the ghost of Hamlet's father ') failed to impress the critics. As Wolsey (when he changed his make-up and padded his costume after the first night) Gielgud did not triumph until the ' fall ', when his bitter, poker-backed, scarlet-robed ascetic (a far cry, it seemed, from the fleshpot-loving butcher's son) collapsed nobly into tears, his fierce pride dissolving into genuine contrition.

Gielgud's more complete successes in Shakespeare include Prospero, although the difficulties of the character -- only Kemble, among the star actors of the past, seems to have made anything of him – proved more intractable than what he has to say. Having played Prospero in 1930 as a surprisingly young turbaned Eastern magician and in 1940 as an embittered Italian scholar-aristocrat, bearded and moustached, Gielgud appeared in 1957 as a kind of hermit in a toga, grizzled, clean-shaven and half naked, fighting against the temptation to give way to his sense of being wronged and to his magic powers, ' first cousin of Timon of Athens but heading towards serenity and release '. Kenneth Tynan, one of Gielgud's less devoted admirers, wrote: ' His face is all rigour and pain, his voice all cello and woodwind: the rest of him is totem pole. But he speaks the great passages perfectly, and always looks full of thinking. The part demands no more.' More was found by a number of other critics. W. A. Darlington went so far as to say that this was the first Prospero who might have satisfied Shakespeare.

The success of Gielgud's Richard II in 1929 has already been noted. When he returned to it in 1937 he gave it a new depth, range, control, simplicity and power, without losing its luxuriant self-pity, singing lyricism and royal authority: the improvement, one critic said, was ' astonishing ', and others, with less amaze-ment, welcomed the maturing process. But that was the end of Richard. Gielgud took much longer before he picked up again another of his early Old Vic roles, Benedick. When he did so in 1950, 1952 and 1955 (first in Stratford, then later in London and New York), it proved to be one of his greatest successes, a triumph of high comedy, especially with Peggy Ashcroft as his Beatrice. In spite of the incongruity between the character's age and the actor's forty-six years, and although Gielgud was somewhat too elegant and genteel a courtier to appear as a young soldier of fortune (when he tried to give Benedick a more martial roughness, in 1955, he dulled the edge of the earlier performances), Gielgud played with an immense gusto for the life of the play as well as its language which overcame most objections. He energized his own production with a stirring gaiety, working radiantly on the lines and between the lines with an ironic relish of the character's situation from outside as well as inside, achieving a comic perfection which has not to date been equalled by another performance in this kind. Gielgud showed a new relaxation, warm and expansiveness in the part, turning his hauteur and remoteness (as in Worthing) into comic virtues, communicating with the audience even on the first night more directly than he usually found possible.

In the same year as his new Benedick, 1950, Gielgud entered a new phase in his development as an artist with his portrait of Angelo in Peter Brook's brilliant production of *Measure for Measure,* dressed in a dark, austere robe, with short-hair wig under a close-fitting black cap. As an icy Puritan who shatters the arrogantly treasured image of his own purity by attempting to barter a man's life for his sister's chastity, he held the stage with a tormented grandeur. It seemed, said Harold Hobson, as if Angelo was ' looking into his soul for the first time '. Gielgud had always been expert in keeping tension highly strung: here the inner agonies which burned behind the arctic authority seemed to flame out of some fresh reserves of power that the actor had tapped in his mid-forties. It was as if, T. C. Worsley wrote later, Gielgud had made a complete break with his Hamlet past and its romantic aura, together with the ' softness ' that derived from an occupational thirst for sympathy. ' Freed from that restriction, he is now discovering in himself new depths of feeling and ranges of voice which did not seem to be there before.'

A third role in 1950 with which Gielgud surprised the critics (and, perhaps, himself) was Cassius, played with a passionate intensity and attack from which, one suspects, he might in his

earlier days have shrunk for fear of ' ham '. *The Times* observed
that he had ' never before shown such sustained vehemence ', and
J. C. Trewin welcomed ' a new, a magnificently forcible Gielgud '.
With a hooded-eyed questing discontent, living between gusts of
fury and depression, flashing reproachful indignation in the tent-
scene with Brutus, this Cassius seemed a man doomed by his own
nature yet imbued with a nobility, a suggested greatness, that
made Brutus's epitaph credible. It is not surprising that Gielgud
was asked to play the role in the 1952 film of *Julius Caesar,* nor
that he stole the picture.

His fourth big role in this *annus mirabilis* at Stratford was
Lear: Anthony Quayle was his co-producer, and acknowledg-
ments were paid to Granville-Barker. This was Gielgud's third
attempt at Everest. After the small-scale and rather fragile Lear
of 1931, his 1940 version – under Granville-Barker – still seemed
too young and lightweight vocally: an ash playing an oak, as his
director had suggested. ' We feel for the words Lear speaks rather
than for Lear himself,' said Herbert Farjeon; but Farjeon also
said that there was a rare clarity of meaning behind every one of
those words. *The Times* praised him for treating as though they
were ' a spontaneous product of the mind ' such phases of the
part as ' the Olympian grandeur, the frets, the rages, the madness lit with flashes of savage irony and broken in upon by
spiritual illumination ', while he attained at the end ' a stillness
of beauty which is rarely achieved on the stage '. In 1950 he had
one of his more disastrous first nights, and nearly every notice
reflects a performance at only half its full potential. He was,
as one critic said, ' showing the speeches to us rather than feeling
them '. Later visits revealed a different Lear, even on the second
performance. As T. C. Worsley wrote:

In the first we were conscious of Mr Gielgud acting: we admired
the grasp, the range, the subtlety, the sureness, the intellectual force,
the largeness of the conception. In the second . . . we were caught up
into the play from the start. This seemed not acting – something
conscious and willed – but the actual enacting itself of events seen
for the first (and only) time, into the heart of which we ourselves
are led, stumbling with the old king down the steep descent.

Gielgud presented, at the outset, a right royal Lear, still active,
sharp and arrogant, who is plunged through shock after shock

of outraged pride, with ebbing strength, into fury, madness and finally – quite perfectly – into the serenity of the reconciliation with Cordelia. T. C. Worsley wrote of that miraculous moment when Lear sighs ' Never, never, never ' over Cordelia's body:

> The second advances so far in intensity from the first that you might think it impossible to produce a third still more intense, still more deeply evocative, and yet he does produce it, and then the fourth again so far beyond that, that it leads into a strangled cry which is at the very brink of death.

Among other peaks of this great performance were the first curse on Goneril, the mock-trial and the recognition of the blind Gloucester. Gielgud's voice was, of course, still too light to rumble his bellyful or thunder through the storm (too loud and gimmicky, initially, in this production), but he brought to the role something that the thunderers cannot generally encompass.

This was 'the text incarnate. What more should anybody ask of Lear?' Ivor Brown asked rhetorically in 1950. Gielgud himself, it seems, still asked a good deal more, and in 1955 he returned doggedly to the part, with a very different directorial approach. In an attempt to establish more clearly ' the timeless, universal and mythical quality of the story ', as the programme explained, he had sought 'a setting and costumes which would be free of historical or decorative associations '. They were commissioned from the American-Japanese sculptor, Isamo Noguchi, whose rubberoid suits, formalized wigs and brightly coloured, enigmatic, abstract devices lowered and hoisted from the flies gave Lear's world a rivetingly alien look which was generally identified as that of a science-fiction landscape. An unusual degree of pictorial unity was achieved, but the production – by Gielgud and George Devine – understandably failed to match the acting with its context. Gielgud himself seemingly attempted to begin again from the beginning, reworking the phrasing without his customary poetic precision, but it appeared to be a misplaced artistic heroism; for while the production aimed far beyond naturalism Gielgud surrendered to it by abdicating his supremacy of voice. Conscientiously refusing the effects of his 1950 performance he deflated Shakespeare's titanic figure, half-person and half-symbol, into a small old man, lacking in his former royalty, terror, sublimity and (until his recognition of Cordelia) pathos.

For most critics, the experiment had failed; although one – hailing the ' psychological truth ' of the portrait – described it as ' the most rewarding interpretation of a great play by a great player that we are ever likely to see '. Is it too much to hope that, before Gielgud retires from the stage, we shall see one more Lear?

Another major performance in the late Gielgud style was Leontes at the Phoenix in 1951, directed by Peter Brook: a dark, fiery portrait with the new voltage and strength that he had first shown in the previous year. By starting the king's insane jealousy at a level of high intensity in a ' naphtha-flare rage ' and maintaining it with controlled energy and perfect technique Gielgud conquered the incredibilities of the character and swept away resistance to the last-act conversion and repentance in a flood of feeling: seldom have his Terry tears – he is a king of weepers – flowed to such effect as in the final scene. The verse, as ever, was spoken with subtle lucidity and delicate balance; and it did not seem too much to claim for the performance as a whole (as I did at the time), ' the profundity of common experience, lit by the incandescent flare of maturing genius '. Professor Sprague wrote later: ' Some great actor of another age, a Macready, say, or a Kean, might have been puzzled by Mr Gielgud's Hamlet. He would, I am sure, have understood and admired his Leontes.'

Yet it is as Hamlet, above all, that Gielgud triumphed in his time. After the first incarnation in 1930 Sybil Thorndike wrote to him: ' I never hoped to see Hamlet played as in one's dreams . . . tonight it was Hamlet complete.' For two generations of playgoers that was Gielgud's achievement: he was *the* Hamlet of his age, although his interpretation of the role naturally changed between his Old Vic début and his last performance sixteen years later in 1946. Looking back from 1970 it is difficult to establish precisely how it changed, for here, as everywhere, there is a cloud of contradictory evidence. The first Hamlet is remembered for his sweetness, sadness, elegance and princeliness, but even more for his neuroticism, aloofness, hysteria, tearfulness, self-lacerating sensibility, for a tendency to lose control of top notes and go shrill in moments of crisis. Yet on one point all are agreed: Gielgud was an unusually young Hamlet – ' so young and so profoundly hurt': at twenty-six he was among the youngest actors to play the role. Forbes-Robertson, as we have seen, was forty-

four when he first acted Hamlet, and John Barrymore, who had
made a great impression in London five years earlier, was forty.
Although people cited the old theatrical adage that the part
could not be mastered until an actor was too old to play it,
Gielgud's youthfulness made an immense impact on the audiences
of 1930 and 1934. With the attack and intensity of youth, he
combined a rare command of the verse, so that he seemed to be
thinking aloud and opened deeper meanings ' in almost every
line '. Agate said: ' You feel that these things are happening
to Hamlet for the first time, and that he is here and now creating
words to express a new-felt emotion.' This was a meditative, not
a passionate Hamlet: he underplayed the cruelty and violence,
while stressing the intellectual side of the prince. He straddled the
old tradition and the new age: he was ' frankly modern ' in
his characterization, as one critic put it, but ' not modern in his
diction '. At the same time he did not appear, in Herbert Farjeon's
phrase, to ' nobilify ' Hamlet, as the Forbes-Robertson school
tended to do (partly by pruning the text): there was a bitterness
and mordancy in Hamlet's horror that reflected the climate
of post-war disillusionment and cynicism. Gielgud emphasized
that Hamlet's failure to act was due to his sense of the futility
of action. He was ' modern ', too, in another respect, pointed
out in retrospect by W. A. Darlington. Looking back in *The
Actor and his Audience,* the *Daily Telegraph* critic wrote that
although he had never seen a better Hamlet and hardly dared to
hope that he ever could, yet Gielgud ' made Hamlet a leading
character in the play rather than its heart's core . . . The actor
was enough product of his own time to be afraid of the theatrical
values of the part.' He was, most probably, ' afraid ' of the ham
in Hamlet, to quote an old stage chestnut – the limelight-hogging
heroics of one mainstream tradition; and it seems likely that his
relative ' avoidance of self-assertion ', as Mr Darlington calls
it, was one important factor, together with his ' extraordinary
feeling for speaking verse as if it were the expression of his own
immediate thought ', in the acceptance of his Hamlet by audiences
' trained in the realistic school of team-acting ' and gentlemanly
understatement in modern dress.

By 1934 Gielgud's performance had become more controlled
and also more naturalistic, to the regret of some critics, who
missed the music of Forbes-Robertson and Henry Ainley. Agate,

who had paid such tribute to him in 1930, complained that
although he had mined a new depth of pathos, he scamped the
prose passages and 'wantonly sacrificed' the play's acting
strength, throwing away 'everything except the highest of its
poetry and the most sensitive of its philosophy'. At the end,
said Agate, Gielgud left the impression of a Hamlet 'who can fly
into the most shattering of pets . . . there is no melancholy in
him, his mind has not the richness of its words, he is not fey or
marked for death, and his talk of ripeness is academic . . .' This
disappointment was not generally echoed in the press: the performance was described as the best Hamlet since the war, one
that made it seem as if the play had never been acted before. But
clearly Gielgud was still growing in the rôle, and the unprecedentedly long run – though a taxing physical ordeal for the actor
– gave him the chance to experiment in his interpretation and to
strengthen his command of the part (in which he was still unchallenged).

In 1936-7, when he captured New York as Hamlet, he still
seemed to Rosamond Gilder – who recorded his performance in
detail in her valuable book *John Gielgud's Hamlet* – 'youth itself,
with its intolerance, ruthlessness, arrogance and self-absorption',
but with nobility, too. The 'pets' of which Agate complained
seemed, convincingly, part of an unresolved psychological conflict
between will and emotion expressed in successive manic and
depressive phases. This inner deadlock was broken in the closet-
scene, and in the last scene this Hamlet appeared to have achieved
the effect that Agate missed in 1934 – of 'an integrated personality', as Miss Gilder put it, who has 'discovered the springs of
his own being'. Miss Gilder had no fault, not a feather of blame,
to find in Gielgud; but her description, though a whit over-
doting, gives an invaluable picture of the actor in command of
his greatest role. She praised his feeling for spatial relationship,
joined with sense of timing; the use of his hands ('he will point
a line, underscore a phrase, emphasize an idea, by a perfectly
timed turn of finger, thumb and wrist'); the expressiveness of his
'tragic mask' (you could read 'every thought and intention' on
his face before he spoke); his ability to listen; his breath-control;
the technical expertise, rich music and deep understanding of his
delivery of the verse. Not all American observers were so en-
thralled. Brooks Atkinson, for instance, complained that this

Hamlet was neither mad enough nor friendly enough (he lacked 'the touch of nature that makes the whole world kin') and that he seemed 'too shallow a vessel for the turbid rancor and scorn'. But none questioned Gielgud's subtlety, intelligence and vocal mastery.

In an absorbing essay, 'The Hamlet Tradition', included in Rosamond Gilder's book and written in 1937, Gielgud said that he had played Hamlet too often in succession 'to do anything like justice to the enormous complexity and the physical demands of the role . . . my mind has been torn in studying the part between a desire to walk in the traditions of the great ones and to carve out some interpretation that I might justly call my own. The result has only satisfied me very spasmodically, and I think perhaps the only really original contribution that I have made to the history of the part has been to play it successfully when I was younger than most Hamlets have been allowed to do.' It was, he said, unlikely that he would ever act it again: Hamlet was not a part for older men of forty or fifty. Two years later, however, he played it at Elsinore, and appeared, briefly, at the Lyceum before going to Denmark. Among those who saw him then was Alan Dent, who said that the performance had passed from 'faulty exquisiteness' to 'something nearly perfect in its way'. In 1944-5 Gielgud returned to *Hamlet* for the last time in his season at the Haymarket (and later toured it in the Far East). By now, at forty, his Prince was not only less youthful but also less shrill, less irresolute, less highly-strung and less tearful. There was more strength, more dignity, and more anger. The Gielgud Hamlet had changed, according to W. A. Darlington, from 'a sensitive youth, aghast at the wickedness of the world which he had just discovered, to a sophisticated man to whom that wickedness is no surprise'. At the end he achieved a greater serenity and poise than in 1934. Now, at last, it was for many people the definitive performance: 'The best Hamlet of our time,' said Agate. Yet to Gielgud himself, in retrospect, his last stage Hamlet was his least successful . . .

Gielgud's limitations as an actor have often been examined, not least by Gielgud himself. He has been charged with lacking animal power, 'virility and strength' (Darlington), 'flesh and blood' (Agate), 'heart and stomach' (Tynan). In movement and mime he is inhibited and constrained. Kenneth Tynan went so far as to say (of his 1957 Prospero) that he was 'perhaps the finest actor, from the neck up, in the world today '. His knees have seemed, on occasion, to be tied together with ribbon (characteristically, it is his own phrase). He lacks muscular ease. He learned late to relax, and showed an uneven ability to make direct contact with the audience. He has seemed, at times, to stand slightly apart from the character with an alienation effect that was neither appropriate nor successful. (That apparent remoteness in modern dress on-stage has led to frequent appearances as a foreigner or a figure from the past.) In his concern for the production as a whole, he has – rare flaw among the stars – failed to mobilize his full solo power when it is needed. He has seemed too ready to compromise with other men's views on his choice of roles, lacking, as far as his own acting goes, a single-minded absolute faith in his own supremacy. At times he has appeared to delight too much in his own verbal music. Moreover, the Gielgud voice, some people maintain, is always the same voice. ('There is always the same lengthening of the open vowels and nasals, the same faint tremolo in the stressed word, a quiver that is not so much excess of feeling as an unvarying trick of speech,' said A. Alvarez.) Other people say that by putting voice before psychology he has confused his priorities: that he is not so much a great actor as a great reciter and verse-reader. He has, certainly, no gift for mimicry or impersonation: he is, *par excellence*, an *acteur*.

Gielgud's virtues have already been touched upon in the preceding survey: they need no elaboration here. He has developed a unique vocal mastery in the music of verse. Lacking brass or percussion, he has deployed his violin, clarinet and viola with unrivalled control of modulation, tone, pace and rhythm, keeping command of the shape as a whole while giving every detail its proper value. You can almost see the line and feel it, too. 'When Gielgud speaks the verse, I can hear Shakespeare *thinking*,' Lee Strasberg is reported to have said. For it is not only the sound but the sense that distinguishes Gielgud's performance. His virtuoso technique, profound knowledge of the theatrical classics and rich awareness of stage tradition combine in a singularly delicate and alert respect for and responsiveness to the text in action. In Peter Brook's words (from *The Empty Space*):

His art has always been more vocal than physical; at some early stage in his career he decided that for himself the body was a less supple instrument than the head: he thus jettisoned part of an actor's possible equipment but made true alchemy with the rest: it is not just speech, not melodies: it is the continual movement between the word-forming mechanism and his understanding that has made his art so rare, so touching and especially so aware.

An aristocrat in the age of Admass, an orator in an era of throw-away mumble, a romantic in a time of realism, a disciple of the word in the world of image-worship, Gielgud appears in some ways to be a magnificent anachronism. In other respects he may be seen as a monumental contradiction: a symbol of the theatre theatrical who is also a custodian of the poetic drama, a star who has not only preached but practised – perhaps more than any other player – the ideals of ensemble playing. 'His uniqueness,' as Kenneth Tynan has said, ' lies in the fact that he is far greater than the sum of his parts ', although in several of those parts he has given some of the outstanding performances of his time.

During the last forty years Gielgud's theatrical intelligence and artistic conscience have been a guiding light on the British stage. He has exemplified a humility of professionalism, a discipline of the actor's ego, a searching perfectionism. He has served Shakespeare, not used him. In that service he has reached greatness.

Sir Laurence Olivier

Sniffing at a red rose, and chuckling softly to himself, the bare-footed, ankleted, blacked-up actor – with thick, mauve-black lips, black moustache and crinkly wig – made his way, saunter-ingly, to the front of the stage in a white, loosely-tied gown, roll-ing his hips and splaying his feet as he walked, with a lounging step that looked as if he was perfectly at ease. Appearances were more than usually deceptive. At fifty-six the artistic director of the National Theatre was playing the hardest part in his career, a part which he had long avoided, a part in which no English actor of the century had completely succeeded: after nearly forty years on the stage he was daring to tackle Othello. The day was the four-hundredth anniversary of Shakespeare's birth-day: 23 April 1964. The place was the Old Vic, where so much Shakespearian stage-history had been made already. The actor was Laurence Olivier.

The performance was, like all Olivier's work, rooted in meti-culous physical preparation. Othello demands gruellingly hard labour, so the actor had exercised for weeks in a London gym and along the Brighton front. Othello calls for a bass, so through months of training Olivier had deepened his voice by almost an octave, in addition to thickening his speech (although the coating sometimes wore thin and the near-baritone veered upwards). With his usual genius for self-transformation he had also remade his whole presence: face, gait and gesture. He looked and sounded like a Negro, almost: a Negro who might be seen in the streets outside the theatre. In making that challenge he alien-ated people who preferred a romantic Arab to what they saw as a London blackie; but for others he reconnected the play to con-temporary reality and recharged the audience's emotional response to the plot.

As in other roles, Olivier seized on one main clue to the character – his self-dramatising narcissism – which helped him to solve
many acting difficulties. This Othello, in the early scenes, was
an arrogantly relaxed, almost complacent soldier, hugging his own
image of himself as a noble hero, a power among the whites he
serves, whose religion he has adopted, and into whose élite he has
married. That match was another confirmation for Othello of his
own mastery; but he was also violently in love. Between Desdemona and him there throbbed, from the beginning, a powerful sexual voltage, pulsating across the stage and into the
audience, which made more plausible the jealousy that was to
come. Olivier's Moor had a massive authority – the kind of
brooding power with which he can mantle a theatre in a minute
– which broke down, with unusual slowness, under the poison of
Iago's lies. Then the confident smile and the open mien vanished,
as he moved darkly into an intensity of torment, racked by
jealousy, rage and anguish. The savagery behind the noble mirror-
image smashed through. It was, said Bernard Levin, 'as though
a wild beast has been sewn up inside him and is clawing to get
out; his whole body writhes and flails, out of control – not the
reeling and grimacing that often passes for passion but the real
thing, directed from within.' In agony and anger he snatched the
crucifix from his neck, flung it away and prostrated himself on
the ground, crouching once again before the tribal idols he had
renounced for the Venetian god. At the end, while still self-
deceiving enough to call himself 'not easily jealous', he commanded a deep tenderness and sublime pathos as he clutched
Desdemona to him, alive and dead. To quote Mr Levin again,
'He kills with such sorrow that it is unbearable; he dies with
such consciousness of waste that it is more unbearable yet.' Inventive to the last, Olivier managed, as always, to die well – and,
in so doing, to spring one final surprise, by stabbing himself in
the neck with a dagger concealed in a bracelet.

The Othello created on that April night in the Waterloo Road
seemed to combine all the qualities whose conjunction, at his
best, had set Olivier through the years apart from other actors
who made do with some of them: magnetic, masculine force;
technical inventiveness; charm; emotional intensity and variety;
a rare impersonative skill; pathos; a vein of humour; wide vocal

range and attack; fury; a sense of tradition, blended with a readiness to experiment; the talent for surprise; a penetrating intelligence; gusto; a capacity for making the most of a character's humanity; the ability to make an audience frightened, make it laugh, make it think, bring it close to tears; eyes that spoke, grew, mesmerized; audacity; and something more as well – that intangible ingredient in a performance which prompts a grateful public to call it ' great '. Not all the critics were in favour. Alan Brien described it as ' a kind of bad acting of which only a great actor is capable . . . the most prodigious and perverse example of this in a decade ', and also, less positively, as ' the last splendid fling of a declining style of acting '. Yet to the majority it seemed that Olivier's performance set the seal on his career and guaranteed his place with Garrick, Kean and Irving. In the words of Franco Zeffirelli, quoted by Kenneth Tynan in his introduction to the pictorial record of John Dexter's production, ' It's an anthology of everything that has been discovered about acting in the last three centuries. It's grand and majestic, but it's also modern and realistic. I would call it a lesson for us all.'

The man who gave that lesson is, offstage, a quiet, compact, grey-haired, spectacled, grey-eyed figure of surprisingly medium height and, for his age, surprising physical grace and stamina, though neither shows in his National Theatre office. Visitors to it are sometimes taken aback to find that a man hailed as the greatest actor in the world has the air, on managerial duty, of an eminently successful and unstuffy City executive or solicitor. He looks and sounds unactorish, out of the theatre – and (usually) in it, too: that is one of his virtues as its leader. There is no sign here of what Alan Brien calls the invisible spotlight that seems to follow him everywhere in every play. Yet it is there as soon as he walks the stage: for that is his kingdom.

' I believe that I was born to be an actor,' Laurence Olivier has said. It happened on 22 May, 1907 in the Surrey town of Dorking, in a middle-class family which had sent its sons for five generations into the Church but had sent none, as yet, on to the stage. His father was a High Anglican clergyman, reconverted to Christianity after a ten-year lapse, a star performer in the pulpit but a remote figure at home. His mother died when he was thirteen ('This was a terrible thing. I think I've been looking for her ever since,' Olivier said in 1963). His future obsession revealed itself at an early age. He made his first stage at seven in his Pimlico nursery, where (as Felix Barker says in his valuable biography, *The Oliviers*) 'he was quite content to take not only the leads but the subsidiary parts as well.' He was fired by the romantic ritual and dramatic sermons of the Church, not least his father's) and by the theatricalism of the 'high' West End choir school, All Saints, Margaret Street, which he attended as a boy. It was run by a schoolmaster-priest with a passion for plays and an eye for talent. At ten, playing Brutus in a school production, Olivier attracted the notice of Forbes-Robertson, Lady Tree, Sybil Thorndike and Ellen Terry (who wrote in her diary, 'The small boy who played Brutus is already a great actor.') At fourteen he was first noticed by the press when he played Kate in *The Taming of the Shrew,* another choir-school production, honoured by the Stratford Memorial Theatre's invitation to play there on Shakespeare's birthday. When he was sixteen Olivier discovered to his astonishment that his apparently aloof father had assumed for some time that he was going to be an actor; and he was encouraged to go the following year for training to the Central School at the Albert Hall, on condition that his father did not have to pay. Olivier won a year's free tuition, a £50 bursary and, later, a cup – with Peggy Ashcroft. He learned a lot, very quickly, under the eye of Elsie Fogerty, the School's formidable and influential director: not least from his first interview with her, at seventeen, when she placed her little finger vertically down the middle of his forehead, and said, 'You have a weakness here, and remember that.' Recalling that over forty years later, Olivier ascribed to it his well-known preference for disguise. ('*Something* made me slap all that putty on my face for years and years afterwards, and I dare say it was that.')

At eighteen, he was out on the market of casual theatrical labour, with no very clear idea what he wanted to do except that he had a burning ambition to act – a drive partly fuelled, he suggests, by the genteel poverty of his background (his father could spare him an allowance of no more than fifteen shillings a week). His other assets included a dark, heavy-browed romantic presence and good looks; a kind of smothered fire and crackling physical energy; and an ability to learn and go on learning at speed, as he has done throughout his stage career. For some months after leaving the Central his lessons were learned from miscellaneous small parts and understudies in and around London. The first milestone came when he appeared as a medieval minstrel (and second understudy to the Saint) in *The Marvellous History of St Bernard*, one of the many productions brought to the West End in the 1920s by the founding father of the Birmingham Repertory Theatre, Sir Barry Jackson, a sharp-eyed talent-spotter and a key figure in recent theatrical history. Jackson sent Olivier on tour for six months as a juvenile lead in *The Farmer's Wife*, the Devonian farcical comedy which was one of his money-making subsidies for more ambitious work; and then invited him to Birmingham for the second half of the 1926-7 season. At nineteen Olivier was where he needed to be: in Britain's leading rep. This was the first building in the country to be erected, thirteen years earlier, as a repertory theatre, planned ' to serve an art instead of making that art serve a commercial purpose'. Ralph Richardson was already a member of the company: Peggy Ashcroft made her stage début there that summer.

During the next two years Olivier appeared in a wide range of plays old and new, both in Birmingham and London. At that time Jackson had three semi-permanent metropolitan bases outside Shaftesbury Avenue, the Kingsway, the Regent and the Court – one cogent reason why ambitious actors were so eager to join the Birmingham Rep – and so Olivier not only learned from the hard labour (and rushed rehearsals) of a fortnightly run at the steep-raked little brown playhouse in Station Street but also gained the experience of holding performances before London audiences for a month at a time. At Birmingham he played, among other roles, Tony Lumpkin, Uncle Vanya, Jack Borthwick in *The Silver Box* and Parolles in modern dress (Jackson pioneered ' Shakespeare in plus fours', beginning with *Cymbeline* in 1923). At the Court, where he also appeared as Martellus in *Back to Methuselah* and in Elmer Rice's expressionistic set-piece, *The Adding Machine*, he played his first leading role in London as the last Anglo-Saxon king of England, Harold, in Tennyson's verse drama. This fifty-two-year-old ' tragedy of doom ' had never before been seen on the stage, for reasons that were soon apparent, but it gave Olivier (wearing a long flaxen wig) the opportunity to show something of his burgeoning quality in handling verse. Critics noticed this and his ' sincerity ',

SIR JOHN GIELGUD. Top:
offstage 1970. Bottom: his
first Hamlet, at 26, in 1929
at the Old Vic.

Left: Gielgud as John Worthing, in the 1939 production of *The Importance of Being Earnest*. Right: as Raskolnikov in *Crime and Punishment*, 1946.

Gielgud at Stratford. Top: as Angelo in *Measure for Measure*, 1950. Bottom: as Prospero in *The Tempest*, 1957.

SIR LAURENCE OLIVIER.
Top: offstage, 1970.
Bottom: as Titus
Andronicus, 1957.

Olivier as Othello, at 57, in 1964.

Top: Olivier as Archie Rice, in rehearsal for *The Entertainer*, 1957. Bottom: his second Macbeth, at Stratford in 1955.

SIR MICHAEL REDGRAVE.
Top: offstage, 1970.
Bottom: as Uncle
Vanya, 1962.

Top: Redgrave as
Sir Andrew Aguecheek,
1938. Bottom: as Antony in
Antony and Cleopatra, 1953.

an intangible theatrical effect which had been observed when he appeared in *Macbeth* as Malcolm, in a grey flannel suit. This early immersion in modern-dress Shakespeare – he also played a dinner-jacketed Lord in *The Taming of the Shrew* – perhaps helped to mould Olivier's later naturalism (*sans* trousers) in the great Shakespearian roles. Yet he was not – unlike many young men in the du Maurier era of anti-ham genteel realism – afraid of looking as if he were acting. For that reason, perhaps, he had been picked out in *The Adding Machine* by St John Ervine (no friend of expressionism) as giving the production's best performance: ' He had little to do, but he *acted*.'

In June 1928, still under Barry Jackson's wing, Olivier moved out of the gymnasium of repertory into the shop-window of a West End run in a modern comedy. For seven months in the Royalty (a Jackson theatre) he played a lovesick juvenile lead – as the son of a Gloucestershire squire who falls in love with an innkeeper's daughter, a role he had created earlier at the Rep – in John Drinkwater's comedy, *Bird in Hand*. Then, in 1929, he was out in the cold again, bidding for hire in the usual way. He got work, off and on; he did not starve; he earned, spasmodically, big money. But as he drifted, like most actors, through the eddies and shallows of the West End, it must have seemed that a promising start was (as so often) petering out with nothing particular to show for it. As far as the West End theatre was concerned, he was a good-looking and virile juvenile: although he was not pejoratively branded as Shakespearian, thanks to the fact that his appearances had been in modern dress, his character roles at Birmingham Rep and the Court were irrelevant to the bread-and-butter demands of the commercial stage. In some particular respects Olivier was prepared for those demands: he had his heavy eyebrows plucked; he brushed back his hair, which grew low on his forehead; he had the gaps in his teeth filled in; he dressed, somehow, well. Moreover, he had – between *Harold* and *The Shrew* – grown a Ronald Colman moustache in order to qualify visibly as a candidate for the romantic Foreign Legion hero of P. C. Wren's best-seller, *Beau Geste,* soon to be translated to the theatre. Against keen competition, he won the race. To play this – his first starring part – he turned down the chance of Stanhope in the West End run of *Journey's End*, a role he had created at a Stage Society performance. But while R. C. Sherriff's

war-drama flourished, *Beau Geste* came off within a month. So
did *The Circle of Chalk,* in which Olivier played (and sang) a
Chinese prince. Two more flops followed in London, a third happened on his New York début, and after the fourth (back in the
West End) he found only four months paid work in eighteen
months – not on the stage, but in a 'quickie' film. Olivier was
saved in 1930 – soon after he married Jill Esmond, his stage
sweetheart in *Bird in Hand* – by Noel Coward's invitation to play
in *Private Lives.* His role as the priggish Victor was woodenly
unrewarding, yet the play was a hit not only in London but on
Broadway; and from New York he went on to Hollywood. It could
not be said that he was missed in the West End, although at least
one critic, Ivor Brown, had singled him out as 'particularly
brilliant' among the younger actors of the year.

For two years Olivier was away from the London stage in
one of those filming interregna which punctuate the careers of
many contemporary actors. After appearing as a romantic lead
with Elissa Landi, Ann Harding and Gloria Swanson he came
close to the Hollywood summits when he was asked to play
opposite Garbo in *Queen Christina.* After a few days on the set
Garbo decided that she preferred another leading man, and one
result of that painful experience was that Olivier turned his back
on Hollywood (and a contract of £12,000 per annum) for five
years, at a time when he might, like so many other London actors,
have deserted the theatre for good. The dangers to his career as
an artist of his success as a personality – a gentlemanly Don
Juan with charm, magnetism and manly beauty – were post-
poned: which was, for the theatre, a great thing. As a romantic
lead he was not exceptional: as a classic actor he later proved
to be unique.

Olivier's luck in the West End casino did not, for some time,
give him much opportunity to test his growing power to the full,
although he enjoyed varying success as an amorous schoolmaster
in *The Rats of Norway;* as a crypto-queer in *The Green Bay
Tree* (on Broadway); as Bothwell in *Queen of Scots;* as the
Barrymore-Fairbanks star of *Theatre Royal,* which won him
praise for his flamboyant and acrobatic zest ('an amazing performance,' said Desmond MacCarthy); as – in complete contrast –
a study in paralysis, a sadistic, ex-actor immobilized in a wheel-
chair in *Ringmaster,* (when in the climax he heaved himself out

and collapsed, writhing, on the floor, the audience cheered); as a homburg-hatted, Eden-resembling politician in *Golden Arrow* (his first venture into direction and management and a resounding flop). Shortly after it closed Olivier started work under a new film contract with Korda, which helped him to meet his theatrical bills; and from now on he frequently used the cinema to subsidize the stage.

Olivier's next big theatrical opportunity came shortly afterwards in the autumn of 1935 when John Gielgud decided to play Romeo and Mercutio turn about with another actor. Olivier was his second choice, after Robert Donat. This friendly open competition continued a tradition of gladiatorial contest going back to Garrick, with one prime difference: that both performances were directed (and, in effect, managed) by one of the contestants. Gielgud and Olivier seemed to present an illuminating contrast in style between classical and naturalistic acting, and the game of comparison between the two young men – only three years apart in age but separated, it seemed, by a far wider abyss of attitude – was to persist for many years, although in this *Romeo and Juliet* the differences may have appeared greater on stage (and at rehearsals) than they were in fact to prove in their full maturity. (Olivier says he has always seen Gielgud and himself as ' reverses of the same coin '.) In 1935, at the New, while Gielgud seemed to stand for the poem, for lyricism, verse-speaking and tradition, Olivier seemed to stand for the love story, realism and action. Against Gielgud's initial direction, he played Romeo as a tousled, impetuous, Italian boy in a fever of adolescent love, groping for words, choked with emotion. A few critics, like St John Ervine and Herbert Farjeon, thought him the best Romeo they had seen; Agate said that he was the most moving Romeo, but could not speak verse; Ivor Brown, in a midway position, judged him a good prose Romeo, ' authentic in suffering, with everything sincere about him '. Most of the press turned down their thumbs on what seemed unpoetic, over-modern, matter-of-fact playing. As Mercutio, however, he scored a more general success (his verse-speaking, said Farjeon, had improved in six weeks); Peggy Ashcroft's Juliet was acclaimed with both her Romeos; and the production broke Irving's record by running for 186 performances. ' I was trying to sell realism in Shakespeare – I believed in it with my whole soul,' Olivier said thirty years later. His fervour was perhaps fuelled by his first experiences in cinematic Shakespeare during the run, playing Orlando to Elisabeth Bergner's broken-English Rosalind.

Later that year – after another ill-fated venture into actor-management, presenting (with Ralph Richardson and the author) J. B. Priestley's satirical-symbolical comedy *Bees on the Boatdeck* – Olivier had a magnificent chance to put his Shakespearian beliefs into practice. Tyrone Guthrie asked him to join the Old Vic, that invitation which, for so many artists, has proved to be an open sesame to their acting selves. As Felix Barker says, ' At twenty-nine he was at a point in his career where he could be a leading man in the West End, a film star, or a theatrical manager. Quite possibly he could even combine all three.' But Olivier hesitantly chose the Alps of the Waterloo Road for £20 a week, instead of £500. He was to play Hamlet for the first time – and virtually whatever else he fancied, in consultation with Guthrie.

It was with a full-length Hamlet (influenced by Freud via his biographer Ernest Jones) that Olivier's Old Vic education began, in January 1937. Consciously turning his back, as in Romeo, on lyricism and tradition, he was found lacking in melancholy, madness and philosophical profundity, the victim of excessive emotion rather than cerebration; he oversimplified Hamlet's complexities; he was thought to fail in the players, nunnery and closet scenes; his suggestions of the Oedipus complex were not readily perceived; and it seemed hard to believe that such a fiery, active prince would have delayed his revenge so long. Predictably, it was his handling of the verse to which most critics objected. He lacked not only verbal music, they said, but variety, rhythm and control. Agate went so far as to say, with characteristic overstatement, ' Mr Olivier does not speak poetry badly. He does not speak it at all.' Yet, with equally characteristic contradiction Agate also praised the ' remarkable cogency ' of the soliloquies, and welcomed ' that too rarely heard thing, a voice up to the demands of high tragedy ', while he said that Olivier excelled any other Hamlet in ' pulsating vitality and excitement '. Apart from the verse-speaking, W. A. Darlington said he did not see how the performance could have been bettered. *The Times* praised it as ' original in the best sense – namely, that Mr Olivier has neither imitated others nor wildly defied convention, but has looked for himself in the part and the part in himself'. What he had succeeded in doing was to project something of the gusto and panache he had admired in Barrymore with his own passionate virility and verve: an athletic man of action, sardonically rated by Agate as the best Hotspur of the present generation, but intensely alive as a character. ' Beyond any other Hamlet in my experience he is a credible and living individual – quizzical, protean, mercurial, leaping in and out of every mood . . . playing a new part every minute with himself for audience. Mr Olivier has as many voices as a ventriloquist, one for each facet of Hamlet's nature,' said Raymond Mortimer. For most playgoers he may not have displaced Gielgud (' I knew I was putting myself up in a kind of stupid rivalry '), but he had shown a confidence of attack and a theatrical virtuosity that augured well for the future.

Next, as Sir Toby Belch, he demonstrated, for the first time, his brilliance in disguise. Since then he has used his make-up box (physical and spiritual) perhaps more thoroughly and inventively than any other British actor. With beaky nose, straggling moustache, bulging red cheeks and pouchy eyes, he seemed ' now and then recognizable,' said *The Times* wonderingly, ' only by a gleam of teeth.' For some critics it was too obviously ingenious, and his acrobatic overplaying – ' a superabundance of comical crawling, stumbling and staggering ' – unbalanced the play. But as Henry v, staged to meet the patriotic demands of the Coronation season of 1936, Olivier felt at first that his trouble was *under*playing, for he intensely disliked the character and his glorification of war. As a result first-night critics noticed a certain vocal monotony and iciness of mien (' unthawed and unthawable '), although Olivier's resemblance to the medieval portrait was admired (he wore a reddish cropped wig above a make-up variously described as ' like a Javanese idol ' and ' Chinese looking '), and he was patted on the back for ' gradually moving towards poetry ', while ' his manliness and chivalry are unimpeachable '. After the play had run for a while he found that he could come to terms with the Star of England as long as he could let the words ' work their own medicine ' and could feel the character. He discovered the key of feeling in a dressing-room tribute by Charles Laughton, who said to him after the performance, ' You are England, that's all ', and so helped to take him into the heart of the role (if not the man). In the cinema Olivier later made one of his greatest successes as this royal warmaker whom he had, initially, been so reluctant to play.

After making several films (he had worked in the studios while at the Vic) Olivier returned to the Waterloo Road in the autumn as Macbeth, in an elaborately stylized and controversial production by Michel St Denis. In 1937 the play's traditional aura of bad luck, even tragedy, seemed to be a superstition more than usually justified: most of all because Lilian Baylis died before the first night. Olivier went so far as to say, in 1966, that the production was 'utter disaster', but this was surely conversational licence: it was not quite as bad as that. *Macbeth* even made a profit at the Vic and, after its fixed run of a month, was transferred to the New (although it closed there in three weeks). Moreover, while Olivier was still patently too light in years and voice, and his uncertainty was reflected in an exaggerated make-up of slanted eyes, highlighted cheekbones, padded gums – in Vivien Leigh's celebrated remark, 'You hear Macbeth's first line, then Larry's make-up comes on, then Banquo comes on, then Larry comes on' – he won near-golden opinions from the press. It was observed that (though over-inclined to force) his verse-speaking had gained in rhythm and strength since his Hamlet. His presence kindled: as Lionel Hale said, 'He has only to walk on a stage to set it alight.' According to another critic: 'Every point is grasped and flourished with a spaciousness that recalls the great actors of the past'. *The Times* said that 'his attack upon the part itself, his nervous intensity, his dignity of movement and swiftness of thought, above all his tracing of the process of deterioration in a man not naturally evil gave to his performance a rare consistency and power.' The last act, wrote Agate, was the best he had seen, 'played at white heat of both imagination and energy'; and although the performance as a whole lacked grandeur and the right voice, it showed not only 'mental grasp' but also 'enough of the character to take one spectator out of the Waterloo Road and set him down on that dubious heath'. When he was twice the age, Agate suggested, Olivier would play Macbeth twice as well. 'Meanwhile he registers another step in a career of considerable achievement and increasing promise.'

The promise did not noticeably increase in *Othello,* when Olivier played Iago to Richardson's Moor. One of the main strands of his performance – the notion that Iago had a subconscious homosexual love for Othello (derived, like Olivier's Hamlet theory, from Freud's biographer) – was lost on the critics, who complained that Iago was 'too cheery', 'too puckish', a practical joker rather than a devil incarnate, and that in soliloquies he maintained this 'excessive liveliness' by continuing 'to be the honest soldier for his own benefit'. Olivier's conversational, throwaway realism was carried too far: so was his sense of comedy. Nor did the new play in this short 1938 season – James Bridie's *King of Nowhere* – offer its leading actor much scope, though Olivier seemed to do all that was needed as Frank Vivaldi, a mad actor who escapes from a mental home and becomes leader of a neo-Fascist campaign to reform the world.

It was as Coriolanus, a role which Garrick ignored and which defeated Kean and Irving, that Olivier seemed to step forward again, partly by stepping back a little into an older tradition. Under the prompting of the play's director, Lewis Casson – Sybil Thorndike was Olivier's Volumnia – he reluctantly subjugated his modern naturalistic detail and humour to a more external, heroic and showy manner. At least one critic observed the strain: 'He seems more concerned with tricks than with sincerity and with imposing pride upon his personality instead of allowing its easy and natural assertion.' But this performance was generally acclaimed with the warmest praise that Olivier had yet received. His faults were all in abeyance, said Alan Dent, and he was 'of a stature to come within the line of the great tradition'. He had, said Ivor Brown, 'grown immeasurably greater since he joined the Old Vic . . . His voice has gained in volume, in reach and passion. It has notes of exquisite appeal, delicate finesse and such attack as makes the syllables shimmer like a sword's blade.' Agate, under one of his pseudonyms, asserted confidently: 'There is now no doubt in my mind that the only sign of a great actor in the making in England today is Laurence Olivier'. Under his own name, Agate acclaimed Olivier's gain in pathos and in vocal depth and resonance and, while complaining about his 'clowning' and his 'excessive make-up', he described Olivier as 'the nearest thing we have today to the heroic tradition. The only thing still to be settled is whether he is going to have the genius, which includes a feeling for poetry.'

Olivier himself was not too impressed by this accolade. It

appears, from Felix Barker's biography, that he rated his first Coriolanus below rather than above his previous performances: what seized the imagination of the press, he thought, was his death-scene, when he threw himself down a staircase in a somersault, rolled over three times and crashed to a dead halt just short of the footlights. In any case, whatever the critics' verdict, he did not give them a chance of passing judgment for a long time. Just at the point when he was being hailed as a great actor Olivier disappeared from the London stage – for no less than six years.

During this period he worked on Broadway, in films, and in the Fleet Air Arm. In filming *Wuthering Heights* he not only became an international star but discovered under William Wyler's direction that there was more to the cinema than merely making money. Although he was (as he considered) a realist in the theatre, he found that he was stagy in the studio: in working out a closer realism for the screen, he may well have influenced his later acting for the stage. He made a Broadway hit in *No Time for Comedy* and a New York flop in *Romeo and Juliet* with his second-wife-to-be Vivien Leigh (they lost all their savings in this disaster). He appeared in films of *Pride and Prejudice, Lady Hamilton, Demi-Paradise* and his own outstanding *Henry V* which could, for once, be accurately described as ' epoch-making ' (even though, inevitably, it could not recapture the vocal resonance and physical excitement of his original stage performance).

The six-year gap – largely, though not entirely due to the war – was finally bridged before the peace in a remarkable way; it was a key event in the history not only of Olivier's career but also of the English stage, and it happened, as so often, through the Old Vic. In 1944 Olivier and his old friend Ralph Richardson (who had persuaded Olivier to join him) were released from the Navy in order to perform a different kind of national service. With a former BBC producer, John Burrell, as their administrative co-director, they organized the return of the Old Vic to London after five years in the provinces – the old Waterloo Road building had been bombed in 1941 – and headed the company which opened that autumn at the New at the invitation of Bronson Albery, one of the Old Vic governors. A new era in English acting seemed to dawn in 1944 at this commercial playhouse in St Martin's Lane, and, although not built for repertoire (no theatre in Britain by 1970 had been so designed) and not big enough to make the most of its successes, the New served, in effect, as the centre of the British theatre for the next five years.

Richardson and Olivier had agreed, in embarking on the enterprise, to share the leading roles between them; and it was Richardson's prime choice, *Peer Gynt*, which opened a season that was to prove triumphantly successful. With spectacular unobtrusiveness Olivier's contribution was the tiny role of the Button-Moulder, to whose one appearance in the last act he gave what was described as 'an unearthly glow'. For surprised cynics the 'unearthly' quality was shared by his sacrifice of customary star-dominance in casting, a much-commended and emblematic decision, paralleled by Richardson in later productions. As the priggish Sergius in *Arms and the Man,* absurd moustache bristling and spurs clicking, his extravagantly funny performance was variously praised as a 'joyous travesty' and a 'museum of invention' (an ambiguity of phrase which, though not apparently intended, perhaps suggests a weakness in the acting). As Astrov in the fourth play, *Uncle Vanya* – the failure (relatively speaking) of the season – he was made up to look remarkably like the author, and for some people he caught the spirit as well as the image of Chekhov; but to others, for all his skill in showing the doctor's charm and conceit, he missed Astrov's rusticity, his deep feeling for the forests and his fundamental inner weakness.

Yet it was on the third play of the season, *Richard III,* that Olivier concentrated his resources. Initially, he was reluctant to take up this role, because Donald Wolfit had made a notable hit in it some eighteen months earlier. At first he could not conceive the part clearly without seeing and hearing Wolfit in the theatre of his memory; and so, in search of guidance, he looked back to Irving (as Gielgud did for his first Macbeth) – or rather, as he says, to the imitations of Sir Henry that he had heard old actors delivering. That was only a starting-point (although Agate found 'a great deal of Irving' in the performance). Other fragments with which Olivier built up the character – 'I work mostly from the outside in' – included the Big Bad Wolf and a New York producer under whom he had suffered. Hitler, too, was not far from his mind. Faced with the monstrous evil of the last decade, the wartime audience was ready for a stage devil, but it had to be a convincing one: the psychologically true portrait of an outsize man who was also exceptionally wicked. He achieved prodigies of self-transformation in spiritual as well as physical make-up, with lank black hair, bright hard lips, a long reptilian nose, pallid warty cheeks, and eyes that shone with inner amusement or glittered with piercing rage; his speech was thin, sharp and precise; but he did not (in the old tradition) overdo the hump or the limp, nor did he loud-pedal Crookback's full villainy from the start. He played it down and he played it almost elegantly, with speed and panache, building up a portrait of paranoiac evil behind the cruel fun. The horrors accumulated, while Richard watched his own devilry with infectious relish, like an actor asking the audience to admire the cunning and impudence of his own performance. Olivier established his dominion at his first entrance, when he limped to the front of the stage to deliver that confessional soliloquy, ' Now is the winter of our discontent . . .', amplified by part of another soliloquy from *Henry VI*. In the words of W. A. Darlington:

As he made his way downstage, very slowly and with odd interruptions in his progress, he seemed malignity incarnate. All the complications of Richard's character – its cruelty, its ambition, its sardonic humour – seemed implicit in his expression and his walk, so that when at last he reached the front of the stage and began his speech, all that he had to say of his evil purpose seemed to us in the audience less like a revelation than a confirmation of something we had already been told.

From then on the game he played – as actor and as character – was staged with remarkable zest and variety, in collusion with the audience, until the slow, convulsive death-throes, writhing with the ferocious animal energy that he had seemed to hold in leash all the way. By his death he had seemed to achieve a kind of grandeur. We were, reluctantly, on his side. Here was a stage monster to the life, but on an emotional scale that a modern audience could tolerate, and within a vocal range that the actor could span without straining for ' big bow-wow ' thunder. It combined, as J. C. Trewin's first-night notice said, ' thinker and doer, mind and mask '. This Gloucester was charged with an electrifying theatricalism which recalled triumphs of the past, yet was founded in contemporary realism: it was both splendidly stagy and brilliantly true, the supreme success of his career to date.

The performance was generally recognized as a milestone in

the history of contemporary acting, and Olivier was hailed in some quarters as the First Player, ousting Gielgud from his fifteen-year supremacy. With characteristic generosity Gielgud showed his own appreciation of Olivier's Richard by sending him a visible embodiment of theatrical tradition: a sword which Kean had used as Gloucester, which was passed to Irving on the first night he played the role, and which Gielgud's mother had given to him some years earlier.

Although Olivier achieved no individual portrait quite on the scale of Richard III for several years, he advanced his reputation for virtuoso versatility during the next Old Vic season with four sharply contrasted performances. His ginger-wigged, ' w '-stammering Hotspur – fierily convincing both as uncouth, braggart warrior and tender husband – showed his talent for bringing a secondary character to bursting life, and spectacular death. After Prince Hal had given Percy a mortal wound on the side of the neck, he stood upright for a few moments while the blood oozed through his fingers, struggling with the last ' w ' of his last word, ' worms ', and then suddenly plunged forward on his face. As Shallow in the sequel he seemed (one American critic said) to have added thirty years and lost ten inches overnight: a wizened, shrill, spinsterly old scarecrow with a sharp nose, a goatee beard and a curiously cracked, quavering voice.

Next, he attempted the heights of *Oedipus Rex* (in W. B. Yeats's translation). Black-curled, thick-voiced, heavy-nosed, this Oedipus was a noble but passionately human victim, with none of that marble classic chill once thought appropriate to Greek tragedy. When Olivier played the role in New York, John Mason Brown described it as ' one of those performances in which blood and electricity are somehow mixed. It pulls down lightning from the sky. It is as awesome, dwarfing and appalling as one of nature's angriest displays. Though thrilling, it never loses its majesty.' He began as an imperious, sullen king, secure in his godlike supremacy, a man above judgment; but behind his eyes there burned the hot violence that was the key to his ruin, flaming out in his conversations with Creon and the Old Shepherd. Looking, as always, for a basic realism of character, Olivier seemed to show that the man's nature was his own evil destiny, and he gradually revealed Oedipus's growing understanding of his doom until, with the final disclosure of his full sin, he threw back his head and uttered two great cries of half-animal anguish and terror, ' as expressive of astounded pain as a woman's cry the moment when her child is born ', ' sounds which speak, as no words could, for a soul torn by horror; for a mind numbed by what it has been forced to comprehend ', coming from beyond shame or guilt – or realism.

Fifteen minutes (and nearly two thousand years) later, after Oedipus had made his last exit with blood streaming from his eyes, Olivier was back on the stage in another false nose (*retroussé* this time), as the foppish Mr Puff in Sheridan's theatrical skit, *The Critic*: tossing snuff in the air and catching it in his nostrils, hoisted into the flies on a painted cloud, clinging to the curtain as it swung down at the end of the piece. The abruptness of the transition from tragedy to farce in this ambitious double bill was widely criticized – it smacked too much of show-off show-manship for some adherents of the Old Vic tradition, while others believed that it damaged the impact of a great play and a great performance. But it could not be denied that Mr Puff was another brilliant feat of comic and acrobatic expertise, and this pheno-menal histrionic double demonstrated again the rare versatility, strength and excitement of Olivier's acting.

As King Lear, with which in September 1946 he opened the third season of the Old Vic under the Olivier-Richardson-Burell triumvirate, he approached the part with his distinctive blend of unexpected humour, humanizing realism and inventive technique, and these (for many people) made up for his lack of height, voice and kingliness. In the early scenes he seemed not so much the impetuous old monarch as a fey, whimsical, almost comic grand-father (with touches of Shallow). To James Agate he was ' a man of infinite fecundity of wit, choleric maybe but resilient and alert, ready in sheer intellectual energy and physical well being for any jest or experimental escapade'. He was 'the quietest Lear in my experience ', noted the veteran playgoer Gordon Crosse. When his experiment of dividing his kingdom went wrong and filial ingratitude struck home, sympathy was drawn less for the king than for the man, a *smaller* man (so objectors felt) than the text requires, in its demand for acting far beyond the limits of realism. Yet a critic like Philip Hope-Wallace, who faulted Olivier's early scenes, said that he began to grow in stature ' just at the point where ferocious and majestical Lears begin to decline'. Others were unreserved in their praise. Alan Dent, acclaiming this as a 'great' Lear, declared that it was faultless throughout – 'it has everything that this hardest of parts should have ideally.' *The Times* could recall no actor who has matched 'the creative stamina which enables Mr Olivier to rise equal to the demands of every phase'. For J. C. Trewin, he was the best Lear yet, faltering only in the hovel scene. Yet there was by no means a unanimous verdict. Judged by the highest standards, as an artist of Olivier's stature must be, this Lear was only a partial success. Agate, who called it 'brilliantly imagined and achieved', and praised Olivier's attainment of 'utter stillness', 'quiet pathos', and 'cosmic grief', yet found something wanting. Kenneth Tynan, one of the actor's keenest admirers, thought the performance, in sum, too lightweight: 'Instead of the pathos of great strength crumbling, he offered the misfortune of bright wits blurred.' For Tyrone Guthrie, in spite of 'moments of extraordinary imagination', it was 'sentimental rather than monumental'.

For two years after *King Lear*'s limited run (forty-eight performances) Olivier was away from the London stage. In 1947 he was engaged on the filming of *Hamlet,* and in 1948, he took an Old Vic company on a ten-month trip to Australia and New Zealand with *Richard III, The School for Scandal* and *The Skin of our Teeth;* Vivien Leigh was his leading lady. (They had married in 1940.) He and Richardson had every intention of continuing with the Old Vic as actor-managers. According to Felix Barker's biography, they had made plans for as far as twelve years ahead to the time when it would become, so it was hoped, the nucleus of a National Theatre. But the governors of the Old Vic had other ideas. During Olivier's Antipodean tour they informed him that they did not wish to renew the contracts of Richardson, Burrell and himself when they expired in 1949. To him and to Richardson this decision came as no less of a thunderbolt than to theatregoers when it was officially announced that they were 'retiring'. The full story of this episode in the history of the Royal Victoria Hall has not yet been told. Clearly, there was resentment that 'the knights' did not appear more often with the Old Vic company, after the first two glorious seasons, and they were accused of extravagance, bad management and concentrating upon their own careers rather than on the creation of a national English ensemble. It had been agreed at the outset that both actors would be free to make a film during their five-year stint; but it so happened that Richardson's film coincided with Olivier's tour, reinforcing charges of absenteeism. One can only say here that the affair provides an illuminating comment upon the difficulties of actors in contemporary management compared with their predecessors in the last century. Who would have thought that after achieving such immense personal success and winning new lustre not only for the Old Vic but for the British theatre as a whole, these two leading actors – at the very top of their profession – should be regarded as expendable and sacked by a board of governors?

There was one more season to go, however, before the split; and in January 1949 Olivier led his company back to the New. Instead of *The Skin of our Teeth*, he presented Anouilh's *Antigone*, in which he took the relatively unrewarding part of the dinner-jacketed Chorus, and Vivien Leigh scored in the title role. Otherwise the programme was as on tour: a revived (and coarsened) *Richard III* and *The School for Scandal* which, with *Antigone*, he directed himself, in addition to playing Sir Peter Teazle. The production seemed generally overdressed, under-played and undermined by sentimental flourishes; and Olivier himself – playing opposite Vivien Leigh in this season for the first time in London – imbued the elderly Sir Peter with such bouncy middle-aged charm that for some critics much of the play's point was destroyed. Although the season enjoyed box-office success, and although Olivier's acting, judged by any standards but those of his own previous performances, was still, dazzlingly, in the front rank, it was not a felicitous end to a memorable, if staccato five-year reign.

Of all contemporary actors, however, none has been quite so concerned as Laurence Olivier with managing theatres – as distinct from directing plays or performing in them. He had already ventured into the West End gamble of producing single plays; he had shared the artistic direction of a state-subsidized repertory company; but he wanted a theatre of his own – and within a year of his return to London he had it. He took an eight-year lease of the St James's, an intimate, inefficient, Victorian playhouse with a rich actor-manager tradition. Sir George Alexander made his fame and fortune there in a twenty-seven-year regime that started in the 1890s, and Olivier seemed determined to restore its former glories.

He opened, starrily and extravagantly, with his own production of *Venus Observed*, a verse play commissioned from Christopher Fry two years earlier; and he himself played the lead as the Duke of Altair, an astronomer-amorist deciding on a second wife between three women he had loved as a younger man. The role demanded little of a man who had played Hamlet, Macbeth, Richard III and Lear, but its urbane, romantic charm gave him an appropriate success for his inaugural appearance as actor-manager. Yet although the play ran for seven months, the economics of the St James's were very different from those of Alexander's and even du Maurier's day. Like all Olivier's productions here, *Venus Observed* lost money; and his dream of re-establishing the personal control of the old actor-managers faded. The productions under his own banner had a boldly distinctive enterprise (they included Dennis Cannan's *Captain Carvallo*, Tyrone Guthrie's *Top of the Ladder*, and the Orson Welles *Othello*), but after the third of these he sub-let the St James's frequently, and it rapidly became – like every other West End theatre – a home for the *ad hoc* ventures of other managers and other actors. After all, the building had to stay open, most of the seats had to be filled (you could not see the stage properly from some of them), and the bills had to be met. Entering the great gamble of West End management on your own, as Olivier did – especially in an uneconomic house which playgoers seemed to think too far off the centre – it was impossible to contract out of the short-term, hit-and-miss long-run system. So Olivier did much more managing than acting. He made films to subsidize his theatre. And he was rarely seen on his own stage. Yet all the time he was accumulating experience that was to come in useful when, in the next decade, he became the top manager of all, staging plays of his own choice, without having to meet the rent from his own pocket.

Olivier leased the St James's until 1956, and the following year it was closed down for 'redevelopment' after a violent public controversy, in which Vivien Leigh played a leading role. The 1950s was the decade not only of the St James's but of 'the Oliviers', a brilliantly glamorous partnership which dominated the entertainment industry. Nine months after *Venus Observed*

Olivier staged – as a special Festival of Britain offering, having failed to organize a *School for Scandal* with Gielgud and Richardson – a starry tandem for Vivien Leigh and himself: Shakespeare's *Antony and Cleopatra* and Shaw's *Caesar and Cleopatra*. As the Egyptian queen in both Vivien Leigh achieved a personal success, and the plays ran for nine months at the St James's and on Broadway. But although Olivier was praised for both his small-scale Antony and his world-weary, somewhat over-elderly Caesar, he seemed – for all the skill and intelligence of his playing – to be well below his best. T. C. Worsley described his Antony as 'exactly right to the last hair . . . not, perhaps, one of his greatest, for Antony needs a Cleopatra to act against, but superb '; yet a more common critical view was expressed by Philip Hope-Wallace, who called this portrait 'lightweight, charming and rather dry '. Olivier was, as Mr Barker suggests in his biography, baffled and tantalized by both roles, but he was reproached with playing them down to make his wife's two Cleopatras shine all the brighter. To sceptical outsiders the great artist seemed subordinated to the loyal husband, and the idea grew that, after scaling the peaks, he had lost interest in his own stage acting in favour of management, direction and the cinema. The notion gained currency from the fact that his only other theatrical part between 1949 and 1955 was the even less rewarding Grand Duke of Carpathia in his own production of Terence Rattigan's featherweight 'fairy tale ', *The Sleeping Prince,* a piece for the Coronation year of 1953 set in the Coronation year of 1911, with a leading role for Vivien Leigh. What was a great actor doing, playing hard – as it seemed – against his charm, as a monocled, muted Balkan stooge in this decorative trifle? The answer was, no doubt, that he was enjoying it: it should be noted that Redgrave and Richardson, among others, have since played the role in other parts of the world. But the public's demands on the leaders of the stage have often been exacting, impatient and even hostile. They wanted Olivier back in big roles; and it looked to many people as if those Old Vic seasons had been not a beginning but an end.

In 1955, however, another turning-point came in Olivier's career with his first season at Stratford. For him it occupied much the same importance, at forty-eight, as the 1950 season had done for Gielgud, at forty-six. He was back, it seemed, where he really belonged – home on the Shakespearian range, in the saddle of great roles, an easy rider but a royal one. Of his three roles at Stratford, the least important was his first, Malvolio, but it gave him an opportunity for some brilliant comic invention, with thick, crinkly hair, a pointed nose, a prissy walk and the uncertain vowels of a social climber wavering through an odd nasal whine. This sour, ambitious and efficient ' Roundhead among Cavaliers ' seemed to some critics too detached from the rest of the play, a performance too conspicuously *voulu* in the engineering of its technical effects; to others it showed Olivier's gift of finding behind the accretions of theatrical tradition a new truth of character expressed in intensely vivid, intensely lived realistic detail. ' He is, very simply, Malvolio,' wrote J. C. Trewin. ' He takes us back to the man's past and makes us speculate about his future . . .'

That capacity to project a character's past in an instant was used, unforgettably, at the first appearance of Olivier's Macbeth, his next role in the 1955 Stratford programme. Taking up his stance on a stage rock – in an attitude evoking, unspecifically but thrillingly, old theatre prints of Kean and Macready – he stood silent, with arms folded, while Banquo questioned the witches. Motionless and waiting, he seemed to radiate a kind of brooding, sinister energy; and one had the curious feeling of glimpsing the black abysses in the man's mind before the play opened and of staying inside his mind as it went along. In a way he had been expecting the witches: this Macbeth had been living fearfully with bloody thoughts for a long time past. From then on Olivier was in full command of the full part, as no other contemporary actor seems to have been – unusually low-keyed and restrained in approach, but also unusually consistent and convincing in effect, uniting (more than most) the soldier, the poet and the hero-villain. He achieved this partly by reducing the emotional scale. Thus he took the soliloquies very quietly, although – as T. C. Worsley said – ' he made every syllable, every consonant and vowel do its maximum of work '. A whole underworld of menace and foreboding was conjured up in his speaking of

> Light thickens, and the crow
> Makes wing to the rooky wood.

The dagger was no surprise to him: he greeted it as if it were ' a fixture in the crooked furniture of his brain '. The scene after

Duncan's killing was played with a deliberate flatness and slowness, and Macbeth talked as if the murder was unreal. The action seemed to be presented not as a blood-and-thunder story, but as a nightmare seen by Macbeth himself – the nightmare of his own life, shared by the audience. Olivier, moreover, found fresh and unifying traits in Macbeth's personality, notably a persistent self-hatred and a pervading sense of doom, mirrored darkly in his wonderfully expressive eyes. 'From Inverness to Dunsinane the eyes are an index of the actor's thought.' In the banquet scene his agonies of apprehension were vividly projected, 'flaming across the darkness with terrifying power,' as *The Times* observed. At Banquo's second appearance he made a splendidly histrionic leap on to the table and advanced on the ghost, with a sweeping movement of his scarlet cloak, in a flourish that not only lit up the courage of the soldier but a chapter of theatrical history. In the last scene, at 'Lay on Macduff', he seemed, inexplicably, to grow; but he resisted the temptation of a death scene to which Garrick and others had yielded, and, faithful to the text, expired offstage. Among Olivier's admirers was Harold Hobson, who described him as making 'a superb leap upwards into glory' after the 'confident badness' of the opening scenes: 'I do not believe there is an actor in the world who can come near him.' J. C. Trewin acclaimed this as much the best Macbeth in our time, perhaps the best since Macready, and, with due caution, very near to great acting. In his second attempt on the role, Olivier had conquered.

Olivier's third Stratford role, as Titus Andronicus, was new not only to him but to nearly all other actors, for although one of the most popular plays of its time, it had, since then, been virtually ignored by the theatre, and Shakespeare's authorship was, until recently, widely questioned. This anthology of atrocities – including thirteen deaths, two mutilations, a rape and a cannibal banquet – was now presented at Stratford for the first time, ruthlessly edited and brilliantly directed by Peter Brook, who with Olivier's help turned a piece of Elizabethan Grand Guignol into one of the outstanding productions of the decade. Olivier began by presenting Titus as an old, grizzled, weary general, whose age, as Mr Worsley wrote, was 'visible in every line of the walk and the stance and the dropping chin'. Returning from yet another triumph on the battlefield, he delivered his

' Hail, Rome ' official speech with a perfunctory and almost ironic detachment. A blunt and tactless soldier, accustomed to a general's authority, he showed his quality by the cheery wave of the hand with which he motioned all the people to kneel when Saturninus was acclaimed emperor: he himself remained proudly standing, thereby adding fuel to the fire of Saturninus's hatred. From this detailed naturalism Olivier moved into a different mode of acting, when Titus's woes began to accumulate and his rant rose in intensity. What he did between the lines was, as often, superb: that moment, for instance, when Titus cut off his hand on-stage, and then, as Philip Hope-Wallace said, ' for an eternity of seconds withheld his howl of pain '. But what he did with the lines was often overwhelming. Speeches that seem mere fustian on the printed page came alive as great rhetoric; other passages seemed to prove beyond all question that Shakespeare was at least partly author of the play. With what Lear-like pathos, for instance, the actor spoke the lines beginning ' O, here I lift this one hand up to heaven '. This is one of the passages which, for Professor Dover Wilson (who has suggested that Shakespeare was writing a burlesque), provide ' most of the fun '; but at Stratford it seemed not ridiculous but sublime. How memorable, too, was Olivier's delivery of the words, ' I am the sea ', when he seemed to engulf the audience in his despairing grief; and his utter stillness, after this long passage of inspired rant, when Titus received the news of his remaining sons' deaths and his own betrayal. He leant against a pillar, head tilted backwards, his face a tragic mask of grinning whiteness, a suffering image of anti-quity. After a pause he said, ' When will this fearful slumber have an end ', with a breathtaking profundity of pathos and weary desperation. ' Now is a time to storm, why art thou still?' asked his brother; and Titus answered with an indescribably gentle, quavering, terrible laugh, a laugh ' all the more ghastly for the long pause that precedes it '. It was one of those moments in which the actor seems to plunge beyond words into the depths of human experience. ' One recognized, though one had never heard it before, the noise made in its last extremity by the cornered human soul,' wrote Kenneth Tynan. From then on you could see, as Philip Hope-Wallace said, a ' crescendo of vengeance taking hold of the body and the whole soul . . . the whole person was transformed '.

The Player Kings

Generally acclaimed as 'one of the great things of his career' (*The Times*), this performance was described by one admirer, Bernard Levin, as 'not so much on the heroic scale as on a new scale entirely, the greatness of which has smashed all our measuring-rods and pressure-gauges to smithereens'. Transcending a bad, bowdlerised play, surpassing the science of naturalism with the magic of theatricalism, Olivier demonstrated the freedoms which sub-standard Shakespeare and Elizabethan kitsch can give to a great actor, who commonly looks in vain to contemporary drama for such opportunities to show man at the end of his tether, in the extremity of agony or knowledge or bliss.

Two years later, however, Olivier found a rare opportunity to demonstrate his now greatly stretched powers in a new play, his best part yet in the contemporary drama: the part of Archie Rice in John Osborne's *The Entertainer*. The production opened in April at the Royal Court for a limited run, and after a gap of several months reappeared in September at the vast Palace, where, in spite of the contrast in size between the theatres, Olivier held the audience (even those who disliked the play) with a virtuoso performance as superb in its way as his Titus, with which he toured Europe that summer. In its freedom of form – variety-turns sandwiched between domestic scenes – *The Entertainer* gave him the chance of composing a realistic portrait with that care for detail in which he excels, and also of creating a symbol of something more, an outsize role, with a bright aureole of significance. Accepting the challenge, at fifty, of the song-dance-and-patter routine of the dying music hall, he was able to make direct contact with the audience of a kind commonly excluded by the modern drama, moving in and out of the conventions as a performer.

The surface detail of Archie Rice seemed definitive: the cheap grey suit, grey bowler and cane, bow-tie, mechanical wink, weary leer and seedy bounce; the slurred rasping voice, mixing Cockney and genteel, scraping the barrel for fake bonhomie and counterfeit randiness; the instinct for the wrong emphasis ('he acts bad acting and indifferent timing with an exactness that is in itself beautiful'). But behind the gin-swilling bravado and the falsity the actor suggested a crippling boredom and desolation: 'making the whites of his eyes gleam with a lost mad emptiness,' as *The Times* said, in challenging the audience with 'You don't think

I'm *real*, do you?', and telling them that he was 'dead behind the eyes'. Far from being dead, a frightened anguish welled up in the long hiss of pain and the hunted look with which Archie Rice greeted the news that his son had been killed in Cyprus; or in that despairing song which, Harold Hobson wrote, 'in a high and beautiful pain unites a sharp and savage irony with an almost unbearable pathos'. This masterly performance (later recreated in the cinema) was acting *about* acting, its shams and realities; it was the personification of a dying theatre and (less certainly) a dying society; but it was also the incarnation of one man's suffering and despair, nonetheless overwhelming in its theatrical truth because the man was a third-rate comic rather than a Shakespearian king.

Eighteen months later Olivier returned to classical kit with another major Shakespearian performance at Stratford, while filming *The Entertainer*. To Richard III, Macbeth and Titus he now added (at his second attempt) Coriolanus, among the roles he has made his own. With smouldering physical power, electrifying voice and penetrating theatrical intelligence in characterization, he brought this figure off its Roman plinth by emphasizing the over-mothered emotional immaturity of Caius Marcius – in his inability to accept praise, for example – and his soldierly loathing of civilian humbug and phoneyness. Here was not so much a monument to patrician pride as a passionate and prickly 'adult boy', a spoiled son seized by a boyish adulation of Aufidius and a boyish spite when the world does not behave like his mother. He won sympathy, and even laughter, by his sullen clowning refusal to play the democratic game and humble himself before the mob. And he cursed the plebeians – 'You common cry of curs' – with such ferocity that (to Alan Brien) every phrase seemed 'a jagged spear of frozen fury', and Laurence Kitchin had 'the bizarre impression of one man lynching a crowd'.

Here, to quote Kenneth Tynan, was 'all-round Olivier. We have the sagging head, the soaring index finger, and the sly, roaming eyes of one of the world's cleverest comic actors, plus the desperate exhausted moans of one of the world's masters of pathos. But we also confront the nonpareil of heroic tragedians, as athletically lissom as when he played Oedipus a dozen years ago.' And here, too, was the master of stage deaths:

At the close, faithful as ever to the characterization on which he has fixed, Olivier is roused to suicidal frenzy by Aufidius's gibe – ' thou boy of tears.' *'Boy!'* shrieks the overmothered general, in an outburst of strangled fury, and leaps up a flight of precipitous steps to vent his rage. Arrived at the top, he relents and throws his sword away. After letting his voice fly high in the great, swingeing line about how he ' flutter'd your Volscians in Cor-i-o-li ', he allows a dozen spears to impale him. He is poised now, on a promontory some twelve feet above the stage, from which he topples forward, to be caught by the ankles so that he dangles, inverted, like the slaughtered Mussolini. A more shocking, less sentimental death I have not seen in the theatre; it is at once proud and ignominious, as befits the titanic fool who dies it.

There was nothing quite like that in the contemporary plays with which Olivier opened the 1960s. In London, indeed, he appeared as ' the anti-hero of the anti-theatre ', to quote A. Alvarez's description of Berenger in Ionesco's confused and inflated parable, *Rhinoceros*. Berenger is an insignificant little-man figure who stays defiantly (but reluctantly) human when everyone else in town has turned into a rhino, and Olivier was praised for the ' rainbow of nuances ' which he produced, while hiding his light so thoroughly under a bushel. Others would have preferred to see the light. They would have had rather more opportunity to admire it in Anouilh's *Becket*, which Olivier played in the USA that autumn, not so much in the title role, perhaps, but later as Henry II, on whom he practised what Mr Tynan described as ' a major act of reinterpretation . . . the actor implied what the character never suspected, namely, that his attachment to Becket was homosexual '. Back in Britain in 1962 Olivier returned to modern dress and little men in David Turner's *Semi-Detached* as an insurance agent in the Midlands, Fred Midway: fast-talking, ruthlessly on the make, mean-souled and generally detestable. It was perhaps Olivier's most unpleasant, antipathetic role, with no redeeming charm or pathos; and although he was very keen on the play, the public failed to share his enthusiasm. Critics even disagreed about his technique: while J. C. Trewin thought Midway's voice ' a masterpiece ', Philip Hope-Wallace described it as a ' terrible amalgam ' of accents which rang ' completely false '.

It may have seemed that this major classical actor might, once again, be in danger of drifting down the swift currents of the entertainment industry towards those whirlpools of show business in which so many artists have disappeared. He did not drift for long. It was in the 1960s that Olivier at last, after thirteen years, found a permanent theatrical home, as actor, director and manager.

First of all, in 1961, while filming in the USA, Olivier was invited to direct the new Festival Theatre at Chichester, the first playhouse with an open stage to be built in Britain since Shakespeare's time. It was a bold venture, especially in a town with no continuing theatrical tradition, but Olivier rose to the bait of artistic experiment, turning his back on safer and richer jobs in show business. The first season opened in 1962 bravely but somewhat shakily with two rare seventeenth-century revivals, but with the third production, *Uncle Vanya* – in which Olivier (who once again played Astrov and directed all three plays) was joined by Dame Sybil Thorndike, Sir Lewis Casson, Michael Redgrave and Olivier's third wife, Joan Plowright, whom he married in 1961 – Chichester became an established success. In that year, moreover, a lifetime's ambition was crowned when Olivier was appointed as the first artistic director of the National Theatre; and in October 1963 (after another successful Chichester season) the new National company opened in his production of *Hamlet* at the Old Vic, its ' temporary ' home.

This is not the place to discuss in detail the merits and failings of the first six years of the National Theatre Company under Sir Laurence's direction. In a deliberately eclectic and empirical policy there have been disappointments and even disasters; the choice of plays and the handling of some classics has seemed, at times, wilfully eccentric and trendy; there is little sign of an *ensemble* in the making, yet sadly inadequate use has been made, for whatever reason, of Britain's leading actors, with such few shining exceptions as Redgrave in *Hamlet* and *Uncle Vanya*. On the other hand, the National has, so far, triumphantly avoided petrifying into a museum, a fate forecast by so many pessimists, while spanning a wide range of plays (including the work of several younger British writers); it has brought on a number of strong, versatile and still-developing players not far below the top; it has sponsored some striking stage-design and theatrical experiment; it has achieved definitive productions of plays both old and fairly recent; and it has done this under physical and financial handicaps in makeshift conditions. On balance, it may be said to have ridden out its first six years with some glory, for which (as for its failures) Sir Laurence must take the prime responsibility.

What concerns us here, however, is Olivier's self-employment as an actor. Othello, his giant single contribution to the National's achievement, has already been briefly described: it has been preserved (with the usual inevitable losses of resonance and superbity) in a film record of the production. For some people, however, his major performance in the 1960s was in Strindberg's *The Dance of Death*, as Captain Edgar, the retired soldier who has never given up fighting his wife through twenty-five years of mutual torture. As always he looked and sounded magnificently right in the role: close-cropped Prussian head, hooded stony eyes, aggressively jutting jaw, a choleric red face which went purple in his fits and seemed to blanch when he was on the point of doing something particularly nasty; Olivier's expertise in quick transitions was displayed in the sudden leap from a brutal bellow to a quiet, lethally polite enquiry, 'Have you ever been to Copenhagen?'; in the fever-chart progress through coarse barrack-room *bonhomie*, cutting arrogance, devilish glee, sly venom, parade-ground pomposity, blazing rage, ferocious hatred and sudden awesome candour, punctuated by abrupt seizures and instant resurrections. There was, as so often in this actor's work, a sardonic underscore of comedy, blended with menace. Among the peak moments were those of Olivier in action, incarnating Strindberg's character without words: the grisly, clumsy little Hungarian dance, in which he seemed both dangerous and funny, and the grunting Dionysiac violence with which he stamped on his hated wife's photograph, tore up her letters and shot at her piano. Here was a brutal, vicious, vulgar, neurotic beast, yet Olivier fused all the apparent implausibilities of what on paper seems a Grand Guignol caricature into the portrait of a man for whom, at the end, one could not help but feel compassion, because he was, in fact, not a monster but a man, blazingly alive.

In his second version of Astrov, for his own near-perfect production of *Uncle Vanya* (brought from Chichester into the National's repertoire for a year), Olivier achieved the complete success that had eluded him in 1945. The doctor's earlier elegance and wit was now, more credibly, subtly coarsened, there was a vulgarity in his bounce, and the soft centre showed behind his charm. But no conspicuous or irrelevant detail, no demonstration of theatrical ingenuity – such as, for instance, a Chekhov-like make-up – was allowed to distract the audience's attention from the reality of this bearded, weary, disillusioned provincial idealist; or, more significantly, from the reality of the other characters in the play. Although Olivier has sometimes overshadowed his company, in effect if not by design, in other National productions, here he kept himself firmly in his place as a member of his unusually starry team. Astrov, almost flawlessly in the round, was indivisible from the world of the play, in which an *ensemble* of rare unity was attained. Acclaiming Redgrave and Olivier, B. A. Young wrote of ' such stunning magnificence that they hardly seem to be *acting*: they are *being*, they *are* Vanya and Astrov. The quality of spontaneity they inject into every movement, every motion, is astonishing.' And Olivier won high hosannas from Philip Hope-Wallace, who described Astrov as ' the very best of his realistic performances and a pitch of perfection which to see once, let alone twice in a lifetime is a reward for which it would be worth going round the world '. Like nearly all productions in the contemporary British theatre, *Uncle Vanya* had, for all its excellence, a short life of less than two years, from season to season. Its dissolution was a particularly sharp reminder of the waste and ephemerality that seems, even now, to be unavoidable on the stage.

Olivier's fourth major part for the National was Solness, which he took over in 1964. Compared with Redgrave's master builder he seemed to lack poetic insight and power: he was less plausibly worried, in his confident bluster, about the rising generation. But his performance bristled, as ever, with realistic detail – in, for instance, the way that Solness lit a cigarette for himself, and not for the visiting doctor – stressing all the everyday human minutiae that could be coaxed out of this craggy role. There was a wealth of studied detail, too, in three small comic parts during the 1960s – Tattle, the mincing gossip in Congreve's *Love for Love;* Etienne, the waiter in Feydeau's farce *A Flea in her Ear;* and, most of all, Captain Brazen in Farquhar's *The Recruiting Officer,* one of the National's most successful productions. This heavy-eyed, red-nosed, lecherous, boozy soldier, a serenely self-

important and absurd fantastic, was a wonderfully funny miniature of controlled flamboyance, right from his first, wordless
appearance – 'a subliminal entrance lasting a split second which
perfectly forecasts the whole of his performance,' wrote Philip
Hope-Wallace. Olivier did not, for all his brilliance, obscure the
rest of the company; although perhaps no production could hope
to stay in balance without other stars (as in *Uncle Vanya*) to
weight the scales.

His 1970 Shylock suffered to some extent from the implausibilities of the 1890s setting in Jonathan Miller's ingenious *Merchant of Venice*: it was hard to believe that, in an age when
Jewish merchant-bankers were pillars of international capitalism
and confidants of the ruling class, this top-hatted, frock-coated
contemporary of Rothschild would have been spat at by so stately
a City gent as Antonio. Yet in spite of that obstacle Olivier
demonstrated once again the abyss that separates good acting
from great acting, even when a great actor is below his summit.
Here was a meticulously worked-out portrait, too conspicuously
studied for some dissenters, of an outsider in the livery of a class
which he despised yet scrabbled to join, straining for old-boy
bonhomie with the wrong kind of joke (at which he laughed,
mirthlessly, himself) and the wrong kind of accent (self-con-
sciously dropping his final g's in search of upper-class gentility).
The detail showed (for those who looked) in those not quite
immaculate, almost baggy trousers, or in the slightly projecting
upper set of teeth which helped him to look both fawning when
he smiled and predatory in repose. This Shylock was crude, immensely unlikeable, and dangerous: not so much in the purple-
faced ferocity of his rages, but in the quiet implacability of his
hatred at the trial and the grim, clumsy jolliness of the sudden
comic dance with which he celebrated the news of Antonio's
losses (reminiscent of his mazurka in *The Dance of Death*, but
none the less right for all that). Yet the badge of sufferance was
real enough; and the centuries-old feeling behind it welled up in
the howl of pain and grief heard off-stage after the broken
Shylock had stumbled from the court-room – a sound of agony
that ranked with Olivier's wordless best.

What next? Olivier has talked, at times, of returning to Lear;
now that he has almost exhausted the big roles of the standard
repertoire he may explore new ones outside it, as he did with

Titus, or take up more minor parts such as Brazen and Tattle; although so few dramatists have risen to the challenge of his talent, there may yet be a new character on the horizon to match Archie Rice. Olivier has already passed the age at which many classic actors of the past left the stage. As he has said, ' Great parts are cannibals. It is a dangerous game.' Perhaps, Felix Barker has suggested, he is waiting to make his own farewell to the stage as Prospero, one of the few roles he has not yet played. But the staff is not yet broken, the game is not over: it is too early to sum up the results.

It is in the cinema, of course, that Laurence Olivier is known to millions now, and will be known to millions more, who have not seen him and never will see him on the stage. Since he began his film career forty years ago, he has made many successful appearances in his progress through the casting generations from juvenile lead to character-bit star. Most of these films are irrelevant to a survey of great acting; and although the screen versions of four Shakespearian productions have, to some degree, preserved for posterity a record of his work – this is not the place to discuss their merits in opening up the cinema to Shakespeare, and opening up Shakespeare to a vast new public – the record is inevitably (as I have suggested) blurred, weakened and distorted. Without a theatre, without a living audience, those performances, adjusted to fit the needs and demands of the cinema, may gain in some particular (in the revelations of close-up and the illustrations of the context), but they have lost that essential something which made people watching them, in the flesh, call them great. Hamlet was not one of Olivier's great roles, and that film, in particular, would give little idea to a visitor from Garrick's London as to why we should rank its hero with the best of all British actors. Beyond that, Olivier's film career is not discussed here; nor do we propose to survey his directing, either in the cinema (*Henry V, Hamlet, Richard III, The Prince and the Showgirl*) or the theatre (a score of productions since 1935, notably at the National, include *The Skin of our Teeth, King Lear, Born Yesterday, Antigone, Venus Observed, Uncle Vanya, The Crucible, The Three Sisters*). In recent years Olivier has concentrated increasingly upon directing. Yet although he has, like Gielgud, sometimes said that he finds it more satisfying than acting, and

although he has some outstanding productions to his credit –
above all, perhaps, *Uncle Vanya* – it has (compared with Sir
John) occupied a less important place in his career and in his
main contribution to the theatre. It is with his stage acting that
we are concerned here. Most of its qualities have already been
listed on pages 205-6, and indicated during the preceding summary. What are the debits?

Olivier has been accused of infusing humour where it is out
of character or outside the text (Agate described him in 1946 as
' a comedian by instinct and a tragedian by art ', although this
distinction, if ever valid, has been obliterated by his later work).
He has, people say, shrunk such figures as Macbeth and Lear to
bring them within his range, vocally and physically; he has been
too acrobatic, too tricky, too apt to decorate a performance with
physical detail; he has dominated the part at the expense of the
whole (and the other parts); he has skimped poetry in favour of
theatrical effect; he lacks the meticulous music and textual
authority of Gielgud; he anthologizes in performance, mixing the
mannerisms of his outstanding roles; he concentrates on the out-
sides of his characters, and neglects their inner lives; he has, in
the last few years, lost some of the subtlety of his middle period.
True? Well, partly.

For Olivier, it has certainly been, in his words, ' Realism first,
beauty second ': or, perhaps one might say, character first, music
second. He has searched for and usually found physical truths
which, in his best performances, light up not only external details
but the whole man: enough of the man to be seen, with the rest
felt, just out of sight but imminent. To him what characters are
has seemed of more importance than what they say: he can speak
Shakespearian poetry with magnificence, as we have seen, but
not all the lines are equally respected or even heard. His comedy
appears to spring out of his own nature, and it helps him to make
characters ' natural '. His acrobatic energy – like his dominating presence – is part of that physicality which has distinguished
him since he first reminded critics of Fairbanks and Barrymore
in the 1930s, and which he has carefully maintained through the
years by training and exercise. Just as Olivier worked through the
decades on his voice, strengthening it, deepening it, expanding it,
so he built up his bodily strength and stamina. It did not come
naturally: like many of the other qualities which make up a

great actor, it had to be developed as part of his craft and his mystery. (Olivier was, he says, 'miserably thin' well into his career, and he was nearly forty before he dared to appear in tights without padding.) If he has seemed, in Alan Brien's words, ' born for action, bred for speed ', it is because he has kept himself in training.

Interviewed on the BBC in 1969, Gielgud summed up that physical foundation of Olivier's success in a characteristic way, recalling his 1935 Romeo:

> I remember Ralph Richardson saying to me, ' When he stands under the balcony you know the whole character of Romeo in a moment because the pose he takes is so natural, so light, so animally correct, that you just feel the whole quality of Italy and of the character of Romeo and of Shakespeare's impulse.' That is an extraordinarily true criticism of his performance, and everything he does is based on that assumption: it gives him enormous power to be able to make his body obey him so well that he can almost characterize straight away.

It is worth recalling here the words of the American critic, Stark Young, in *Theatre Practice* (1926):

> One of the first tests of an actor's talents is in the identity of his body and his mind. Not the actor's voice, not his brain, are the parts of him by which he becames a medium for his art; it is his whole make-up, body, brain and voice; it is the man you see before you on the stage. In fine acting the words and the body are at supreme moments inseparably one, and they can be said to be interchangeable in meaning and significance . . . the idea that moves within becomes one with the outward form.

How to sum up the unfinished? By quoting Sir Laurence's own words, in conversation with Kenneth Tynan on television in 1966, about the two things that are, he said, ' absolutely necessary to an actor. One is confidence, absolute confidence, and the other is an equal amount of humility towards the work. That's a very hard equation.' It is an equation in which he has triumphed, repeatedly, where other great talents have failed.

✠✠✠9✠✠✠

Sir Michael Redgrave

At twenty-six John Gielgud was established, after nine years in the theatre, as the leading Shakespearian actor of his generation; at twenty-six Laurence Olivier, with eight years' experience, had made a name in the West End and on Broadway, and was playing romantic leading roles in Hollywood; it was not until the same age that Michael Redgrave made his first appearance on the professional stage. Generations of actors on both sides of the family tree helped, perhaps, to seed his flowering. Greasepaint in the blood showed at an early age. Within only two years of his début he was, in his turn, at the Old Vic, and was soon tipped for stardom. But it took nearly twenty years more to realize his full power; and even now, no doubt, his place in this book will be questioned by readers who may not have seen him realize it. Redgrave's very success, in the cinema and on the stage, was a check to the kind of progress with which we are here concerned. Although, like Olivier, he has used films, in which he has worked for four decades, to subsidize his stage career, they have used him more often and more conspicuously; and this professional dualism – bringing both penalties and rewards unknown to a Kemble or an Irving – has, like the belated start at twenty-six, retarded the growth and broken the continuity of his work in the theatre.

Yet this slow maturing behind the almost instant success is a striking reminder of an unpalatable theatrical maxim. In an age of mushroom reputations on the stage, the cinema and television screens, when the showbiz landscape is littered annually with the obsolete star-models of the year before last, little attention is paid to the adage that it takes twenty years to make an actor. Michael Redgrave's career to date is an illuminating commentary not only on that truth but also on the complexities of a contemporary player's development, a mirror of some central problems in theatrical art and organization.

Michael Scudamore Redgrave (knighted 1959) is six foot three inches tall, above the average acting height, a fact which has had a marked influence on his career in the entertaiment industry. Blue-eyed, brown-haired, with Nordic good looks that have weathered uncommonly well, he looks offstage, in public, like a gentle patrician born to give orders and never to make a scene: it is not surprising that much of his film career has been spent in uniform as a high-ranking officer. But his background is far from being conventionally upper-class, and his easy charm masks an acting self which has shown a special skill in presenting haunted and divided men on the edge of breakdown and madness.

He was born on 20 March 1908 in theatrical digs in Bristol, where his mother, Margaret Scudamore, had arrived on tour. His actor-father, Roy Redgrave, who was then working in London, left for Australia a few weeks later in a touring company. His wife and son caught up with him down under, where Michael Redgrave first appeared on the stage, at the age of two, in his father's arms. But when he was three his parents split up, he sailed back to England with his mother, and he never saw his father again. (A broken home, or the early loss of a parent, seems to be a recurrent factor in the childhood of actors.) Back in England he grew up in the backstage nursery of the old touring theatre, with no settled family life and an interrupted education; but when his mother married again the nine-year-old boy moved suddenly into a different social world, achieving a new financial, but not emotional, security. His stepfather undertook to send him to public school and university, on the tacit understanding that he would never become an actor. The prohibition was urged by Redgrave's mother and endorsed by him. He had other ambitions, and had already seen too much of the business to be stage-struck. He acted throughout his schooldays at Clifton (notably as Lady Macbeth), and made his début on the professional stage at thirteen when he walked on at Stratford in *Henry IV Part 2* (his mother was in the company). But acting, like music, was only a secondary hobby for him: he was determined to be a writer. During his four years at Cambridge he made a university name for himself as a poet and editor; and although he also distinguished himself with the ADC and the Marlowe Society (his Edgar in *King Lear* won high praise from London critics in 1929) he still had no intention of becoming an actor when he left Magdalene in 1931. For one thing, he was convinced that he was too tall.

Instead of going into the theatre, Redgrave went to a Surrey public school, Cranleigh, as a teacher of modern languages and stayed there for three years. During this time, however, he was allowed to carry out a theatrical self-education of a rare kind. Encouraged by the headmaster (who had been his chaplain at Clifton) he staged a series of school plays – *As You Like It, Samson Agonistes, Hamlet, The Tempest, King Lear* – in which he was director, manager, designer and leading actor, not much hampered by considerations of time, expense and temperament, with a guaranteed audience and a malleable cast. These Cranleigh plays – 'an exhilarating break in the tradition of school dramatics', said *The Times* – attracted an unusual amount of notice among critics and scholars. At *Lear,* for instance, Wilson Knight praised the profound understanding of the production ('I have seldom, if ever, known more poignant moments in a theatre') and J. Dover Wilson described Redgrave's King as 'unimaginably beautiful, a lifelong possession'. By this time Redgrave had decided to go on the stage – as a director. He was influenced not only by tasting his own power in these school productions, but also (like Gielgud) by the example of the Compagnie des Quinze.

After persistent lobbying Redgrave was given an audition at the Old Vic and was offered a small-part contract for the 1934-5 season. But instead he went to the Liverpool Repertory Company, using the London offer as a weapon. He knew that he needed experience in the bread-and-butter drama under orders, and there were few places better suited to his further education than the Liverpool Playhouse, which enjoyed a three-weekly change of bill, a continuity of direction (William Armstrong had been in charge for the past twelve years) and a record of prosperity which were all then virtually unique. In a surprisingly short time this novice on the professional stage, who until now had chosen his own roles and directed his own acting twice a year, established himself as one of the company's leading men, rehearsing all day and playing at night for some forty weeks a year. During his two seasons at the old playhouse in Williamson Square, Redgrave played twenty-seven roles, most of them in modern dress from the theatre of comfort; wrote two plays; and found a wife, Rachel Kempson, who had made her stage début as Juliet two years earlier at Stratford. Thirty years later their remarkable family all emerged as successful young players – Corin, Lynn, and Vanessa, herself ranked by some critics as a great actress in the making.

At the end of Redgrave's second season both he and his wife were asked by Tyrone Guthrie to join the Old Vic. Redgrave's roles were relatively secondary – the King of Navarre in *Love's Labour's Lost,* Mr Horner in *The Country Wife,* Laertes and Orlando – but he gained a deal of primary experience, not least from his forty-eight-year-old Rosalind, Edith Evans, who helped him from her own great artistry to understand his new acting self and its problems, both technical and psychological. Critical bouquets for his Laertes – 'an ideal performance', said Raymond Mortimer – included the tribute that with 'a voice that could not be bettered . . . he has an unusually wide emotional range for an English actor, and is therefore a useful acquisition to the Vic.' As Orlando he was acclaimed as one of the white hopes of the English stage – 'he . . . has the power to speak verse, and also – which is rare these days – knows how to wear costume and still look a man,' one critic observed alarmingly – but it was as a juvenile lead and a romantic personality actor that Redgrave was welcomed by the press. There was, as yet, no sign of the classic *comédien.*

Redgrave's stay at the Old Vic was unusually brief, for after five months he went with *As You Like It* into the West End (under Bronson Albery's banner) for a short run. Three mediocre West End parts followed, with a short stint in the Waterloo Road to replace the Chorus in *Henry V.* But he did not have to mark time for long.

That spring of 1937 Redgrave made a discovery of decisive importance: he read Stanislavsky's *An Actor Prepares.* At twenty-nine, with less than three years on the stage, he had considerable leeway to make up. Lacking any grounding in the cliché and trickwork so often identified with acting 'style', he did the right thing by instinct – but he wanted to know how and why. He found that he had the power, rare among novices, to

The Player Kings

' hold ' a characterization, but he was dissatisfied by the way in which he was expected to relate to the part. He wanted guidance, in first and last things, the knowledge that could only come from acting experience – and in *An Actor Prepares* he found a storehouse of such experience, concentrated and analysed by a great artist with the authority of many years in a permanent company. Redgrave had read about the Russian director and his ' system ' since Cranleigh days, in *Theatre Arts*. Now that he studied it for himself many of his immediate problems were on the way to being answered. He was helped not only to compensate for his belated start in the profession and to escape from the inhibitions of an English middle-class education but also to hold the mirror up to nature more closely in modern-dress parts and to cut his way through to the great classic roles.

In the autumn another door opened for Redgrave, thanks to John Gielgud, who, on the strength of his Orlando, engaged him for his starry team in his season at the Queen's. As Bolingbroke in *Richard II,* a beefish soldier with a conscience, as Charles Surface and as Tusenbach in *The Three Sisters* – pimply-faced, sentimental, dithering and doomed – he was suddenly recognized as a character actor of rare distinction. In Chekhov he had the stimulating experience of direction by Michel St Denis, another major influence on his career. As the Baron, said one critic, Redgrave's very bones seemed to shape themselves differently and his physical habits adapted themselves to the character's mental habits. The Stanislavsky system appeared to be working well, applied by a master director. With the rest of that brilliant *ensemble* the ex-schoolmaster reached the heights: he had seen his dream of an English Compagnie des Quinze coming true, and he was in the dream. Yet he asked to leave the company before the season's end, giving up his role of Bassanio in *The Merchant of Venice* to take up a temptingly lucrative five-year film contract – a decision which he later regretted as disloyalty.

Redgrave came back to the stage in the autumn of 1938 to join a new venture launched by St Denis, in partnership with Bronson Albery. St Denis sanguinely proposed an ambitious programme at the Phoenix with a ' permanent ' company under his own direction, supplemented by the more promising graduates of the London Theatre Studio which he had set up in 1936. He was aiming high, at the English version of his own Compagnie des

Quinze which Gielgud's season at the Queen's had prefigured, and he had hoped to reunite many of that team at the Phoenix, with Olivier, Richardson and Edith Evans: a company of all the talents. But the French director underestimated both the temperamental and the economic difficulties, while he overrated the readiness of a London audience for what he had to offer. After a few months the scheme collapsed, though not before Redgrave – who shared the main acting honours with Peggy Ashcroft – had won plaudits in two sharply contrasted roles: as a stiff-backed, tender-hearted, neo-Chekhovian officer in a play about the Russian Civil War, *The White Guard,* and as a witty, wily, deliberately self-fantasticating Aguecheek in *Twelfth Night* ('a magnificent piece of clowning,' said Agate, although he disapproved of the reading.) Within a year St Denis was swallowed up in the war, leaving a flock of disciples in search of a leader.

' I want to go on experimenting and learning, playing character parts as often as "straight", gradually growing to the size of the big parts,' Redgrave told a reporter in 1938. After the breakdown of the Phoenix season, he was given a prestigious but perilous opportunity in T. S. Eliot's *The Family Reunion,* as that upper-class English Orestes, Lord Monchensey. Ashley Dukes suggested that Redgrave faced ' perhaps the hardest task that any young actor has set himself in our generation. For not only is the play a modern verse-drama, requiring to be spoken with a tonal expression completely foreign to the uses of our stage but his part is as urgent as Hamlet's in its questioning of all values in life and eternity . . .' The questioning of the theatrical values proved particularly intractable, for the actor had to cope with Eliot's camouflaged poetry – breaking from semi-naturalist conversation into public soliloquy – and the shadowy characterization of a tragic hero in modern dress haunted by the Eumenides. Although Redgrave won favourable notices from many critics, he felt that his failure to present Monchensey's aura of suffering right at the first entrance showed that he was still only a *serious* and not a *tragic* actor.

Later that year Redgrave was asked to rejoin the Old Vic, after making two films, for the second part of the 1939-40 season. He was to play Richard II, Uncle Vanya and either Romeo or Macbeth. It could have occupied in his career the role of the 1929-30 season in Gielgud's development. But war broke out, and it was ten years before he played again in classic repertory. In retrospect Redgrave believes that the collapse of the Old Vic plan was for the best, because he wasn't ready for it and would not have lived up to his 'exaggerated critical reputation'. He had, moreover, a relatively comfortable war: his Navy service was short, he continued to star in British films and he scored individual successes on the London stage. Yet his progress towards the heights was inevitably deflected by that vast hiatus which the war opened up in everyone's work and life. Great plays breed great acting, and although the war years gave Redgrave time to 'grow to the size of the big classic parts', his opportunities on the stage were haphazard and disconnected. Instead of consolidating his experience in a classic repertory or a coherent group he acted in the theatre when he could find the time, the part and the play. In the next decade he played ten roles on the stage and sixteen in the cinema.

Most of his stage roles were in new plays, but in 1940 Redgrave appeared with romantic dash as the singing high-wayman, Captain Macheath, in *The Beggar's Opera*. This represented another milestone in his development, because a Hungarian coach from Glyndebourne, Jani Strasser, taught him diaphragm breathing and so helped him to extend his range and reinforce his power, gaining strength and stamina for verse-speaking when the chance came again. In the same year he made a personal hit in Robert Ardrey's *Thunder Rock* as a disillusioned writer who regains his faith in humanity and progress after talking to the ghosts of nineteenth-century immigrants. When Redgrave returned to the stage two years later, after four films and a brief career as an Ordinary Seaman, it was as a director, realizing his old ambition for the first time since Cranleigh in 1934. His inaugural production was a short-lived naval drama, *Lifeline*, and he then directed Patrick Hamilton's *The Duke in Darkness*, a play of more significance but not much better luck. Redgrave had not intended to act in it, but in solving an emergency casting problem he gave an outstanding performance as Gribaud, the dangerously unreliable servant of a medieval duke planning to escape from fifteen years of captivity in the castle of his bitter enemy. The actor who in *The Family Reunion* had been described by a dissenting critic as 'too healthy to be hag-ridden' appeared memorably here as a hysterical neurotic on the edge of lunacy, whose reason crumbled visibly into nameless horrors. Redgrave explored at high tension the dark underside of the personality, learning the way to embody the greater terrors of Macbeth. But he did not have time to explore it for long. The play – over which the critics split – came off in a few weeks, and he was not seen in the role again.

He stayed for a while in the theatre, however, and his next role, two months later, was one to which he has returned several times as actor and director: Rakitin in Turgenev's *A Month in the Country*, which turned out to be a box-office success. In Stanislavsky's own role – ' Rakitin can never be fully credible to an Englishman,' observed *The Stage*, dismayed at this resident lover of four years' unrequited experience who is content with adultery in thought alone – Redgrave was faced with very different problems from those presented by Gribaud. After a study in hysterical abandon, he produced a study of rigid self-control – too rigid, indeed, for many London critics. Thus, although Desmond MacCarthy paid tribute to the performance as ' intelligently tender, sadly ironical and beautifully considerate – just what he should be ', he complained that there were moments when Rakitin ought to *lose* self-control. But high praise also came from Alan Dent, who commented that he could now see why Stanislavsky chose this unshowy part instead of the apparently more rewarding role of the doctor. Redgrave was, he wrote, ' at once still and turbulent, like a deep brook whose channel is too narrow for its content. His is a performance of great tact and technical adroitness, full of passion kept icily under control.'

In the same year Redgrave directed two more plays: Peter Ustinov's *Blow Your Own Trumpet* and Maxwell Anderson's *The Wingless Victory*. Both – like *The Duke in Darkness* – were ambitious attempts to break away from the clichés of naturalism in form and language. Both were also flops. His next production, *Uncle Harry*, was far less ambitious but far more successful. It ran for a year, and it gave Redgrave the material for one of his best performances, greeted with unanimous hosannas from the press. With the help of Stanislavsky he took the opportunity in the title role for a remarkably convincing transformation of his stage personality in minute, truthful detail, as a neurotic bachelor who secretly poisons one of his dominating sisters, pins the blame on to the other, and is later haunted by his guilt. Critics praised

' the sickly-sad voice, the gestures, gait, and glances of the evil weakling, and the little physical hints of a cunning which appals by its artless humility ', with ' marvellously handled ' spectacles, ' ghastly sympathy-provoking smiles, and winning intonations '. This ' subtle exposure of moral cowardice ', a kind of realistic Grand Guignol, was perhaps Redgrave's most complete success on the stage in a decade.

After another West End flop – as an aristocratic Polish refugee in his own production of S. N. Behrman's Broadway hit, *Jacobowsky and the Colonel* – Redgrave was out of the theatre for over two years: another break in his development as an artist. He was busy making films in England and Hollywood, with one outstanding role as Eugene O'Neill's nineteenth-century Orestes, Orin Mannon, in *Mourning Becomes Electra*. An indication of his market value at that time is that Rank agreed to give him £20,000 to £25,000 a picture, and the right of veto over scripts, compared with the £300-£400 a week that he might earn in the West End or the £50 a week at Stratford or the Old Vic. The money was plainly tempting, but he embarked on this intensive filming partly to strengthen his position in the theatre, looking forward to classic acting in the kind of *ensemble* that had been so briefly established before the war and which Gielgud and Olivier, in their different ways, approached in 1944-5. He has found it once only to date.

When Redgrave came back to the stage in December 1947 it was in one of the great roles that he had nearly played in the Waterloo Road eight years earlier. But it was not for the Old Vic or for an experimental *ensemble* that he now took up the challenge of Macbeth. He was invited to play it in the West End by Hugh Beaumont (who had offered him a job while he was still at Liverpool). Beaumont also asked Redgrave to direct the play, but the actor chose an independent director, Norris Houghton, an American student of the Stanislavsky system at work in Russia. As often in Redgrave's career, the performance and the production split the critics. *The Times* dismissed the cast as ' not particularly serviceable ', but T. C. Worsley praised them for playing as a group, ' subordinated to the overriding pressure of an idea which they appear to share, an idea of the play as a whole '. It was for his ' subordination ' of virtuoso technique that Mr Worsley admired Redgrave's Macbeth. Others, who wanted more insubordination, agreed that the actor was defeated by his own theories. In order to achieve the soldierly realism which had so often eluded earlier Macbeths he roughened his voice, and flattened the verse; and although he achieved an unusual degree of psychological consistency he sacrificed too much of the poetry, the terror and the tragic emotion on the altar of Stanislavsky. Yet in the final scenes at Dunsinane, when actors so often collapse, Redgrave triumphed. ' I have never known any Macbeth begin worse or finish better,' said Alan Dent. Philip Hope-Wallace wrote that he ' suddenly leaps into the vividest life and instead of the usual staggering hoarse death-rattle, gives us a cuttingly clear and painful picture of a great soul going down to perdition . . . Does that make a " great Macbeth "? Some of it anyway.'

In spite of the mixed notices *Macbeth* ran in the West End, and even made a profit. When Redgrave took it to New York after three months' run (with a new Lady Macbeth, Flora Robson) critical opinion was again divided. Among the objectors was George Jean Nathan, who described Redgrave's Macbeth as ' a circus side-show wild man ', while the most notable of this Macbeth's champions was Brooks Atkinson: ' No one else in the contemporary theatre has drawn so much horror and ferocity out of it.' Joseph Wood Krutch argued that Redgrave was at his best when he played scenes down ' almost to the naturalistic level ', and that in making a neurotic demand for absolute security virtually the central fact of Macbeth's personality he had ' humanized ' the character in a new way.

Although Redgrave's first attempt at the Shakespearian heights on the professional stage missed complete success, it taught him valuable lessons. Redgrave and Houghton set out with the high ambition of creating an *ensemble* united in a common aim, but they underrated the common West End difficulties of fusing a company together in four weeks' rehearsal and six weeks on tour with an inexperienced director; and also of staging the result in an unsuitable theatre, because by the luck of the London draw it was the only one that happened to be available. They put, moreover, an exaggerated value on psychology. In his search for plausible consistency Redgrave distorted his own potential and the full Shakespearian character. He was too much under Stanislavsky's influence to realize the theatrical needs of Shakespeare's impressionism: ' I was trying to rationalize and understand Macbeth, instead of just presenting him.' This was, perhaps, an inevitable mistake; having made it, and – several years later – having understood *why* he made it, Redgrave was able to close one chapter in his acting life and to begin the next with greater range and fuller power.

Initially, however, the reception of his Macbeth was a sharp check to Redgrave. It seemed like a signpost pointing back to the film studios. This was followed, moreover, by another only half-successful assault on a big part: the Captain in Strindberg's *The Father*. As this monster of misogyny badgered into madness he continued the exploration of pathology for which he had by now made a name on both screen and stage. Until the last-act climax of violence he gave a performance of impeccable skill, showing the weakness of the lonely neurotic behind the Captain's sham virility: but although the fuse was laid with immense care the final explosion went off at half-cock. Redgrave won high praise, but he had not scored a complete success. He was now forty, and in spite of his glittering start twelve years earlier his staccato stage career had not flowered with the full bloom of a Gielgud or an Olivier. Candid friends advised retreat to the wealth and security of the film studios. But for Redgrave films had mainly been a means to an end – the dazzling Alps of the actor's art, which could be scaled only in the living theatre; and he had climbed too far to turn back. Although he did not realize it at the time, the summit was in sight.

In 1949 Redgrave was asked, once again, to join the Old Vic. The programme had already been largely chosen, and it offered no major challenges: but Redgrave knew it was high time for him to work in classic repertory again, and he agreed to return to the Vic (temporarily housed at the New) on condition that *Hamlet* was included. It was, with memorable results.

After opening the season in *Love's Labour's Lost* with a zestful, sunny and strongly characterized Berowne, Redgrave appeared as Young Marlow in *She Stoops to Conquer* and so destroyed something of a theatrical myth, in which he himself had almost come to believe. Six years earlier, in the course of a spirited correspondence, James Agate had instructed him that he must never, on any account, attempt to play comedy: Young Marlow, for instance, was quite outside his range. Forgetting the early Aguecheek, it had become one of Agate's settled convictions that (like Gielgud) Redgrave was, as an actor, devoid of humour; and this conviction was shared by others who, in the past decade, had seen him habitually earnest or close to madness. If Agate had been alive, Redgrave said, he would probably not have dared to play Young Marlow, but he did so now with signal success. In a performance which *The Times* described as ' accurately pitched and beautifully staged on the note of high comedy ', he presented a character who was romantic, likeable, deliciously funny and still in period. Part of the comic effect came from Marlow's subtly timed stutter on the letter ' m ' (justified by his reference to ' this stammer in my address '). ' While scarcely a sound escapes his lips,' wrote Harold Hobson, ' he manages to suggest that an earthquake is shaking him inside, without for a moment disturbing the sartorial splendour of his appearance.' Yet it was not only on such a device, however justified, that Redgrave depended for his victory over the ghost of James Agate. He showed that he was a comedian as well as a *comédien*. And then, after a second Rakitin – subtler but chillier and less popular than his romantic 1943 portrait – it was time for Redgrave's Hamlet, in which he made his London début a few weeks before his forty-second birthday.

At his first entrance Redgrave set the key of bitter, filial sorrow with such immediate effect that – as it seemed to Harold Hobson – ' a single glance at Mr Redgrave, the first sad sound of his hopeless voice, made meaningless the teasing puzzle of why Hamlet found such difficulty in killing Claudius. Before the curtain rose, this Hamlet's will was paralysed by sorrow . . .' The intensity of the Prince's love for the dead king rang out on the battlements in the heart-broken cry of ' Father! ' to the unresponsive Ghost. The revelation of Claudius's crime convulsed Hamlet with a violent hysteria that was, for most critics, too epileptic to be apt. But once his grief was overcome, ' the desperate inaction of a man appalled ' was succeeded by a clear acceptance of the way ahead; for this Hamlet, as Hobson said, seemed to be ' a man who spiritually grows '. After the crucial scene with his mother, where he behaved with an angry tenderness free from any Freudian readings, and the killing of Polonius (' his shocked misery at the sight of the body . . . with all to do again and every nerve to be summoned up once more, was a terrible thing to see ') he showed the hard-won inner serenity of a man at peace with himself, a self-mastery sustained to the last. This Hamlet was no vacillating, introspective dreamer, but the true son of a king, a formidable enemy to Claudius, a man born to command who would, indeed, have proved most royally had he been put on. Redgrave played down not only Hamlet's indecision but his cruelty and the intensity of his love (as often represented) for both the Queen and Ophelia; and he showed a sweetness of temper in ' princely unbending ' towards the grave-digger and the players (in which he was said to equal Forbes-Robertson).

To many people, as to T. C. Worsley, it seemed that Redgrave's prime virtue was his ' absolute mastery of the vocal line. He is beautifully sensitive to the words as poetry and gives us, from the very start, the assurance that he will value at its full worth every nuance of every phrase, every supporting syllable of the whole poetic structure. And he keeps his word. It is an exemplary performance as a piece of verse-speaking, without tricks, mannerisms or affectations, but immensely various, always absolutely true, always perfectly in tune.' He never forgot that the great soliloquies and the prose were all part of the dramatic action; he spared the audience both the reciting voice and the naturalist gabble; and he gave the sense, time and again, of discovering the words for the first time as a man thinking aloud.

There was a change in Redgrave's acting noted by Worsley:

In the past few years we have sometimes felt that his feelings were not coming out as clean as they should. His laughter seemed too distorted: grief, when he wanted to express it, remained half-strangled in his throat. But now his acting is almost entirely free from these constrictions. He moves with a new grace and certainty. His voice, musical and flexible, has discovered in itself a new richness.

The change was not generally observed on the first night; for some critics then, while praising the virtues of the performance, complained that it failed to take fire. Yet even by the second night it was ablaze; and the critic of *The Times*, seeing Redgrave some months later when he appeared at Elsinore, remarked on ' the wonderful difference . . . between a part which had been carefully thought out but not completely felt and a part with

which the actor's self has been securely identified.' The fact
is that, like Gielgud, Redgrave is a notoriously slow starter. He
can seldom give of his best when he ' opens cold ' (as with this
production), and his performances grow and deepen as the run
of a play proceeds. The structure is, of course, unchanged, but
the ' flesh and the nerve ' may, as he has said, be transformed
within ' a very narrow margin '.

' No one but a fool can fail with Hamlet,' Redgrave had
written in 1930, with all the humility of a Cambridge under-
graduate; or, in the words of Macready, ' A total failure in Hamlet is of rare occurrence.' Redgrave's mastery of the role at the
New none the less surprised those who had thought of him
primarily as a film-star and, on the stage, as an excessively
' psychological ' actor. In gaining new freedom, strength and
confidence from the challenge that only the great roles can
offer, he broke down many of those barriers which had sometimes seemed to block full communication in the theatre. This
Old Vic season seemed, indeed, a self-renewal for Redgrave; and
the process continued at Stratford in 1951 in a cycle of Shakespearian histories to which, at his proposal, was added *The
Tempest*.

As Richard II he sought a new consistency of character – after
another flat first night of non-communication – in a production
which emphasized, in stressing the historical context of the
drama in the Shakespearian cycle, that it was not only a personal
but a political tragedy. One critic, Richard David, who thought
this emphasis went too far in subordinating Richard's royalty,
gave a vivid verbal picture:

Michael Redgrave's performance as Richard was technically brilliant. His make-up followed the traditional portraits, but with every
outline softened and blurred. The fine golden fur of beard dissolved
the line of the chin; the hollows and shadows of cheek and brow were
toned down into dimples and colourless uniformity. This was a face of
putty, a watery face over which the fleeting expressions chased each
other – the most constant being an uncertain smile, half self-approving
half placatory, that appeared whenever smiles were least in season.
The indecision of the face was reflected in the nervous gestures, the
handkerchief picked at and flaunted, the self-consciousness of gait
intended as a sign of assurance but revealing an acute lack of confidence. As a portrait of a wayward weakling, painfully cockering him-

self up to exhibitions of arbitrary power, it was superb; but it lacks a quality essential to Shakespeare's Richard.

Instead of Gielgud's kindly, lyrical victim, Redgrave presented a harsh, unsentimentalized portrait, sharp with cruelty, spite and envy; yet the feline homosexual of the early scenes was, for all his malicious weakness, a right royal Plantagenet. Indeed he was in one respect, said Harold Hobson, more credible than any other Richard, ' and quite new . . . this is the only Richard I have ever seen who could conceivably have suppressed Wat Tyler's rebellion.'

Redgrave's next role in the cycle, Hotspur, was, like Richard, trimmed of its traditional romantic limelight, in the interests of the tetralogy. In a production devoted to Harry Monmouth's exaltation as the ' Star of England ' it had to be quite clear that the best man had won at Shrewsbury if we were to appreciate his true glory at Agincourt, and the player of Hotspur was asked to co-operate in keeping him firmly in his place. Building up the character with his usual scrupulous regard for detail, Redgrave assumed a Northumbrian country accent which had the double virtue of contrast not only with Richard II, whom he played in each preceding performance, but also with Prince Hal. This brogue helped, in addition, to strengthen the warmth and home-liness of the scenes with Lady Percy. Redgrave also showed again his talent for the transformation of gait, gesture and mannerism. ' Here was a man,' wrote Richard David, ' whose restless spirit never allowed him to be still. His hands were always busy, point-ing, emphasizing, demonstrating or merely gesturing impatience that speech should be so slow to express his driving emotions: when he moved it was in starts and quick turns. Most effective of all perhaps was his continual half-conscious flexing of the knees, the instinctive action of one who spent most of his life in the saddle and the rest of it dreaming what he might do there.' He brimmed with gaiety and humour, yet never too much to out-shine Prince Hal. Subtly but unmistakably the actor indicated that the hot Percy's roughness and bravado were signs of deeper flaws; his faults were those of a vain and violent border raider who might prove a danger to the state. As Mr Worsley wrote:

It was a triumph alike for producers and actor to have caught this delicate balance to a hair's breadth. In Mr Michael Redgrave's

Hotspur there was spirit to the highest degree – in his impatience he could hardly ever come down off the balls of his feet; yet in that very spirit there was just this unamiable excess of pride. There was a rough violence of humour that was genuinely comic; but it brought up also the faintest whiff of the crude that fell short of real nobility. There was a virility and vitality and attack which raised the blood; but it was somehow just a little too self-interested, just a shade egomaniacal.

Redgrave directed the next play in the cycle, *Henry IV Part 2*, and appeared as the Chorus – an eloquent commentary and not a character – in *Henry V*; but it was outside the histories, in the role of Prospero, that he made his most important discovery of this Stratford season. In working out his own solution to the problems of acting this ' characterless, stupid old proser of common-place ', as Macready once described the exiled Duke of Milan, Redgrave found that Stanislavsky was no help. It was pointless to construct a dossier for Prospero's experiences before the play opens, to examine too closely the ' perspective of the role ' or to paint a portrait with the kind of detailed realism he had used in Hotspur. Rejecting the romantic approach which had influenced him at Cranleigh twenty years earlier, Redgrave presented Prospero as a very old man whose magic had been painfully acquired and who lifted his wand apprehensively, as if unsure that it was going to work, knowing that he was near to death and had little time in which to carry out his plans. Just as Prospero appeared as an ' empirical magician ' (as Peter Fleming called him), so Redgrave from then on became a more empirical actor, realizing to the full the inadequacy of Stanislavsky's psychological approach to Shakespeare. It seems significant that this was the first role (at forty-three) in which he used a false nose.

In the following year, when Redgrave returned to the contemporary drama with a major performance in a six-month West End run, his relationship with Stanislavsky changed still further and his education as an actor took another step forward. As Frank Elgin, the central figure of Clifford Odets's backstage drama *Winter Journey* (*The Country Girl* in the USA), he played a treacherous self-pitying dipsomaniac actor who has drunk himself out of the theatre: one of those hysterical, divided men who frequently appear in the Redgrave portrait gallery. It was not, however, Elgin's moral problem that attracted Redgrave to the role so much as his professional reputation: that of a great actor who has gone to seed, a 'natural' whose power is not reinforced by technique. The play's success depended to a large extent on a demonstration of Elgin's buried glory in the opening scene, when he is brought out of obscurity by a young director who believes in his redemption. He stumbled awkwardly, abjectly through an audition until the broken-down ham was suddenly transferred into a great player. Here was a challenge for any actor – and to Redgrave it was especially significant at that point in his career. For Elgin seemed to be the contradiction of all that Stanislavsky stands for, the opposite kind of actor to the one Redgrave was supposed to be; and the director in the play and of the play, Sam Wanamaker, was, like Redgrave, a champion of the Method.

All Elgin's past seemed to be revealed when Redgrave first stepped on to the stage for his rehearsal, and from that first memorable scene up to the queasily happy ending he gave a bravura performance of exquisitely studied detail, high theatrical voltage and penetrating understanding. Here was, as Ivor Brown put it, 'a capital essay in flabby degeneration of the moral fibre: the puffy aspect, the half hysterical transitions from despair to hilarity, the muddled self-deception and nervy domestic fraudulence are all brilliant contributions to the portrait of a likeable louse' – but not too likeable to obscure the fact that he was a humbug, a liar and a coward. The weaknesses of the man seemed to be linked with the weaknesses of the actor. This Elgin was a man out of control, snatching at inspiration, misunderstanding his own fitful power, and the egotism that was one essential factor in his stage success had turned in on him in his defeat and eaten him away. Yet at moments he could still speak with tongues of fire; and the ability to move so swiftly into this state of rapt authority, after the rapidly changing moods of blustering *bonhomie*, self-hatred and quivering despair, was one of Redgrave's notable achievements in the role. It was, as T. C. Worsley said, 'a triumph of naturalism' – in presenting theatricalism.

In assuming this character Redgrave seemed to have advanced still further into that new theatrical freedom which was first apparent in his Hamlet, as if the task of presenting a type of playing to which he was opposed in theory had revised both his theory and his practice. To Kenneth Tynan he appeared to be battling to free himself from ' the technical preoccupations which have been disfiguring his work ', and the result was ' the best serious performance he has given us for years '. Almost as important as the play was the quarrel that it caused between Redgrave and his director, who turned out to be a much more devout disciple of the Method and whose zeal prompted Redgrave to the discovery that in modern drama, as in Shakespeare, you can take Stanislavsky too far. During his battles on and off the stage he learned to place more trust in his own capacity and less in the Method, although, as he says, ' it still floats superbly in the right waters '.

After *Winter Journey* Redgrave returned, in 1953, to the gruelling demands of a Stratford season in three major roles. His Shylock, with which he opened, showed a new explosive attack and power. Resisting the pressures to romanticize and fantasticate the character or to play for sympathy – pressures reinforced by the wartime proximity of mass-murder – he presented an uncompromisingly menacing, sardonic, ferocious villain, guttural and asthmatic, ' as fanatically full of race hatred as his persecutors and the kind of Jew whose Jewishness invites persecution '. As *The Times* said, he showed that ' though there may be something sublime in the Jew's passion for revenge it is something which must be crushed at all costs ': yet his performance was not felt to be anti-Semitic. It was a characteristically bold attempt, executed with characteristic intelligence, although it was generally reviewed with something less than fervour, thanks to an equally characteristic first-night failure to achieve instant mastery.

In *Lear,* which he tackled in July, Redgrave appeared in the opening scene as a Blake-like Ancient of Days, very old and weary, but still unreconciled to his loss of power and vitality. You could believe that this ruin'd piece of nature had once been a terror of the battlefield. Although he seemed to grow still older – for Redgrave emphasized his age in increasing detail – his former strength came back in sudden gusts of fury; yet, like Kean, ' his warmest bursts of passion never removed him from the weakness of age.' He lacked the heroic bass of a Macready or the singing lyricism of a Gielgud, but his handling of the great vocal score displayed remarkable variety, control and endurance, rumbling, whimpering, raging and keening through its many moods, giving full value to the words without being tethered by the technical detail. He conveyed, time and again, that sense of rapture which Agate prescribed as one essential for Lear, 'a quality of ecstasy . . . in which the soul stands beside the body' (a most un-Stanislavskian posture); and he maintained throughout a distinguishing consistency and humanity, flowering in the last act. Philip Hope-Wallace, describing it as 'the most satisfying' interpretation since the war, observed that although other actors had discovered more striking power or more simple poetry in the part, none had found 'an interpretation at once so full (in the sense of histrionic volume) and so consistently bringing all the aspects of the part together, without any shirking or pruning away of what is inconvenient'. Robert Speaight and T. C. Worsley suggested that he was the finest of modern Lears. And Kenneth Tynan wrote:

In simple roles Mr Redgrave is often in the predicament of a higher mathematician asked to add two and two together; he may very well hum and haw and come to the conclusion that in certain circumstances they may make five. But give him a scene, like this at Dover, which is the higher mathematics of acting, and he solves it in a flash: here, and throughout the last act, was the cube root of Lear, 'the thing itself'.

Not all the critics were so impressed: they did not reach a unanimous verdict on Redgrave's acting between *Uncle Harry* and *Uncle Vanya*. Yet it seemed to many people, as it did to me, not only the best Lear, in some ways, since the war, but the best performance that Michael Redgrave had yet given in the theatre. It was, in my view, matched, if not outshone, by his other great role in this season of 1953, a role which he had refused at the Old Vic in 1951 and was reluctant to play at Stratford: Antony. The part has baffled some actors and repelled many more. Garrick and Phelps failed in it; Irving and Kean avoided it; Macready found his own performance 'hasty, unprepared, unfinished'; Gielgud and Olivier did not succeed in bringing alive this 'titanic embodiment of adult passion', as William Archer called him. But Redgrave minted an Antony as definitive, in its Shakespearian completeness, as Olivier's Richard III or Gielgud's Angelo.

The open secret of his success lay first in his height, physique and voice: from the first entrance the look of this Antony was so right – with a careless, laughing magnificence – and when he spoke, one seemed to see his past and future spread around him like his scarlet cloak. Here indeed was a triple pillar of the world, a demi-atlas of the earth; and the full magnitude of that rhetoric had to be projected in performance if one were to feel the nobility, the shame and the ruin of the man – a world-sharer in a fever of love, consumed by jealousy and self-reproach (' I have lost command '), yet still great-hearted and heroic. He was an outsize poetic figure (' the greatest soldier in the world '), yet he was at the same time intensely human, as a lover, a drinker and a comrade; and by making Antony so visibly the arena of a fierce battle between pleasure and duty, Redgrave avoided that shrinking of the man which is caused by presenting the battle as already lost before the play begins. He could boom with rage and defiance, but he could meet the exquisite music of the text with a rich choice of voices. The command of detail in which he, as ever, excelled was indivisible here from the character, and the character was incarnate in the verse. This was no self-analyzing Antony, no intellectual voluptuary: Redgrave presented the character in a portrait that, while founded upon mastery of naturalism, went beyond naturalism. In the words of *The Times,* he aimed at the terrific and attained it.

This Antony was not unanimously acclaimed, and full honours from its admirers were not earned until it came to London later in the year, when critics registered the transformation of the first-night performance. Redgrave himself was fairly astonished by its success. 'Perhaps I've always *tried* too hard. I didn't in Antony,' he said some years later. But as he wrote in 1950 in *The Actor's Ways and Means*: ' " We only really begin to act," I have heard our greatest native actress say, " when we leave off trying ". But some have to try much longer than others and the moment to leave off dictates itself, cannot be chosen.'

Within four years Michael Redgrave had played eleven roles in classic repertory, in addition to a West End run. He had come into his theatrical inheritance at last. But financially the inheritance was damaging, and between 1954 and 1958 he made a dozen films to redress the economic balance. He also found three successful new roles under commercial auspices in contemporary plays (although only one of these was in modern dress). Most notably, he appeared in London and New York as Hector, the pacifist soldier-hero of Giraudoux's *Tiger at the Gates* (in a new translation by Christopher Fry), a part he had been cast to play twenty years earlier in St Denis's abortive season at the Phoenix. Giraudoux's rhetoric demands actors who can handle big speeches with the precision, music and variety of vocal effect learned in Shakespeare, but can deliver them through smaller, more ambiguous characters. Redgrave found the right compromises between naturalism and formalism, with delicate adjustments of scale and mood in the language and the character. As Brooks Atkinson wrote of the London production, he gave ' a heroic performance of distinction and power . . . Although the part is classical, he keeps the human being alive and responsive inside the classical formalities. The dimensions of his acting are big, but the humanity is warm and simple.' Harold Clurman, the director, proved to be the biggest influence on Redgrave since St Denis, although the Stanislavsky method, of which Clurman had for years been a prime champion, was recognized by both director and star to be irrelevant in Giraudoux's Troy.

During this period Redgrave directed on Broadway *A Month in the Country* and Rattigan's featherweight comedy *The Sleeping Prince,* in which he took Olivier's role. Later, in the West End, he made a hit in N. C. Hunter's *A Touch of the Sun,* as a puritanical headmaster suddenly translated to Riviera comfort, whose idealism has congealed into priggishness, and who comes to see his true image in the mirror. Never playing for sympathy but gaining enough of it all the same, Redgrave gave one of his most subtle, touching and truthful character studies, a model of technical skill and theatrical sensibility in what T. C. Worsley rightly described as a ' skin-deep ' part.

It was five years before Redgrave returned to the Stratford classic repertory, principally to play his second professional Hamlet: daringly – too daringly, perhaps – at fifty. After a witty, elegant Benedick in nineteenth-century costume – a bearded, cigar-smoking, straw-hatted and white-toppered anachronism – he came back to Elsinore in a smaller, colder, more naturalistic but above all less romantic portrait. There was high praise, again, for his intelligence and command of the text. ' No Hamlet has ever understood so fully and few can have felt more deeply the meaning of the words that he is given to speak,' said W. A. Darlington, who ranked it among the very best Hamlets he had seen. ' No one gives us, as Mr Redgrave does, such a feeling of having an absolute intellectual grasp of the whole of a part and every detail in it; and you can be quite sure with him that every minutest one of these details has been calculated for a special effect,' said T. C. Worsley. Yet Worsley added that although this Hamlet was 'perfectly done', 'we' could not 'respond' to it; and Felix Barker, who praised it as a 'great' Hamlet, said that it was, all the same, 'not a memorable one'.

For Tynan the trouble was the old bogey of non-communication. Redgrave 'has in abundance all the attributes of a great actor,' he wrote, 'without the basic quality necessary to be a good one . . . getting into emotional touch with others.' Yet for those who saw Redgrave's performance after his usual first-night wall of reserve had melted, a more convincing explanation why the 1958 Hamlet fell short of greatness (and below the level of 1950) was the one given by Worsley. He argued that the universality of Hamlet depended upon its conception as a wholly romantic role . . . 'In the last analysis, what wins him to us is an essentially youthful property, the ability to romanticize his predicaments and to do it brilliantly.' Redgrave was too anti-romantic, and too old, at fifty. (Yet when he played it later in Leningrad and Moscow – with a new wig and costume – the age-barrier seemed less significant, and he scored a personal triumph.)

Another new chapter opened for Redgrave in 1959: as manager, author, director and actor in one. He went into management (in collaboration with Peter Daubeny) to present his own production of his own brilliant adaptation of Henry James's *The Aspern Papers*, which he had written twelve years earlier. He himself appeared as the New England intellectual in the Venice of 1885, wheedling a literary cache from the mummified mistress of a dead celebrity. With a remarkably sure sense of period Redgrave achieved the difficult feat of creating gripping theatre which was still true to the essential James: a triumph, both as writer and actor, of subtle intelligence, delicate control and exact technique. In the following year he played an Oxbridge philosopher-don converted to private and political commitment in Robert Bolt's *The Tiger and the Horse*: a good part finely acted, but incompletely realized by the author and somewhat beneath Redgrave's full stretch. His next West End role, in 1962, was in a very different and oddly rewarding vein: as Lancelot Dodd in *Out of Bounds*, a vague, tousled, cricket-mad prep-schoolmaster who turns out to be the double of an international spy and is involved in farcical misadventures of a familiar kind. In this entertaining trifle Redgrave displayed a thistledown comic expertise which converted at least one critic. 'I used to think that Michael Redgrave was incapable of comedy,' wrote Harold Hobson, 'but either I was wrong (as is probable) or he has enlarged his field. Bumblingly passionate for Lord's, giggling with pride over Eton, wide-eyed at a succession of strokes of stupendous luck, Sir Michael's Lancelot is a rich comic creation.' Meanwhile, at Chichester in the summer of 1962, he had achieved a great tragi-comic creation as Uncle Vanya.

Since his Tusenbach twenty-four years earlier Redgrave had, surprisingly, played no Chekhov; but this vanished yet still curiously contemporary Russia seemed now to be his natural home. In Vanya his command of naturalistic detail, his vocal expertise, his psychological penetration, his capacity for subtle half-tones and delicate balances, his gifts for comedy and pathos found a new, electrifying fusion: the parts of his performance had sometimes been conspicuous at the expense of the whole, but here the technics were transcended. Forelock straying over his temples, this tall Vanya stumbled clumsily through his continual frustrations with a physical awkwardness that semed to be an emblem of his failure to cope with life. 'An ungainly, muscular figure, built for action but habitually bowed in an apologetic stoop, he seemed constantly at odds with his own body; and even at the climax of his anger, his fists turn into harmless flappers when they come within reach of the target,' said *The Times*. For such a man to miss when he tries to shoot the Professor seemed inevitably right, heartbreakingly funny. 'Torn between self-assertion and self-deprecation,' Kenneth Tynan wrote, he took over the stage in 'a tottering, pigeon-toed stride that boldly amalgamates both.' His ineffectual menace and violent jealousy often seemed, like his defeated gloom, comic as well as touching. But behind his visible misery there was a deeper charge of banked-up despair, under precarious control, which kept an intensity of apprehensive feeling throbbing through the audience; his proposal to Ilena had a muted stillness of hopeful humility that made its pathos all the more piercing; and mixed with his absurdity he kept throughout a curious gentle dignity. You could almost see the waste of the past and the waste to come – the wilderness to which, in the last scenes of this great play, Vanya seems resigned

Sir Michael Redgrave

with a chilling, deadly calm. With a cast including Dame Sybil Thorndike, Joan Plowright, Rosemary Harris (in 1963), Sir Lewis Casson and Laurence Olivier, this *Uncle Vanya,* produced by Olivier, was a miracle of team acting; and Redgrave was, seamlessly, part of the *ensemble.* Yet even in such triumphs of harmony some performances are more perfect than others: Redgrave's was outstanding, growing richer from year to year. It was, arguably, one of the outstanding performances of our time.

In the opening season of the National Theatre Company at the Old Vic in 1963-4 Redgrave played, apart from Vanya, Henry Hobson in *Hobson's Choice* (strange miscasting, tackled with skilful technique in heavy beard and padding, but not quite overcome); Solness in *The Master Builder* (Redgrave's first stage Ibsen: a performance of towering neuroticism, subtly strong, but not one of his main successes); and Claudius in the company's inaugural *Hamlet,* conspicuously the best acting in that unfortunate production. Instead of the too obviously villainous upstart who often occupies the throne of Denmark, he achieved a definitive portrait of the king as a ruddy, genial careerist, hiding an amoral opportunism behind his sleek façade of mock-bluffness and real charm.

Since then Redgrave has not – at the time of writing in 1970 – been seen again in classic repertory. He has appeared in only one role on the West End stage, as Rakitin once again in his own production of *A Month in the Country,* with which in 1965 he opened the Yvonne Arnaud Theatre at Guildford in a season under his direction. (He also revived his old Cranleigh role of Samson in Milton's dramatic poem.)

In spite of all his achievements, he has remained an actor in search of a theatre and a drama. His absence from the stage for so long is a disturbing symptom of its perennial inability to make proper use of our major acting talent, and, reciprocally, of that talent's failure to use the stage.

' I went into films against what I thought was my better judgment,' Redgrave has said, and although he has stayed there, off and on, for over thirty years he has in the last resort (or so he has maintained) learned nothing as an artist from the cinema. ' I can't help feeling that you're simply selling what you've learned in the theatre. The traffic is entirely one-sided.' In that viewpoint, perhaps, he is speaking for his own generation: cinematic changes in recent years have brought an enlargement of acting opportunities and a shift of focus, so that actors going into films in the 1970s often take a very different attitude from Olivier and Redgrave in the 1930s.

Since his 1938 début in that apparently indestructible Hitchcock comedy-thriller *The Lady Vanishes*, Redgrave has played his way through a wide variety of roles: Kipps; a Regency smuggler; a Ramsay MacDonald-type leader in *Fame is the Spur*; a French lawyer; a Polish junk-dealer; a comic con-man; John Worthing in Anthony Asquith's *The Importance of Being Earnest*; O'Connor, the (renamed) Investigator in Orwell's *1984*; W. B. Yeats; Mr Peggotty; a Borstal governor; a surgeon; a British journalist in Vietnam in *The Quiet American*; and many more, including senior officers of the British Army or RAF, farcically funny or dead serious. Among the most remarkable were Orin Mannon in *Mourning Becomes Electra*; Crocker-Harris, ' the Himmler of the Lower Fifth ', in *The Browning Version*, the scientist Barnes Wallis in *The Dam Busters*, and – a classic performance, this – the schizophrenic ventriloquist in *Dead of Night*. Yet, for all his achievements in films, and despite their economic importance in his career, the cinema seems to have been of relatively minor significance in Redgrave's development as an artist.

Television, on which he has appeared half-a-dozen times (films apart), has been a minor fringe activity of the past decade. And in the theatre he has given little time to his early ambition of directing: barely a dozen productions in thirty-five years. This is partly due, perhaps, to his failure or refusal either to establish himself (like Gielgud) in continuous association with one West End management, or (like Olivier) to set up in management on the commercial or subsidized stage. In spite of his pre-war dreams, it was not until he was fifty that he formed a producing company, which staged, among other West End productions, his own *Aspern Papers* and Coward's *Waiting in the Wings*. Redgrave helped to bring Theatre Workshop to London for the first time in 1952; he has directed two productions at Glyndebourne; and he played a main role in establishing the Yvonne Arnaud Theatre at Guildford, leaving the National Theatre in order to run its inaugural season, in which he served as actor, director and impresario. But it is as an actor that he has made his principal contribution to the theatre and for that (with his writing) he will be remembered.

If Redgrave's work has often sharply divided critical opinion, it is partly because his career reflects, more vividly in some ways than that of either Gielgud or Olivier, the problems of actors of his generation tugged between behaviourism and theatricalism, psychology and tradition, cinema and stage, the long run and the classic repertoire; working against the paralysing effect of English middle-class emotional etiquette, with its exaltation of understatement, against the persistent anti-theatrical strand in intellectual life, against the deflationary pressures of post-Freudian, post-Marxist conditioning; attempting personal solutions to the challenges presented by the eclecticism of contemporary style, the general sterility of acting values in new drama, the anarchy of the trade.

For some people there is one central flaw in Redgrave, considered as a top-rank actor. It is reflected in his honours degree, his schoolmaster's stint, his occasional plunges into public controversy, his championship of Stanislavsky, his lectures, books and plays. The charges are that he is an intellectual, and that it shows in, for instance, his communications problems of 'opening cold' on first nights; that he thinks too precisely on and around the event; that he concentrates overmuch on detail; that he is preoccupied by technique and ideas about technique, by what an actor ought to do, not by what he, personally *has* to do; that in his acting there is too much naturalism and not enough nature.

On the credit side, as this summary survey has shown, Redgrave appears to combine some of the distinctive virtues of Gielgud and Olivier. As a verse-speaker he is second only to Sir John: as a 'character actor' (how curious and revealing that label is) he shares Sir Laurence's skills in impersonation. Yet he is, at his best, in a class on his own, harmonizing naturalism and theatricalism, *acteur* and *comédien*, vocalizing and humanizing, tradition and experiment. He has both scrupulous taste and, on occasions, Dionysian power. He is a bold soloist, but he can also submit himself to the *ensemble*. He is a subtle miniaturist, who knows how to fill the full stage. He has been Lear, Hamlet, Macbeth, Shylock and Antony. His career is – it seems to me – a rebuttal of Hazlitt's proposition that 'no actor becomes great by improvement.'

✦✦✦ 10 ✦✦✦

To be concluded

If, as Granville-Barker said, ' the art of the theatre is the art of acting, first, last and all the time ', then the art of the British theatre should, by now, have attained a state of rare felicity. During the forty years since Gielgud's début at the Old Vic the stage has flowered with splendid if staccato crops of acting talent in both classic and contemporary drama. Yet a great deal of that talent has failed to remain on view, in bud and in the theatre. Much of it has gone into the cinema, and many leading players who began on the stage are now seldom, if ever, seen there: a modern tradition of retreat, which has been vigorously maintained from the era of Hardwicke, Donat and Laughton to that of O'Toole and Burton by such illustrious deserters as Jack Hawkins, John Mills, Harry Andrews, Dirk Bogarde, Anthony Quayle and Trevor Howard. As theatre acting has increasingly become a part-time occupation, top actors of different generations – such as Michael Redgrave, Ralph Richardson and Alec Guinness from the 1930s, Paul Rogers, John Neville and Eric Porter from the 1950s and Albert Finney, Tom Courtenay and Nicol Williamson from the 1960s – appear only for limited runs and at long intervals. The provincial reps and the national companies have trained many fine actors, fulfilling on a wider scale the role that Oxford, Birmingham and the pre-war Old Vic played in the growth of Gielgud and Olivier; but when these actors leave the National or the Royal Shakespeare, they are likely to find more frequent employment in films and television than on the stage. And it is only on the stage that great acting, as I have attempted to outline it, can be achieved – in the presence of, with the collaboration of, a living audience.

Greatness has, however, frequently been acclaimed in the

theatre, not merely by agents, columnists and PROs for their clients and favourites, and not only for the three knights singled out in the preceding chapters (whose choice would not, perhaps, be unanimous in a national referendum). Several artists in recent years have – more persistently than the rest – been cited as candidates for immortality. The short list is headed by three superb actresses: Dame Edith Evans, Dame Sybil Thorndike and Dame Peggy Ashcroft. Their long and brilliant careers have been closely intertwined with those of Gielgud, Olivier and Redgrave, to many of whose successes they have richly contributed. Yet as I am obliged to leave this trinity – with Sarah Siddons, Ellen Terry, and other leading ladies of the British stage – to be given their due honour and glory in another book, I must pass on briefly in this final chapter to four leading favourites and ex-favourites among actors in the last three decades.

First comes the man who has most often been ranked at the summit with Gielgud and Olivier since he appeared at the Old Vic seasons at the New in 1944-6. According to Harold Hobson, the fact that Ralph Richardson is a great actor has never afterwards been questioned. Richardson's elusive talents include a gift for suggesting a deep-rooted kindness and tenderness behind a stolid ultra-English reserve. As Desmond MacCarthy said of his Sheppey, in Somerset Maugham's 1933 play, he seems to project ' a rare understanding of goodness, and a rare restraint in expressing it ', and this is one of the most intransigent of virtues on the stage. With similar restraint he can evoke the fantasies and despairs behind the façade of suburban life. Some of his greatest successes have been made as failures – especially drunken failures – such as Charles Appleby, the whisky-tippling actor of Priestley's *Eden End;* the boozy, self-deceiving insurance man of Robert Bolt's *Flowering Cherry;* or the despairing doctor with a taste for too much gin in N. C. Hunter's *A Day by the Sea.* At his wordless best Richardson is remembered in such crises of domestic life as the moment in Graham Greene's *The Complaisant Lover* when the pompous, cuckolded, practical-joking dentist learns of his wife's adultery: in Harold Hobson's words, ' Sir Ralph's face turns colder than stone; it becomes a generation older in a few seconds; and when it breaks into irresistible tears the effect on the audience is tremendous.' Getting the audience into sympathy with unsympathetic characters is one of his specialities: partly, perhaps, because – in contrast with a Gielgud or an Olivier – he has seemed to be so conspicuously and reassuringly average, unheroic and unactorish, one of us, or *them* (depending on your point of view). But Sir Ralph also has an unrivalled and mysterious flair for maintaining a halo of universality around those apparently ordinary men in whose distresses he has, over the years, made something of a sublime corner. That was one reason for the success of his Peer Gynt, his prime choice in 1944 when he asked Olivier to join him in actor-management at the Old Vic. Throughout the fantasies of Peer's progress he kept the play tethered by the firm, friendly, earthy humanity of his personality; yet, while English to the core, he wore the aura of Everyman – just as he combined pathos and comedy, simplicity and cunning, rhetoric and poetry.

In his earlier career Richardson was particularly identified with J. B. Priestley's plays. He has acted in five, and has praised, twenty years after his last stage appearance in one of them, the 'considerable music' of Priestley's prose and the 'great beauty' of what the actor describes as 'his particular form of simplicity'. Richardson's own apparent simplicity conceals, like Priestley's, a continent of complexities. He makes poetry out of prose, and prose out of poetry. Like Priestley, again, he has often appeared to be a man between two worlds – naturalism and the other side. One Priestley play in particular, written with him in mind, symbolizes part of Sir Ralph's peculiar specialism. In *Johnson over Jordan* (1939) he was cast as 'a man of our time, an ordinary citizen of the suburbs' who is dead but in limbo, watching his past life unroll before him in half-fantastic, half-realistic episodes, linked in a strong undercurrent of nostalgia and pathos, until he marches out bravely into Eternity with bowler hat and briefcase. Richardson has frequently managed to suggest, somehow, that he is out of this world or not all there, and that this is somehow theatrically significant. It is not altogether irrelevant that his prime role in *Hamlet* has been the Ghost, and that he played two West End roles by R. C. Sherriff in the 1950s, as a concussed bank manager who had lost his memory (*Home at Seven*) and as the spectre of a commuter blown to pieces before the play started (*The White Carnation*). On this occasion Kenneth Tynan dubbed him as 'the best supernatural actor of his generation'; and if you take that accurate gibe seriously, you might well rank him as the best super-naturalist actor – in naturalistic plays. An other-worldly halo, combined with an everyday façade, has helped him to raise his role of suburban man – visibly not too far removed from the ones watching him in the stalls – to the heights of some exceptional, almost extra-terrestrial feeling. That is one reason why throughout Sir Ralph's fifty years on the stage you will find repeated invocations of the moon by critics attempting to describe what, precisely, the actor radiates that transcends what he is saying and doing. It is one of those endlessly renewable con-tricks that we rightly dignify by the name of magic; and, in Sir Ralph's case, it seems to be irrefutably white magic. Although the character he plays may seem to be in touch with the infinite, he is still (one feels) in love with his wife: and he is never too distant to be either pathetic or funny, and frequently both.

In West End drama Richardson's acting seems to soar far above the needs of naturalism, towards the Alps of great art; yet when it is actually confronted with the summits it usually drops like a stone. Out of modern dress he is, essentially, a prose actor. As he has grown older his light, feathery voice has become increasingly mannered and eccentric; and he has seemed even less well-equipped to tackle in maturity the tragic roles which he failed to conquer as a young man. It was not for want of experience. By 1970 he had played more parts on the stage than Olivier or Gielgud. He started earlier in the profession, back in 1920 – he was born on 19 December 1902 – and for his first four years he played dozens of roles in dozens of towns, first with a semi-amateur troupe and then with a Shakespearian touring company, before he joined the Birmingham Rep in 1926. He worked at the Old Vic in 1930-2 and again in 1944-8, during his co-management with Olivier and Burrell. He played a season at Stratford in 1952, returned to the Old Vic in 1956 to play Timon, and later appeared as Shylock in the West End. But Richardson's prime successes, far back, were in the secondary roles, when he played, Kent, Caliban, Enobarbus and Bolingbroke to Gielgud's Lear, Prospero, Antony and Richard II, or Richmond to Olivier's Crookback. As Shylock, Timon, Prospero and – worst of all – Macbeth and Othello he seemed sadly out of his depth, and both the poetry and the play sank with him. For all his technical expertise and his long seasoning in the Shakespearian repertoire, he could not master the verse. Without an adequate sense of rhythm, phrasing, timing, tone, tempo and (at times) meaning, he could not hold the stage and bring the characters alive. He had crossed the boundaries where his naturalist magic stopped working.

In comedy it has been a different story. Richardson scored as Sir Toby and Bottom in the 1930s; in the 1940s as Cyrano, Falstaff and Face in *The Alchemist;* and in the 1960s, more marginally, as Sir Peter in *The School for Scandal* and Sir Anthony in *The Rivals.* Falstaff was, perhaps, his greatest Shakespearian achievement. With a wild halo of white hair above his pale, lean head and a surging mind above his sagging, rather implausible paunch and Rowlandson-like legs, this Falstaff was no cross, farcical buffoon, but a witty, dry and even dignified knight. ('His principal attribute was not his fatness but his knighthood,' wrote Kenneth Tynan). Rich in humour, gusto, pathos and intelligence, the performance was generally acclaimed as definitive; in the past twenty-five years no actor has been recognized as Richardson's equal in the role; and, perhaps together with his Peer Gynt, it is by its creation at the Old Vic in 1944-6 – never, unhappily, repeated – that Richardson will most assuredly win his niche in the hall of theatrical fame, although later generations know him best through the many films he has made since his cinematic début in 1933. He is, if probably not a great actor, a great eccentric, and perhaps something of a genius.

Like Richardson, Sir Alec Guinness is better known to the general public on both sides of the Atlantic as a film star, an international technician in the manufacture and servicing of character parts; yet he grew up, as an actor, in that same extraordinary theatrical forcing-house of the 1930s where Gielgud, Olivier, Redgrave and Richardson – together with Peggy Ashcroft – came to flower, and in earlier days he appeared to be in the direct line of succession to the throne. He made his name, under the tutelage of Gielgud and Guthrie, with remarkable speed and without any exposure to the provincial gymnasium. After only a score of parts in the West End he was playing Hamlet at the Old Vic, at twenty-four, within four years of his theatrical début – he was born on 2 April 1914. He worked with Harcourt Williams and Guthrie at the Old Vic, Gielgud at the

To be concluded

Queen's, Olivier at the New. But after 1947, when he made his first film (*Great Expectations*), Guinness appeared in barely a dozen stage roles, once he had finished at the Old Vic: and since 1948 he has never worked in repertoire with one of the national companies. Although it is, of course, by the quality rather than the quantity of his roles that an actor's greatness must be judged, Guinness's persistent absenteeism, coupled with his deliberate rejection of the Shakespearian traditions without apparently presenting coherent alternatives, has discouraged those who hoped that he would, in his turn, be a leader of the English stage.

Guinness has shown himself to be an expert in the presentation of men with double lives, watchful men with secrets to hide, the ultimate secret being their identity. Inaccurately labelled as ' faceless ' because of his versatility in the cinema, he has excelled in remaking himself in a series of recurrent moulds: simpletons (Aguecheek and Abel Drugger), scientists (in *The Human Touch* and *Under the Sycamore Tree*), near-saints and sages (*The Prisoner* and *The Cocktail Party*), near-geniuses (*The Ascent of F6* and *Ross*); as the cold joker or eccentric enjoying his private game with the world; as the proud victim, hugging his suffering in silence; as the lonely leader, numbed by a sense of responsibility; as the secular monk tormented by a sense of difference. (His conversion to Catholicism, one suspects, is a clue to that difference.) The common denominator of most of his temporary selves is that their lines of communication have frozen up. The whole man is in hiding, behind a chosen role or mask. In the cinema, without a live audience in circuit, this is no disadvantage: Guinness's anonymous, secretive disguises triumph before the camera. But the actor seems to be over-wary, in the theatre, of showing off, acting up, giving out; he is a master of emotional understatement and control, but he turns his back on the outsize, the extravagant and the Dionysian; he can suggest unspoken and unspeakable depths, but he will not plumb them. He shares the veiled, aristocratic remoteness that Gielgud and Redgrave sometimes display, without their ability to relax, to soar and to sing. He has something of Olivier's self-transforming skill, without that exaltation in the commingling of personality and part that seems to help distinguish great acting from fine acting. Deliberately and adventurously anti-romantic and anti-heroic in his approach to Shakespeare, both in his 1951 Hamlet and his 1966 Macbeth,

269

Guinness has so far generally failed in performance to eclipse – or even to equal – the more orthodox, rhetorical, traditional effects of his predecessors with his own cool, ironic, contemporary naturalism. Yet he is, if not a great actor, a considerable artist; and the absence of his lucidity, intelligence, sensibility, authority and integrity is a great loss to the stage.

In the postwar generations of actors, one man marked as a possible candidate for greatness was Richard Burton. The twelfth of a Welsh miner's thirteen children, he was seen to represent the accession of a new class as well as a new age-group; he was acclaimed for his earthiness and masculinity; and he brought to the stage a presence that was sometimes explained as 'Celtic', although others were content to welcome it as 'star quality'. Burton made his stage début, in a Welsh juvenile role, at seventeen (he was born on 10 November 1925), but it was not until 1948, after some years at Oxford and in the RAF, that his career began in the West End. Like Guinness, he never worked in the provinces: he started near the top, under the umbrella of John Gielgud and Hugh Beaumont; and he made his film début in the very same year of 1948.

For eight years, while continuing to make films, Burton appeared at Stratford, the Old Vic and in the West End, almost entirely in Shakespeare, and in three verse-plays by Christopher Fry. Stocky, watchful, unsmiling and still, with dark-green unwinking eyes, he had a contained passion and energy that, in spite of his technical inexperience, made some critics reach uneasily for their superlatives. Even when not actually in play, he radiated a smouldering authority. He was the kind of actor you could not help noticing, and by 1951 at Stratford – where he played Prince Hal and Henry V – the word 'greatness' was already being used, with caution, after only three years. T. C. Worsley wrote, 'If he works at his art long and humbly, he has every chance of becoming a great actor by the age of forty.' Yet by the time Burton was forty, he seemed – in effect – to have given up the stage. By 1970 he had played barely a score of roles in the theatre, but he had become, for a time the world's highest-paid film actor.

Like Olivier, by whom, as by Gielgud, he was inevitably influenced, Burton projected a kind of physical authority and attack, notably in the roles of Coriolanus and Henry V. He was, essentially, *acteur* rather than *comédien,* although at the Old Vic he made an efficient attempt to disguise himself as Sir Toby and Caliban. Like Guinness, he radiated a kind of privacy, that was expressed most obviously in the rapt, far-away gaze which, though somewhat too frequently directed at the middle distance, usually had a telling effect upon the audience. Like Guinness, too, he is a cool, detached, heretical actor; but, unlike Guinness, he rose to the vocal and theatrical challenge of the verse without apparent scruples about romanticism, faking and succumbing to tradition. His Othello, at thirty, not surprisingly failed; but his Iago – alternating with John Neville in the same Old Vic season of 1956 – was a plain yet wily portrait; and his Hamlets of 1953 (Edinburgh and Old Vic) and 1964 (North America only) were, in their various ways, praised for strength, stamina, vocal power, theatrical intelligence and, of course, personal authority. Although Burton had spent most of the intervening decade in films he had not ceased, it seems, to develop as a stage actor by the mid-1960s.

Richard Burton showed from the outset of his career the kind of instant authority over the audience and the text that some actors strive desperately and unsuccessfully to achieve through twenty years of hard theatrical labour. It went surprisingly easy for him. If he, too, had spent twenty years on the stage, he might perhaps have achieved true greatness beyond that immensely marketable mesmeric charm and power. If he comes back, perhaps he could still do it. Meanwhile he must be regretfully written off as another loss to the theatre.

In the 1950s Burton was seen by some critics as the prime challenger to one outstanding contemporary as a rival candidate for the royal theatrical succession. To use an inaccurate parallel of the time, the Gielgud to his Olivier was cast as Paul Scofield – it was Scofield who was originally to play Othello and Iago turn-about with him at the Old Vic – but after Burton's disappearance to Hollywood no other actor of his generation emerged to oust this brilliant artist from the place on the dais that he has long occupied as heir-apparent to the knights. Scofield is unmistakably – if somewhat uneasily – an inheritor of their tradition. Remote from the naturalism of the 1960s, he seems as far removed as it is possible to be in the contemporary theatre from fashions in publicity and pontification, a man on his own, unique and withdrawn; yet his acting has nearly always been, in its way, electrifying in touch. Since his stage début in 1940 – Scofield was born on 21 January 1922 – he has made what looks like a rigorously deliberate progress, punctuated by frequent rejections of show-business offers to which less single-minded actors would have succumbed. He did not appear in a film until 1955, fifteen years after he became an actor, and fifteen years after that, at forty-eight, he was quoted as having said that he had just begun to enjoy them. He learned his craft in the provinces: it was only after two seasons at the Birmingham Rep and three seasons at Stratford – ten years in all – that he took his first starring part in London (Alexander in Rattigan's *Adventure Story*). Since then he has worked almost entirely in the West End, and at Hammersmith in Gielgud's 1952-3 season, under the management of H. M. Tennent, the Royal Shakespeare Company and the English Stage Company. Unlike Olivier, Gielgud and Redgrave he has worked only as an actor, never venturing into direction or management (although he was for a time on the RSC's panel of artistic directors).

Scofield's range has been carefully eclectic, moving between classics and moderns, and seldom putting a foot wrong – at least on the lower slopes – though seldom taking his talent to full stretch. In the contemporary drama since 1949 his roles have included the elegant heroes of Anouilh's *Ring round the Moon* and *Time Remembered*; the wizened, hunted ' whisky priest ' in the stage version of Graham Greene's *The Power and the Glory*; Harry Monchensey, the English Orestes in Eliot's *The Family Reunion;* Sir Thomas More – ' at once wily and holy ', as Kenneth Tynan said – in Robert Bolt's *A Man for All Seasons*; Laurie, the wry, monologuing script-writer of John Osborne's *Hotel in Amsterdam;* and a homosexual barber in *Staircase*. In the classics his early successes included the Clown in *The Winter's Tale,* Don Armado, Aguecheek, Mercutio, Young Fashion in *The Relapse,* Witwoud in *The Way of the World* and, some fourteen years later, Gogol's *Government Inspector*. What unites most of these parts, including some of the comic ones, is Scofield's brooding aura of melancholy and despair, salted with irony. With his sculptured, curiously uncontemporary, grieving face, his darkly haunted, hooded eyes, and his sad, oddly monotonous voice, suddenly cracking and splitting into veins of gold or tin, he looks and sounds, as Clive Barnes wrote, ' as if the world is gnawing at his guts, and it gnaws away whatever costume you ask him to wear, whatever lines you ask him to speak, or whatever thoughts you ask him to express ', or as if, in Harold Hobson's words, he radiates ' a basic non-understanding of the universe, a deep, though sometimes masked, distress '. It was that deep sadness which distinguished his two Hamlets of 1948 and 1955 (the latter seemed to be distinguished by little else). An even more profound despair was incarnated in his superb 1962 Lear, although the titanic agony of the King was scaled down and stilled to meet the Beckett-based approach of Peter Brook's masterly production. For some people (though not for me) Scofield's apparently congenital sorrow swamped his Richard II in 1952; and a surfeit of melancholy marred his 1967 Macbeth, a good man grieving over the ambition which led him astray. Played against comic situations, rather as Gielgud has played his gravity, the submerged distress can have memorably funny effects : that rueful countenance has the lined beauty of a clown's mask. Although in his 1970 Uncle Vanya, the comedy was (for me) paralysed by his grief-frozen face, this performance was warmly praised for achieving the right mixture of laughter and tears.

In major classic roles Scofield – for all his shining reputation – has not enjoyed unanimous acclaim, except for his sterling, romantic performance of Pierre, the straightforward hero-victim of *Venice Preserv'd*. He has been criticized for excessive understatement and studied immobility or impassivity; for the level, toneless delivery with which he flattens out long stretches of dialogue, suddenly picking on one phrase or passage to make it glow and pulse in the air around the theatre: for the occasional self-conscious theatricalism of his effects, when he seems to show the actor acting, with a kind of fastidious detachment. Although his first Hamlet at Stratford – elegant and romantic in Victorian dress – was widely praised for its promise, his second was gabbled, dull, monotonous and actorish. Yet the promise, tantalizingly, remained. ' Potentially,' said Kenneth Tynan, he still seemed to be Olivier's ' natural heir '. And he made a further claim to the inheritance with what is to date, perhaps, his best performance: the magnificent, earthy, heartbreaking Lear of 1962, full of particularity and pathos in the details of old age, but achieving a universality and a freedom from the actor-self which has else-where eluded him.

The fact is that there is something about Paul Scofield which for the past twenty years has recurrently brought out that word 'greatness'. It is not only his stillness, his weary authority, his mesmeric *mana,* his eloquent eyes or his capacity to touch the heart and surprise the mind. To quote W. A. Darlington: 'In Scofield today, as in Irving a century ago, there is a force which transcends argument. When he plays Shakespeare, however oddly, Shakespeare is there to meet him.'

And in the generation after Scofield are there any great ones in the making? It is, of course, too early to say: even to start talk-ing about greatness, when nobody has yet played enough great parts. But the disquieting fact is that people do start talking about it – because they think they see its halo and feel the touch of its wings, because they *want* great acting, even before the actor has begun to learn his trade. All too often the star career takes over, the basic training is never completed as it should have been, and the full talent doesn't flower, because it can't.

Today comedy, farce and the musical are the ruling forms in the Shaftesbury Avenue system: tragedy, melodrama, the play of ideas, sentimental situation-drama, costume drama, even the matinée play of prewar years, are in conspicuously short supply, with obvious effects on the acting range of the commercial stage. Wider opportunities may be offered by such American imports as Miller and Albee, by such British actor-dramatists as Osborne and Pinter, or by the now-rare revivals of classics staged in the West End. But in general the actor's vocabulary inside the industry is still largely governed by a stylized reflection of middle-class manners. This kind of West End formalism, framed by the proscenium arch, is the dominant theatrical mode for a domi-nantly middle-class audience; and commodity acting to match it is still in demand.

Moreover, TV and films have encouraged the reductionism which had been a marked trend in acting since the death of Irving: the contraction of gesture, the lowering of volume, the miniaturization of signals, the flattening of emphasis, the fear of overdoing it in general. Watched by the camera, you need only let a tremor touch your cheek where once, watched by the gallery, you would have had to put your whole face into play. In close-up you can wince instead of shrieking, whisper instead of projecting your voice fifty yards up into the back circle, economizing in every department of theatrical effect. On the stage, you must have presence: on the screen and the box, you cannot afford to look stagy. It could be said that, in some respects, you learn to do less and less, for more and more. Television acting tends to be from the neck up: ' The rest of you might as well be in plaster ', as one leading TV player says; and a theatre director has complained that ' after five years in television they are finished: communication ceases at the end of the third row '. In films the actor works in fragments, and the fragments may be out of sequence, emotionally, psychologically and structurally; he cannot usually give a performance, continuously, as a whole; and his timing, pauses and reactions are controlled and changed by directors and editors. He is less in command of his own acting, and he is disconnected from the living audience.

Yet both media have, in some ways, encouraged an extension of the actor's opportunities as well as of his income. The cinema has, at its best, promoted a kind of intimate truthfulness which the conventional stage can scarcely match; and, with television, it may offer openings – in fantasy, romantic drama, neo-documentary, and other forms – that are seldom available in the theatre. Among the younger generation of stage players the influence of American film models often seems more powerful than that of the West End *farceur* tradition or the Shakespearian line of descent from Burbage to Gielgud; and an earthier, less inhibited and more explicit style of speech and behaviour has reverberated in the theatre, notably in the classic tradition of speaking verse. Young actors are likely to be more concerned with looking and sounding real than with practising realism. They are inclined to put meaning before music, humanity before nobility, topicality before tradition.

Inside the ' non-commercial ' theatre, moreover, a broader range is open to the actor now than between the wars, and a wider vocabulary of performance is spasmodically in use. In rep he must be ready to adapt himself to several kinds of style in a couple of seasons: say, to Farquhar and Orton, Ibsen and Beckett, Osborne and Brecht, Pinter and Sheridan, as well as to Shakespeare and to whatever new plays may be introduced.

Instead of having to remain content with the sedentary under-statements of conventional West End realism, he will probably be given the chance to stretch his vocal, physical and intellectual limits, to regard himself less as a soloist than a team-member, less as an artiste than a social worker, a doer as well as a talker.

Today a younger actor's style may be compounded of many influences: acting in rep in Restoration comedy and Strindberg, acting in a film spectacular about the Napoleonic Wars and a television soap opera, acting in the West End run of a Neil Simon hit and a Sunday-night happening. He will probably keep an open mind about Grotowski and Brecht, Stanislavsky and Artaud, Simon and Garfunkel, Morecambe and Wise. New plays are more likely to be important in his growth than they were in the working lives of the Gielgud-Olivier generation. Whereas a Macready or a Kemble was most at home in costume drama, while a Hawtrey or du Maurier was at his best in contemporary clothes, there are now, perhaps, more actors than ever before who have worked both in the leading classics and the more or less significant contemporary drama and who can move freely (when given the chance) between their several worlds – across a far greater potential span of experience, technique, imagination and understanding.

If I had to pick as a candidate for greatness one name from the talents to emerge in the 1960s, it would be that of Nicol Williamson; but the major reputation he had already made by 1970 rests upon only a handful of stage performances – notably, his brilliant marathon solo of frustration and failure in *Inadmissible Evidence* and his compelling but superficial, over-hurried Hamlet. Has he the stamina to stay in the theatre and go on learning? Where will he – and others like him – find the experience and discipline they need?

What is still conspicuously lacking in the British theatre, in spite of reorganizing progress in recent years, is concentration of development and opportunity, continuity of growth, direction and policy, full employment *on the stage* for all our leading players. Promise is marketed before it can bear fruit. Brilliance is scattered and diffused, under the drive for novelty. The fear of over-exposure buries great performances all too soon. The power of fashion increases with the accelerating speed of change. It is hard for the younger generation to believe that it takes twenty years to make an actor, when stars are so often said to be made overnight – and can show their notices (and tax returns) to prove it. It is even harder for managers to keep artists inside the disciplines of the stage when instant freedom and fortune sometimes seem to beckon from the film and television studios, when the turnover of parts in the theatre is so relatively small and the chances of success so relatively uncertain. One of the most powerful traditions of the profession – in spite of long-established lip-service to the *ensemble* and in spite of the growing economic pressures of overcrowding and unemployment – is still short-term compromise, empiricism, 'muddling through' and all the waste that goes with it. For actors, as for writers, the theatre plainly suffers from the transitional problems of its mixed economy and even more mixed aesthetics: it is still dominated, in spite of current processes of renewal, by an ageing audience and a fossilized architecture, complex economic burdens and the penumbra of a bygone social order.

Yet whatever forms the theatre of tomorrow may take, whatever kinds of drama, acting and production may emerge in the 1980s, we may be sure of two things: that the school of Shakespeare will continue to be the school of truth and greatness, outside all fashions in theatrical ideology, beyond all social and technological change; and that it is through great plays, greatly acted, that the theatre will continue to survive at the centre of our experience.

Postscript

My gratitude is due to many people and many books: to Sir John Gielgud, Sir Laurence Olivier and Sir Michael Redgrave for their courtesy in allowing me to consult their collections of cuttings and to quote their written and spoken words; to Ronald Hayman, for generously permitting me to read, in draft form, his forthcoming biography of Gielgud; to Mrs Joan Hirst, Mrs Mollie Sole, Mrs Legh, George Nash and the staff of the invaluable Enthoven Collection, for helping me in research; to Edward Thompson and Felix Barker, for reading parts of this book, and to Sir Julian Hall, for reading all of it and for giving much valuable advice; to Hamish Hamilton, who originally asked me to write a book about great acting (*Six Great Actors*) which, in a revised and extended form, constitutes most of Part 1 of this book; to Tony Godwin, who encouraged me to expand it into a new work; to Helen Dawson, who suggested the title; and to all those critics who have contributed to this record by their personal testimony over the years.

Among the books which have gone into the making of this survey, several biographies and autobiographies have been indispensable: Margaret Barton's *Garrick* (1948), Herschel Baker's *John Philip Kemble* (1942), J. C. Trewin's *Mr Macready* (1955), Laurence Irving's *Henry Irving* (1951), Sir Johnston Forbes-Robertson's *A Player Under Three Reigns* (1925), Sir John Gielgud's *Early Stages* (1948 edition), Felix Barker's *The Oliviers* (1953), and my own *Michael Redgrave: Actor* (1956). For details and analysis of acting I am indebted to A. C. Sprague's *Shakespearian Players and Performances* (1954); *Lichtenberg's Visits to England* (1938), translated by M. L. Mare and W. H. Quarrell; William Hazlitt's *A View of the London Stage* and his essays on the drama in 'The London Magazine'; *Dramatic Essays by Leigh Hunt* (1894), edited by William Archer and R. W. Lowe; *Leigh Hunt's Dramatic Criticism, 1808–1831* (1950) edited by L. H. and C. W. Houtchens; William Robson's *The Old Playgoer* (1854); *The Diaries of William Charles Macready* (1912), edited by W. Toynbee; G. H. Lewes's *On Actors and the Art of Acting* (1875); *Dramatic Essays by John Forster and George Henry Lewes* (1896), edited by William Archer and R. W. Lowe; Bernard Shaw's *Our Theatres in the Nineties* (1932); Gordon Craig's *Henry Irving* (1930); *We Saw Him Act: a Symposium on the Art of Sir Henry Irving* (1939), edited by H. A. Saintsbury and Cecil Palmer; W. Graham Robertson's *Time Was* (1931); Ellen Terry's *The Story of My Life* (1908); C. E. Montague's *Dramatic Values* (1910); Sir Max Beerbohm's *Around Theatres* (1924); Rosamond Gilder's *John Gielgud's Hamlet* (1937); James Agate's *Brief Chronicles* (1943) and *Red Letter Nights* (1944); T. C. Worsley's *The Fugitive Art* (1952); Kenneth Tynan's *He Who Plays the King* (1950), *Alec Guinness* (1953), *Curtains* (1961), *Tynan Right and Left* (1967); *John Gielgud: An Actor's Biography in Pictures*, edited by Hallam Fordham (1952); Sir Michael Redgrave's *The Actor's Ways and Means* (1953) and *Mask or Face* (1958); *Shakespeare's Histories at Stratford, 1951*, by J. Dover Wilson and T. C. Worsley (1952); J. C. Trewin's *Paul Scofield* (1956); B. L. Joseph's *The Tragic Actor* (1959); several editions of *Shakespeare Survey*, and many newspapers and magazines.

Among other useful books I have drawn upon *An Apology for the life of Colley Cibber* (1889 edition); *Letters of an Unsuccessful Actor* (1923); Arthur Murphy's *Life of David Garrick* (1801); James Boaden's *Memoirs of the Life of John Philip Kemble* (1825); Giles Playfair's *Kean* (1950 edition); William Archer's *William Charles Macready* (1890); Alan Downer's *The Eminent Tragedian* (1966); *Macready's Reminiscences, and Selections from his Diaries and Letters* (1876 edition), edited by Sir Frederick Pollock; Westland Marston's *Our Recent Actors* (1890); W. G. Pollock's *Impressions of Henry Irving* (1908); Henry James's *The Scenic Art* (1949); W. A. Darlington's *The Actor and his Audience* (1949); *Great Acting*, edited by Hal Burton (1967); *Othello: The National Theatre Production* (1966), edited by Kenneth Tynan.

For permission to quote at length from copyright material my thanks are due to the Public Trustee and the Society of Authors (for various excerpts from G. Bernard Shaw); Richard David and the Cambridge University Press, publishers of *Shakespeare Survey, 6;* Chatto and Windus, publishers of *Dramatic Values;* Hurst and Blackett, publishers of *We Saw Him Act;* Kenneth Tynan and Longmans, publishers of *He Who Plays the King, Curtains* and *Tynan Right and Left;* W. A. Darlington; and T. C. Worsley.

Index

Films, plays and theatres are listed under separate headings after the main index

Abingdon, Frances, 35
Addison, Joseph, 13, 59
Agate, James, 146, 175, 176, 182, 188, 192, 194, 199-201, 211-13, 215, 220-1, 236, 243, 248-9, 256
Ainley, Henry, 175, 199
Albee, Edward, 274
Albery, Sir Bronson, 181, 182, 216, 241, 242
Alexander, Sir George, 138, 141, 159, 222, 223
Alma-Tadema, Sir Laurence, 139, 152
Alvarez, Al, 202, 230
Anderson, Mary, 157
Andrews, Harry, 264
Angelo, Henry, 76, 100
Anouilh, Jean, 222, 230, 272
Archer, William, 103, 108, 116-17, 119, 130, 136, 142, 146, 149, 150, 160, 168, 256
Ardrey, Robert, 244
Armstrong, William, 240
Arnold, Samuel, 79
Artaud, Antonin, 276
Ashcroft, Dame Peggy, 183, 186, 189, 195, 207, 208, 211, 243, 265, 268
Ashwell, Lena, 145
Asquith, Anthony, 262
Aston, Anthony, 13
Atkins, Robert, 172
Atkinson, Brooks, 191, 200, 247, 258

Baddeley, Angela, 183
Bagnold, Enid, 188
Baker, Herschel, 69, 71
Bancroft, Sir Squire, 156-8
Baring, Maurice, 143-4
Barker, Felix, 207, 212, 216, 221, 224, 235, 259
Barnes, Clive, 273
Barry, Spranger, 34-5, 45

Barrymore, John, 199, 210, 213, 236
Bateman, Hezekiah, 129-32
Bateman, Isabel, 129-30, 134
Baylis, Lilian, 171-3, 214
Beaumont, Hugh, 184-5, 246, 270
Beckett, Samuel, 273, 275
Beerbohm, Sir Max, 10, 139, 142, 144, 146, 159, 161
Bennett, Alan, 188
Bensley, Robert, 35
Benson, Sir Frank, 168, 170, 174, 177
Benson, Lady, 177-8
Bergner, Elizabeth, 212
Betterton, Thomas, 13, 14, 30, 37, 49, 50, 59, 131, 161, 192
Betty, Master William, 62-3, 78
Boaden, James, 57, 59, 71
Bogarde, Dirk, 264
Bolt, Robert, 259, 265, 272
Booth, Edwin, 137
Boswell, James, 46
Boucicault, Dion, 128
Brecht, Bert, 275, 276
Brien, Alan, 206, 229, 237
Brook, Peter, 185, 195, 198, 202, 226, 273
Brown, Ford Madox, 152
Brown, Ivor, 175-6, 179, 181, 192, 197, 210-11, 215, 254
Brown, John Mason, 9, 219
Browning, Robert, 105-6
Buckstone, J. B., 156
Bunn, Alfred, 104-5, 116
Burbage, Richard, 10, 14-15, 19, 192, 275
Burne-Jones, Sir Edward, 139, 158
Burney, Fanny, 40
Burrell, John, 216, 220-1, 267
Burton, Richard, 170, 265, 270-1
Byam Shaw, Glen, 183
Byrne, Muriel St Clare, 140
Byron, Lord, 68, 74, 102, 106, 116

Index

Calvert, Charles, 154
Campbell, Mrs Patrick, 158
Cannan, Denis, 223
Capon, William, 57
Carey, George, 76
Carey, Nancy, 76
Carlyle, Thomas, 105
Casson, Sir Lewis, 215, 231, 261
Catalani, Angelica, 63
Chekhov, Anton, 170, 179, 180, 189, 190, 217, 233, 242, 260
Cibber, Colley, 13, 14, 25, 28, 30, 35, 57, 96, 132
Clive, Kitty, 35
Clurman, Harold, 258
Coleridge, S. T., 60, 88
Colman, Ronald, 209
Congreve, William, 13, 41, 59, 189, 190, 233
Cons, Emma, 171
Cooke, George Frederick, 55, 61-2, 65, 73, 84, 95, 100
Copeau, Jacques, 183
Coppée, François, 159
Courtenay, Tom, 264
Coward, Sir Noel, 169, 180, 188, 210
Cox, Robert, 82
Craig, Gordon, 120, 139, 143, 145, 170, 172, 177, 186
Craven, Hawes, 139
Crosse, Gordon, 137, 161, 220
Crouch, Mrs, 57, 58
Cumberland, Richard, 32, 59, 60

Daly, Richard, 53
Darlington, W. A., 169, 176, 192, 194, 199, 201, 212, 218, 258, 274
Daubeny, Peter, 259
Davenant, Sir William, 14, 41
David, Richard, 251-2
Davis, E. D., 126
Dent, Alan, 193, 201, 215, 221, 245, 247
Devine, George, 183, 186, 197
Dexter, John, 206
Dickens, Charles, 103, 123
Donat, Robert, 211, 264
Downer, Alan, 108, 111, 117
Downes, John, 13
Doyle, Sir A. Conan, 136
Drinkwater, John, 209
Dryden, John, 57
Dukes, Ashley, 243
Dumas, Alexander, *père*, 91

Du Maurier, Sir Gerald, 169, 209, 223, 276

Eliot, George, 128
Eliot, T. S. 243
Elliott, Gertrude, 158
Elliston, R. W., 79, 81-2, 100
Ervine, St John, 209, 211
Esmond, Jill, 210
Evans, Dame Edith, 186, 189, 192, 241, 243, 265

Fagan, J. B. 178-9
Fairbanks, Douglas, senior, 210, 236
Faraday, Michael, 108
Farjeon, Herbert, 196, 199, 211
Farquhar, George, 233, 275
Faucit, Helen, 105
Fawcett, John, 97, 107
Feydeau, Jacques, 233
Ffrangcon-Davies, Gwen, 179
Finney, Albert, 264
Fitzgerald, Percy, 38
Fleetwood, Charles, 30, 32
Fleming, Peter, 253
Fogerty, Elsie, 207
Forbes-Robertson, Sir Johnston, 141, 147-63, 198, 199, 207, 250
Forrest, Edwin, 108
Forster, John, 97, 107
Fox, Charles James, 62
Freud, Sigmund, 212, 215
Fry, Christopher, 188, 223, 257, 270

Garbo, Greta, 210
Garrick, David, 10, 12, 21, 24-48, 49, 55, 57-60, 62, 66-7, 72, 74-5, 79-81, 83-5, 91, 103, 107, 109, 111, 116, 118, 131, 142, 155, 160, 182, 189, 206, 211, 215, 226, 235, 256
German, Sir Edward, 139
Gielgud, Sir John, 12, 170, 173-203, 211, 213, 217, 219, 224, 235-7, 238, 242-3, 246, 248-9, 251-2, 255-6, 262-3, 265-273, 275-6
Gielgud, Val, 179
Giffard, Henry, 29, 32
Gilder, Rosamond, 176, 200, 201
Giraudoux, Jean, 257-8
Granville Barker, Harley, 170, 172, 174, 178, 186, 193, 196, 264
Gray, Thomas, 26
Greene, Graham, 188, 265
Grein, J. T., 149, 161, 175
Grotowski, Jerzy, 276

Guinness, Sir Alec, 183, 268-70, 271
Guthrie, Sir Tyrone, 212, 221, 223, 241, 268

Hale, Lionel, 214
Hamilton, Patrick, 244
Harding, Ann, 210
Hardwicke, Sir Cedric, 264
Hare, Sir John, 157
Harris, Augustus, 127
Harris, Henry, 94-7
Harris, Rosemary, 261
Harrison, Rex, 170
Hawkins, Jack, 264
Hawtrey, Sir Charles, 276
Hazlitt, William, 13, 15, 66-70, 74-5, 84-9, 102, 113, 117-18, 144, 263
Henderson, John, 13, 21, 34, 51, 55, 99
Herbert, Louisa, 128
Hillebrand, H. N., 73-4, 83, 86
Hobson, Harold, 193, 195, 226, 229, 249, 252, 260, 265, 273
Hood, Thomas, 129
Hope-Wallace, Philip, 192, 220, 224, 227, 230, 233-4, 247, 256
Horne, R. H. 98, 113
Horton, Priscilla, 105-6
Hoskins, William, 126
Houghton, Norris, 246-7
Howard, Trevor, 264
Hunt, Leigh, 58, 66-8, 70, 75, 87-8, 90, 95, 97, 111, 113, 115, 117-18
Hunter, N. C., 188, 258, 265

Ibsen, Henrik, 141, 167-8, 178, 261, 257
Incledon, Charles, 76
Irving, Edward, 127
Irving, Sir Henry, 10, 12, 120-46, 147-8, 150-1, 154, 158, 160, 170, 172, 175, 179, 182, 186, 188-9, 191, 206, 211, 215, 217, 219, 238, 256, 274
Irving, Laurence, junior, 133, 136-7
Irving, Laurence, senior, 144

Jackson, Sir Barry, 178, 208-9
James, Henry, 19, 137, 143-5, 154, 159, 259
Jephson, Robert, 54
Johnson, Samuel, 28, 30, 36, 37, 43, 46
Jones, Henry Arthur, 133, 137
Jonson, Ben, 15
Jordan, Dorothy, 101
Jouvet, Louis, 66

Kean, Charles, 74, 77, 84, 100, 108, 132-3, 136, 139, 160
Kean, Edmund, 10, 12, 21, 55, 65, 67, 72-93, 94-6, 103-4, 111-19, 140, 145, 147, 157, 160, 170, 171, 179, 189, 192, 198, 206, 215, 219, 225, 255-6
Kean, Mary, 77
Kean, Moses, 76
Keats, John, 87, 90
Kelly, Fanny, 94
Kemble, Charles, 52, 94, 96, 102, 103, 111
Kemble, Fanny, 113
Kemble, John Philip, 21, 49-71, 72, 78, 82, 84, 86, 91-2, 95, 96-7, 100, 104, 107-19, 147, 154, 157, 160, 186, 194, 238, 276
Kemble, Roger, 51-2
Kempe, William, 20
Kempson, Rachel, 241
King, Thomas, 35, 54, 56, 59
Kitchin, Laurence, 229
Knight, G. Wilson, 240
Knowles, Sheridan, 97, 102, 106, 115
Komisarjevsky, Theodor, 180, 186, 189
Korda, Sir Alexander, 211
Kotzebue, August, 59

Lacy, James, 33
Lamb, Charles, 59
Landi, Elissa, 210
Laughton, Charles, 213, 264
Lawson, Wilfred, 13
Leary, Timothy, 11
Leigh, Vivien, 214, 216, 221-4
Levin, Bernard, 205, 228
Lewes, G. H. 10, 13, 87, 91, 111, 115-19, 168
Lichtenberg, G. C. 39, 41, 45
Liston, John, 94, 100
Lytton, Lord (Edward Bulwer), 103, 105-7, 156

MacCarthy, Sir Desmond, 181, 192, 210, 245, 265
Mackenzie, Ronald, 181-2
Macklin, Charles, 13, 29-31, 34, 40, 44, 72, 99
Macready, W. C., 21, 67-8, 82, 84, 94-119, 125, 130, 139, 140, 144-5, 147, 154, 155, 160, 162, 170, 174, 198, 225-6, 251, 253, 255, 256, 276
Macready, William, senior, 99-101

Index

Mankiewicz, Joseph, 186
Marston, Westland, 106, 111, 115-17
Martin Harvey, Sir John, 141
Massinger, Philip, 61, 83
Mathews, Charles, 67, 168, 170
Miller, Arthur, 274
Miller, Jonathan, 234
Mills, John, 264
Mitford, Mary Russell, 117
Modjeska, Helena, 157
Montague, C. E., 162
Moore, Nellie, 129
Morgan, Charles, 192
Mortimer, Raymond, 213, 241
Mossop, Henry, 34
Motley, 186
Munden, Joseph, 94, 100
Murphy, Arthur, 40, 44-5

Nathan, George Jean, 247
Neilson, Terry Phyllis, 178
Neville, John, 264, 271
Nietzsche, Friedrich, 92
Noguchi, Isamo, 197
Noverre, Jean-Georges, 42

Obey, André, 182, 188
Odell, G. C. D. 58, 163
Olivier, Sir Laurence, 9, 10, 12, 37, 47, 176, 182, 193, 204-37, 238, 243, 246, 248, 256, 261-3, 265-73, 276
O'Neill, Eliza, 94, 114
O'Toole, Peter, 264
Otway, Thomas, 13, 41, 59

Parsons, William, 35
Partridge, Sir Bernard, 175
Payne, J. H., 84
Pearson, Hesketh, 151
Perry, John, 183-4
Phelps, Samuel, 21, 92, 105, 126, 130, 152, 154-5, 157, 160, 162, 256
Pinero, Sir Arthur, 157-8
Pinter, Harold, 274-5
Pitt, William, 26, 35
Playfair, Giles, 83
Playfair, Sir Nigel, 178
Plowright, Joan, 231, 261
Poel, William, 170, 172
Pollock, Sir John, 143
Pope, Alexander, 26
Pope, Jane, 35
Porter, Eric, 264
Powell, William, 34-5

Priestley, J. B., 180, 212, 265-6
Pritchard, Hannah, 35, 41

Quartermaine, Leon, 183
Quayle, Anthony, 183, 196, 264
Quin, James, 21, 26, 28, 30, 32, 35, 41, 47, 66

Rattigan, Terence, 224, 258, 272
Redgrave, Corin, 241
Redgrave, Lynn, 241
Redgrave, Sir Michael, 176, 183, 231, 233, 238-63, 264-5, 268-9, 272
Redgrave, Roy, 239
Redgrave, Vanessa, 241
Reynolds, Sir Joshua, 37, 69
Rice, Elmer, 208
Richardson, Sir Ralph, 187, 208, 212, 214, 216-7, 220-2, 224, 237, 243, 264, 265-8
Robertson, Graham, 134, 143, 158
Robertson, Tom, 23, 156
Robinson, H. Crabb, 87
Robson, Dame Flora, 247
Robson, William, 58, 67
Rogers, Paul, 264
Rossetti, D. G. 153
Rowe, Nicholas, 41, 77
Royde-Smith, Naomi, 180
Russell, Edward, 134
Ryan, Lacy, 31

St Denis, Michel, 183, 189, 214, 242-4, 258
Saintsbury, H. A., 142
Scofield, Paul, 271-4
Scott, Clement, 168
Scott, Sir Walter, 57, 83, 102
Scudamore, Margaret, 239
Shaffer, Peter, 188
Shaw, G. Bernard, 148-9, 150-1, 158-9, 162-3, 167-8, 176, 178, 224
Sheridan, Richard Brinsley, 37, 56, 59, 60, 62, 81, 190-1, 220, 275
Sheridan, Thomas, 55
Sherriff, R. C., 209, 266
Shuter, Ned, 35
Siddons, Sarah, 35, 49-50, 52-4, 63, 65, 67, 91, 101, 114, 155, 265
Simon, Neil, 276
Smith, William 'Gentleman', 52, 54-5
Speaight, Robert, 256
Sprague, A. C., 198
Stanfield, Clarkson, 103, 106

Stanislavsky, Konstantin, 114, 241-2, 245-8, 253-5, 258, 263, 275
Steele, Sir Richard, 13, 14
Stephens, Kitty, 94
Strasberg, Lee, 202
Strasser, Jani, 244
Strindberg, August, 232, 248, 276
Sudermann, Hermann, 159
Sullivan, Sir Arthur, 139
Swanson, Gloria, 210
Swinburne, A. C., 152

Talfaurd, Thomas, 103, 105
Talma, Francois Joseph, 61, 113
Tarleton, Richard, 20
Tate, Nahum, 43-4, 57, 106
Tearle, Sir Godfrey, 169
Telbin, William, 139
Tennent, H. M., 183-4, 272
Tennyson, Lord, 132, 136-7, 208
Terry, Ellen, 131, 133-5, 138-9, 142-4, 151-2, 154, 157, 175, 177, 207, 265
Terry, Fred, 177, 182
Terry-Lewis, Mabel, 192
Thorndike, Dame Sybil, 198, 207, 215, 231, 261, 265
Tieck, Ludwig, 67, 118
Toole, J. L. 129
Tree, Sir Herbert Beerbohm, 141, 159, 170, 172
Trewin, J. C., 110, 119, 196, 218, 221, 225, 230
Turner, David, 230
Tynan, Kenneth, 176, 191, 194, 201, 203, 206, 221, 227, 229, 230, 237, 254, 256, 259-60, 266, 268, 272-3

Vanbrugh, Violet, 142
Vandenhoff, George, 92
Vestris, Eliza, 94

Walbrook, H. M., 133
Walkley, A. B., 142
Wanamaker, Sam, 254
Watson, Ernest Bradlee, 107
Welles, Orson, 223
Weston, Thomas, 35, 40-1
Whiting, John, 190
Wilde, Oscar, 189-190, 192
Wikinson, Tate, 53
Williams, Emlyn, 182, 188
Williams, Harcourt, 172, 174, 180, 183, 186, 268

Williamson, Nicol, 264, 276
Wills, W. G. 130, 136, 153
Wilson, J. Dover, 227, 240
Woffington, Peg, 33, 35
Wolfit, Sir Donald, 13, 182, 217
Woodward, Harry, 35
Worsley, T. C., 191-2, 195-7, 224-5, 246, 250, 252, 254, 256, 258-9, 270
Wren, P. C., 209
Wycherley, William, 59
Wyler, William, 216
Wyndham, Sir Charles, 141

Yates, Mary, 35
Yeats, W. B., 219, 262
Young, B. A., 233
Young, C. M., 82, 94, 96, 101-2, 118
Young, Stark, 237

Zeffirelli, Franco, 185, 206
Zoffany, John, 39

FILMS

Becket, 186
Browning Version, The, 262
Charge of the Light Brigade, The, 186
Dam Busters, The, 262
Dead of Night, 262
Demi-Paradise, 216
Fame is the Spur, 262
Great Expectations, 269
Hamlet, 235
Henry V, 216, 235
Importance of Being Earnest, The, 262
Julius Caesar, 186, 196
Lady Hamilton, 216
Lady Vanishes, The, 262
Mourning Becomes Electra, 246, 262
1984, 262
Pride and Prejudice, 216
Prince and the Showgirl, The, 235
Queen Christina, 210
Quiet American, The, 262
Richard III, 186, 235
Wuthering Heights, 216

Index

PLAYS

Adding Machine, The, 208-9
Admirable Crichton, The, 178
Adrienne Lecouvreur, 157
Adventure Story, 272
Ages of Man, The, 185
Alchemist, The, 39, 268
Alexander the Great, 78
Androcles and the Lion, 175
Antigone (Anouilh), 235
Antony and Cleopatra, 224
Arms and the Man, 217
Ascent of F6, The, 269
Aspern Papers, The, 259, 262
As You Like It, 240-1

Back to Methusaleh, 208
Battle of Shrivings, The, 188
Beau Geste, 209-10
Becket, 186
Bees on the Boatdeck, 212
Beggar's Opera, The, 244
Belle's Stratagem, The, 128
Bells, The, 120-4, 129, 130, 143-4
Bird in Hand, 209, 210
Blot on the 'Scutcheon, A, 106
Blow Your Own Trumpet, 245
Born Yesterday, 235
Bridal, The, 115
Bride of Lammermoor, The, 126
Brutus: or, The Fall of Tarquin, 84

Caesar and Cleopatra, 159, 224
Captain Carvallo, 223
Careless Husband, The, 31
Cato, 59
Charles I, 130, 132
Cherry Orchard, The, 179, 190
Circle, The, 191
Circle of Chalk, The, 210
Cocktail Party, The, 269
Complaisant Lover, The, 265
Constant Nymph, The, 180
Coriolanus, 57, 58, 107, 138
Corsican Brothers, The, 136
Count of Narbonne, The, 54
Country Girl, The (Winter Journey), 253
Crime and Punishment, 188
Critic, The, 220
Crucible, The, 235
Cymbeline, 208

Dance of Death, The, 232, 234
Dan'l Druce, Blacksmith, 156

Day by the Sea, A, 185, 188
Dead Heart, The, 136
Dear Octopus, 183, 188
Distrest Mother, The, 101
Dr Faustus, 41
Douglas, 59
Duchess de la Vallière, The, 105
Duke in Darkness, The, 244

Eden End, 265
Entertainer, The, 228-9

Fair Penitent, The, 32
Family Reunion, The, 243-4, 272
Farmer's Wife, The, 208
Father, The, 248
Faust, 136, 139
Flea in her Ear, A, 233
Flowering Cherry, 265
For the Crown, 159, 160
Forty Years On, 188

Gamester, The, 41
Government Inspector, The, 272
Green Bay Tree, The, 210
Golden Arrow, The, 211
Good Companions, The, 180-1

Hamlet, 36, 49-50, 61, 70, 72, 115, 135, 152, 159 175, 182, 201, 221, 231, 240, 248-51, 261, 266
Harold, 209
Henry IV Part 2, 239, 253
Henry V, 106, 173, 241, 253
Henry VI, 218
Henry VIII, 59, 139, 157, 184
He Was Born Gay, 188
High Bid, The, 159
Hobson's Choice, 261
Home at Seven, 266
Hotel in Amsterdam, 272
Human Touch, The, 269
Hunted Down, 128

Ides of March, The, 188
Importance of Being Earnest, The, 191
Inadmissible Evidence, 276
Ion, 105
Iron Chest, The, 88
Isabella, 54
Ivanov, 190

Jacobowsky and the Colonel, 246
Jane Shore, 41, **77**
Jealous Wife, The, 102, 115
Jewess, The, 104
Johnson over Jordan, 266
Journey's End, 209

Index

Julius Caesar, 186

King Arthur, 157-8
King John, 55
King Lear, 21, 36, 42-3, 57, 106, 152, 173, 221, 235, 240
King of Nowhere, 215
Lady of Lyons, The, 106
Lady of the Camelias, The, 157
Lady's Not For Burning, The, 188
Last Joke, The, 188
Lethe, 29, 38
Light That Failed, The, 159
Louis XI, 133
Love for Love, 13, 179, 191
Love's Labour's Lost, 248
Lyons Mail, The, 132

Macbeth, 34, 41, 54, 59, 63, 70, 72, 86, 106, 108, 114-5, 159, 175, 181, 209, 247
Magda, 159-60
Maitlands, The, 182, 188
Malade Imaginaire, Le, 174
Man For All Seasons, A, 272
Marino Falioro, 106
Marvellous History of St Bernard, The, 208
Mary Queen of Scots, 153
Mary Stuart, 157
Master Builder, The, 261
Measure for Measure, 184, 195
Merchant of Venice, The, 29, 72, 159, 174, 183, 234, 242
Merry Wives of Windsor, The, 155
Mice and Men, 159
Michael and his Lost Angel, 160
Midsummer Night's Dream, A, 36, 155
Miss in her Teens, 38
Money, 156
Month in the Country, A, 245, 258, 261
Mountaineers, The, 59, 77
Mourning Bride, The, 41
Mrs Grundy, 160
Much Ado about Nothing, 139, 157
Musical Chairs, 181-2, 188

New Way to Pay Old Debts, A, 61
Noah, 182-3, 188
No Time for Comedy, 216
Notorious Mrs Ebbsmith, The, 158
Nude with Violin, 188

Oedipus Rex, 219
Olivia, 139
Orphan, The, 41

Othello, 84, 90-1, 159, 215, 223
Ours, 156
Out of Bounds, 259

Passing of the Third Floor Back, The, 159-60
Patrician's Daughter, The, 106
Patriot, The, 180
Peer Gynt, 173
Pelléas and Melisande, 159
Perouse, La, 77
Pickwick, 121
Pizarro, 59
Potting Shed, The, 188
Power and the Glory, The, 272
Prisoner, The, 269
Private Lives, 210
Profligate, The, 157
Provok'd Wife, The, 39

Queen of Scots, 210

Raising the Wind, 130
Rats of Norway, The, 210
Recruiting Officer, The, 31, 233
Rehearsal, The, 31
Relapse, The, 272
Revenge, The, 59
Rhinoceros, 230
Richard II, 174, 183, 194, 242, 251-2
Richard III, 24-6, 32, 57, 74-5, 104, 141, 221
Richard of Bordeaux, 181-2, 188
Richelieu, 107, 127, 130
Ringmaster, 210
Ring Round the Moon, 272
Rivals, The, 56, 268
Rob Roy, 102
Romeo and Juliet, 173, 182, 186, 211, 216
Ross, 269

Sacrament of Judas, The, 160
Samson Agonistes, 240, 261
Scarlet Pimpernel, The, 182
School for Scandal, The, 56, 116, 159, 183, 191, 221, 224, 268
Semi-Detached, 230
She Stoops to Conquer, 248
Silver Box, The, 208
Skin of Our Teeth, The, 221-2, 235
Sleeping Prince, The, 224, 258
Spring 1600, 182
Staircase, 272
Story of Waterloo, A, 136
Strafford, 105

Index

Stranger, The, 59
Suspicious Husband, The, 38
Sweet Nell of old Drury, 182

Taming of the Shrew, The, 207, 209
Tartuffe, 185
Tempest, The, 57, 106, 240, 251
Tiger and the Horse, The, 259
Time Remembered, 272
Theatre Royal, 210
Three Sisters, The, 183, 189
Thunder Rock, 244
Tobacconist, The, 39
Top of the Ladder, 223
Tosca, La, 157
Touch of the Sun, A, 258
Twelfth Night, 243
Two Roses, 129

Uncle Dick's Darling, 129
Uncle Harry, 245, 256
Uncle Vanya, 217, 231-6, 256, 261
Under the Sycamore Tree, 269

Venice Preserv'd, 13, 41, 59, 192, 273
Venus Observed, 223, 235
Vicar of Wakefield, The, 136
Virginius, 97, 115, 182
Vortex, The, 180

Waiting in the Wings, 262
Wat Tyler, 173
Way of the World, The, 191, 272
Werner, 102
Wheel, The, 178
Wheel of Fortune, The, 59
White Carnation, The, 266
White Guard, The, 243
William Tell, 102, 115
Wingless Victory, The, 245
Winter Journey, 253-5
Winter's Tale, The, 36, 157, 272
Woman's Wit, 106

Zara, 41

THEATRES

Astor Place Opera House, N.Y., 108

Birmingham, 77, 99-100, 128
Birmingham Repertory, 169, 208, 209, 264, 267, 272
Blackfriars, 14
Bristol Old Vic, 185

Chester, 100
Cheltenham, 77
Chichester, 231, 260
Covent Garden, passim, 22-119, 154, 170

Drury Lane, passim, 22-119, 154, 159, 170

Edinburgh, 127-8
Exeter, 73, 78

Gaiety, 155
Garrick, 157
Glyndebourne, 262
Goodman's Fields, 24, 43, 75

Haymarket, 156, 184-5, 191, 201
His Majesty's, 181

Kingsway, 208

Liverpool, 51, 53, 128
Liverpool Repertory, 169, 240, 246
Lyceum, 89, 120, 129, 135-42, 147, 151, 157-8 170, 201
Lyric, Hammersmith, 184-5, 272

Manchester, 99-100, 128, 154-5

New, 181, 211, 214, 216-7, 222, 248, 269

Old Vic, 171-6, 180-1, 184-5, 187, 193, 198, 204-6, 212, 214, 216, 220-2, 231, 241, 243-4, 246, 248, 251, 256, 264, 267-71
Olympic, 79, 156
Oxford Playhouse, 178, 186-7, 191, 264

Palace, 228
Phoenix, 191, 198, 242-3, 258
Prince of Wales's, 156
Princess's, 127, 153

Queen's, 183-4, 185, 191, 242-3, 269

Regent, 178, 208
Royal Court, 208-9, 228-9
Royalty, 209

Sadler's Wells, 125-6, 176
St James's, 128, 159, 222-4
Smock Alley, Dublin, 53-4
Stratford-on-Avon, 184, 193-4, 207, 224-5, 239, 246, 251, 256, 258, 269-70, 272

Wyndhams, 181

Yvonne Arnaud, Guildford, 261-2